D0919205

FLORIDA STATE
UNIVERSITY LIBRARIES

FEB 0 8 2001

TALLAHASSEE, FLORIDA

Redesigning Democracy

FLORIDA STATE
UNIVERSITY LIBRARIES

JAN 9 2001

TALLAHASSEE, FLORIDA

For Louis, Robin, Siobhan and Elisabeth,
to help them remember.
And to the memory of Gwyn Alf,
who helped us all to remember.

FLORIDA STATE
UNIVERSITY LIBRARIES

JAN 9 2001

TALLAHASSEE, FLORIDA

Redesigning Democracy

The Making of the Welsh Assembly

Kevin Morgan & Geoff Mungham

seren

seren is the book imprint of
Poetry Wales Press Ltd
Wyndham Street, Bridgend, CF31 1EF, Wales

JN
1157
.m67
2000

© Kevin Morgan & Geoff Morgan, 2000

ISBN 1-85411-283-X

A CIP record for this title is available from
the British Library

All rights reserved. No part of this publication
may be reproduced, stored in a retrieval system,
or transmitted at any time or by any means
electronic, mechanical, photocopying, recording
or otherwise without the prior permission
of the copyright holder.

Cover: detail from a photograph by David Hurn,
taken in Newport during the referendum hustings.
Reproduced by permission of Magnum Photographs.

*The publisher works with the financial assistance of the
Arts Council of Wales*

Printed in Plantin by WBC Book Manufacturers, Bridgend

3 1254 03519 2992

Contents

Preface

This is one of those unfortunate books which was fated to be over-taken by events whilst in press. Perhaps this is not wholly surprising when one considers the protean world of Welsh politics in recent years. But the forced resignation of Alun Michael – the first First Secretary of the National Assembly and Tony Blair's personal favourite for the Labour leadership in Wales – registered throughout the UK. Why? Because it suggested that the devolved administrations might want to think and act for themselves, rather than degenerate into cowed and passive bodies whose sole function is to rubber stamp decisions made in Downing Street.

What was to be done about such a significant political event? Fortunately, and without any prompting, Mick Felton – the publisher at Seren – invited us to write a Postscript to bring the book 'up to date', a forlorn hope since devolution is a process not an event, as Ron Davies famously remarked. However, we readily agreed to write a postscript on one condition: that the rest of the book remained exactly as we had written it before the resignation crisis. In other words there has been no attempt on our part to revise the analysis or amend the tone of the original eight chapters.

To avoid any misconceptions about the focus of the book we should say at the outset that it aims to tell two stories: the first concerns the long campaign for a Welsh Assembly, with all its trials and tribulations; the other concerns the schizophrenic role of the Labour Party in this process, and how it has facilitated and frustrated devolution at various points in its history. Strictly speaking then, this is not so much a book about Welsh politics as a book about Labour politics in Wales. Although Labour has dominated Welsh politics since the 1920s, this distinction has become more important with the advent of democratic devolution.

Astonishing as it may seem, the story of the Welsh Labour Party has never been properly told despite the fact that Wales is probably the most durable electoral heartland of British Labourism. Confined as it is to devolution, this book is too particular in its focus to provide more than a partial account of the Labour Party in Wales, but hopefully it will stimulate others to fill the void with a more substantial study.

A great many people have helped us to tell our stories. In particular, activists reflected on their personal experiences; politicians spoke to us, on and off the record, about their role in the devolution battles; civil servants offered judicious insights; and friends and family recounted their memories of the events described in this book. Because some people have requested anonymity we can only thank the following by name here: Dave Adamson, Andrew Bold, Kevin Brennan, Alun Burge, Sue Essex, Cynog Dafis, Wayne David, Andrew Davies, Ron Davies, John Davies, Mark Drakeford, Ceri Evans, Val Feld, Paul Flynn, Peter Hain, Annabelle Harle, Michael Hines, Ken Hopkins, Gareth Hughes, Mari James, Carwyn Jones, Ieuan Wyn Jones, Jon Owen Jones, Richard Wyn Jones, Brian Morgan, Rhodri Morgan, John Osmond, Adam Price, Sue Taylor, Dafydd Elis-Thomas, Terry Thomas, David Waterstone and Dafydd Wigley. Needless to say none of the aforementioned bears any responsibility for the views contained in this book.

We are grateful to Diane Tustin for her administrative skills.

Particular thanks are due to Peter Stead, who read the whole manuscript on behalf of the publisher, and to our friend and colleague, Kevin Williams, who can always be relied upon to find a cloud in every silver lining of Welsh politics.

Introduction

Stateless nations like Wales cannot express their national identity through the political apparatus of an independent state so they use surrogates when they wish to do so. This is surely why sport and culture are expected to carry such a large share of the 'national burden' in Wales, where the people who excel in these fields are popularly perceived to be ambassadors for Wales at home and abroad. If civic or cultural nationalism is not too strong a word for it, this diffuse sense of Welshness should in no way be confused with political nationalism, a narrower and far more specific phenomenon. If Plaid Cymru, the Welsh nationalist party, is the obvious vehicle for the latter, there is a wide array of vehicles for civic nationalism, including the Labour Party, even though party officials have always been extremely nervous and deeply suspicious of any kind of national sentiment. In fact, one of the founding fathers of the Labour Party, Arthur Henderson, even tried to abolish Wales from the party map.

The 'Welsh Question' took a long time, and not a little effort, before it was recognised as such in British politics. No one has done more to chart this process, the national awakening in Wales after the Great Election of 1868, than K.O. Morgan, whose classic study, *Wales in British Politics*, carries two important lessons for us today. First, it proves that we can learn "new truths about the nature of society and the struggle for political authority by turning away from the centre to the periphery" (Morgan, 1970). Indeed, the entire book can be read as a critique of metropolitan provincialism, the conceited mindset which treats British political issues as glorified Westminster issues. In other words the Celtic nations, to say nothing of the English regions, rarely appeared on the radar screen of London-centred political analysts other than for scandals and idiosyncratic human interest stories.

Second, it serves to remind us that, unlike Scotland, no significant tradition of independent statehood survived in Wales after the so-called 'Act of Union' with England in 1536 (a misnomer if ever there was one because the Act was never ratified in Wales and it announced not a new union but confirmed a union which it claimed had always existed). If Scotland retained some important institutions, in the form of the Kirk, the legal system and the educational structure, the struggle for national recognition in Wales had to begin almost from scratch after 1868, not least because the very idea of Wales "was in itself a cause of speculation" (Morgan, 1970). But the struggle for national recognition expressed itself not so much through the conventional political demand for Home Rule, though this was part of the story, as in other ways, like pressure for the disestablishment of the Church of England in Wales, the defence of the Welsh language and the campaigns for educational equality and land reform. This helps to explain why the struggle for national recognition began to pay dividends in the cultural and educational spheres long before it did in the political sphere, with more than a hundred years between the creation of the University of Wales in 1893 and the birth of the National Assembly in 1999.

Nothing better illustrates the extent to which Wales was politically assimilated by England than the notorious injunction in the ninth edition of the *Encyclopaedia Britannica*: 'For Wales, See England', an ignominious entry for any self-respecting nation. Generation after generation became so inured to that geo-political amalgam we call 'England and Wales' that an act of will was required to think of Wales in and for itself. In a subversively titled essay called 'Wales and England' Raymond Williams suggested that this administrative assimilation left the Welsh "with some of the most radical identity confusions of any modern people" (Williams, 1989). His namesake, Gwyn Alf Williams, the distinguished Welsh historian, went further. In an essay called 'When Was Wales?' he said:

> the problem of identity has been desperate from the beginning. In recent centuries we have progressively lost our grip on our own past. Our history has been a history to induce schizophrenia and to enforce loss of memory... We have no historical autonomy. We live in the interstices of other people's history (Williams, 1979)

In the same essay Gwyn Alf notes with some surprise that the very survival of the Welsh as a people "has been a kind of miracle" given the pressures of assimilation. Miraculous or not a distinctive Welsh identity survived against the odds because, over the last century in particular, being 'British' did not preclude being 'Welsh'. Indeed, as we'll see in chapter one, the stability of the UK as a multi-national state is partly due to the fact that successive governments have had the wit to recognise, rather than suppress, these multiple identities. Though it may not be fully appreciated, the territorial stability of the UK also owes a great deal to the Labour Party, the only party of the 'Celtic fringe' which has been resolutely committed to preserving the integrity of this multi-national country.

As the Celtic nations recalibrate their national identities within the UK it often seems that they are having fewer problems doing so than the English, many of whom are genuinely confused by this 'identity thing'. When you account for over eighty per cent of the population, and when your nationality has never been compromised by a larger neighbour, then your national identity is a bit like your health, some-thing that is taken for granted until it is threatened. Make no mistake, democratic devolution may have been driven by the Celtic nations, but the implications are just as profound for England and the idea of 'Britishness'.

In a survey of constitutional change in the UK *The Economist* claimed that the cumulative impact of Labour's reforms will be noth-ing less than revolutionary because they will change "not only the way in which Britain is governed but also the meaning of 'Britain' itself" (*The Economist*, 1999). The survey noted that the Union Jack, the most potent symbol of a certain kind of Britain, "no longer does the business". As a superimposition of emblems – the crosses of St George for England, St Andrew for Scotland and St Patrick for Ireland – the Union Jack signals two very clear things: that Britain is not a single nation and that Wales is conspicuous by its absence. But what attracted most attention in the survey was the finding that a large majority in Wales (81%) and Scotland (72%) now identified with their own nations, compared with how many identified with Britain. Only in England, it found, did a small majority put British identity first. Although we should not make too much of this small poll its findings are confirmed by other surveys; so much so that this has provoked an epidemic of anxious texts from the Right like 'The Death of Britain' by the Conservative MP John Redwood and 'How To Be British' by Charles Moore, the editor of the *Daily Telegraph*. What these angst-ridden custodians of the Union forget is that the renaissance of national identity in Scotland and Wales may be incom-patible with a centralised Britain, but it is not necessarily inimical to a more pluralist kind of Britishness.

In recent years the upsurge of national consciousness in Wales has been associated less with political developments as with popular culture, though both are implicated in the phenomenon of 'Cool Cymru', a media-induced celebration of things Welsh. As the self-proclaimed national newspaper of Wales intoned:

> Call Cool Cymru a cliché but our rugby team is riding high, our musicians and actors dominate the charts and the big screen, our language is enjoying a resurgence and our new devolved politics means Wales is taking control of its own destiny (*Western Mail*, 12 July, 1999).

Leaving aside the fact that at least one of these claims was wrong at the time, there is no doubt that popular culture, and Welsh pop bands in particular, have been the most important catalysts for the renaissance of national consciousness among young people in Wales, however fickle this might seem to older generations. Indeed, the unlikely columns of the *New Musical Express* became the forum for a debate on the meaning of Welsh national identity under the banner headline 'Is Wales the New Germany?' This followed the 1999 Morfa Stadium gig by the Stereophonics, a band from Cwmaman, at which a Welsh flag was draped over the stage and fans were invited to participate in a (rugby) song called 'As long as we beat the English we don't care'. A number of English fans complained to the *NME* and the latter ran an editorial which rebuked the Welsh for excessive national pride. Silly for some, symbolic for others, the *NME* controversy showed that the upsurge in Welsh national consciousness among young people is perceived to be 'anti-English' even if that is not the intention.

The conventional response to the Cool Cymru phenomenon *within* Wales is highly polarised: either it is celebrated as an expression of self-confidence in a small nation which desperately needs it or it is dismissed as wishful thinking on the part of a fickle and self-referential metropolitan clique. The truth is somewhere between these poles: it is not that Cool Cymru is wholly without substance, but rather that it gives such a partial view of Wales, essentially a Cardiff-centric view of a country which is bedevilled with enormous regional imbalances. The 'economic miracle' which the Welsh Development Agency likes to present to the international investment community flatters to deceive: admittedly this picture has some substance in the high growth region of south-east Wales, but there is 'the other Wales', where we encounter some of the most deprived communities in western Europe, and needless to say there is nothing 'cool' about acute poverty (Morgan and Price, 1998). In 1999 large swathes of Wales, in the west and the valleys, qualified for Objective One status, a form of regional aid awarded to the very poorest regions of the European Union. In the same year Oxfam appointed a full-time officer to work in Wales, another symptom of the stubborn levels of poverty which scar this country of contrasts. What this means is that modern Wales, like the UK generally, is an economically differentiated and socially divided country.

A cultural and political renaissance may be underway but economics, that dismal science, seems coy about joining the party. The birth of the National Assembly of Wales may be an important date in the political calendar, but 1999 witnessed disquieting news on the economic front: for example, Wales bucked the UK trend towards lower unemployment in the second quarter; the rate of business failures in Wales was substantially higher than elsewhere in the UK; and serious setbacks occurred at some of the biggest names in the Welsh economy, like Ford, LG and Laura Ashley. These trends pose major problems for the Welsh Assembly because, ultimately, it will be judged on bread and butter issues like jobs and public services.

But politics, too, will have its part to play. The Labour Party can take great credit for introducing democratic devolution to the UK because it would certainly not have happened otherwise. In fact one of the arguments in this book is that the main debate about democratic devolution in Wales actually occurred within the Labour Party, even though it was influenced by voices outside the party.

Within two years of coming to power, however, New Labour had scaled the heights and plumbed the depths in Wales, its premier electoral heartland in the UK. Having delivered on its election pledge to create a Welsh Assembly after a referendum, it quickly squandered all the political capital it had painstakingly acquired by employing shamefully undemocratic tactics to decide the Labour leadership in Wales, tactics which demeaned and affronted the new era of democratic devolution and precipitated the worst crisis in the history of the Wales Labour Party.

This book aims to tell the story of how and why the National Assembly for Wales was created in 1999 and, as regards the role of the Labour Party, it can be read as a case study in the uses and abuses of political power. Like all good stories it contains its high points, and we see the creation of the Assembly as the culmination of a long and laudable struggle for a more democratic and accountable political system in Wales, a system which might eventually afford better opportunities for public debate and popular participation. Since the UK is not over-endowed with democratic and accountable political structures, this is the best defence of the Assembly in the face of critics who suggest it is not worth having because its powers are so modest.

But the story has its low points too, like the way in which Labour's machine politicians, in London and Wales, sought to place their favoured candidates in an Assembly which was supposed to signal a new democratic era. Seasoned politicians will smile at the naïveté of anyone who expected anything else. Nevertheless, it is worth documenting the manifold ways in which a formally democratic process could be subverted by politicians who had 'the knowledge', a shorthand for Labour Party insiders who controlled such seemingly prosaic things as the names and addresses of party members, the timing and venues of party meetings as well as the services of local party workers who defied the rules (with impunity) to solicit postal votes for favoured candidates. Unless one understands the micropolitics of the process, especially with regard to the pre-election candidate selection process, one cannot possibly understand how some low calibre insiders triumphed over higher calibre outsiders.

The saga of the Welsh Assembly is also a story about the limits of one-partyism in Wales. With the possible exception of the Ulster Unionists no party in the UK has exercised such a durable political hegemony as the Labour Party in Wales, the ideological birthplace of British Labourism, where voting Labour was more a social habit than an individual decision, and where some of the foremost names in the Labourist pantheon were based, like Keir Hardie, Nye Bevan, Jim Griffiths, James Callaghan, Michael Foot and Neil Kinnock, the last three successive party leaders. At the party's 1999 conference Tony Blair paid tribute to this record, saying "I don't think there's any part of the UK where the Labour Party means more, or has worked harder than in Wales". But on the eve of the centenary year of all years Wales went and spoiled the celebrations by giving Labour its worst electoral results since the 1920s, including the spectacular loss of Rhondda, Islwyn and Llanelli, heartland seats if ever there were. Experienced political analysts saw the wider significance of these results, namely that there are limits to political loyalty, even in a heartland, when one treats voters with contempt. In an open letter to New Labour the founding director of Charter 88 wrote: "Even the Welsh, the most traditional Labour tribe of all, proved more modern than you are and deprived you of a majority in your assembly" (Barnett, 1999).

Democratic devolution may seem a modest institutional innovation by the standards of federal countries, but it nevertheless signals a major challenge for a London-centric political culture which, until now at least, has been impervious to campaigns to extend democracy and participation. This is as much a challenge for devolved bodies, like the Welsh Assembly and the Scottish Parliament, as it is for central government itself, though the latter has yet to realise this. If the Labour Party holds sway one imminent problem for democratic devolution could be the combination of the *old* mindset of one-party-ism in Wales and the new culture of control in Millbank and Downing Street.

Let us take Wales first. The ideology of one-partyism, born of prolonged electoral dominance, pervades the Wales Labour Party and this is what sustains the belief that Labour has no need to forge pacts or alliances with others, be they political parties or social movements. As we show in chapter three, the Wales Labour Party has resolutely eschewed any campaign for devolution which involved working with others, especially Plaid Cymru. At bottom this is why Wales had nothing like the Scottish Constitutional Convention, which helped to build a wider constituency for the cause of democratic devolution in Scotland. What further distinguished the two Celtic countries was that a Scottish Parliament was seen as a 'claim of right' from a historic nation whereas in Wales the Labour Party tried to smuggle an Assembly into being as part of its proposals for local government reform. The ideology of one-partyism explains the refusal to work with others, and a reluctance to campaign openly on the Welsh national question led to what we call the *smuggler's road* to devolution, all of which helps us to understand why the Welsh referendum result was so close.

In Wales the mindset of one-partyism lingers on for a number of reasons, not least because Labour continues to dominate Westminster politics and because party managers hope and believe that 'normal service' will be resumed shortly, that is to say that the voters will return to the fold. In chapter eight we consider the argument that Wales has a *monist* rather than a *pluralist* political culture, so that within parties, unions, councils and even chapels, dissent is regarded with suspicion. This argument seems most compelling when applied to the Wales Labour Party, where there is little or no capacity to tolerate and take advantage of differences within itself, hence these *differences* (between British Labour and Welsh Labour for example) could deepen in the future. But this narrow tolerance for debate inside the party is compounded by the narrowing of opportunities for debate in Wales more generally on account of the concentration of media ownership. Geraint Talfan Davies, the former Controller of BBC Wales, puts it succinctly when he says that in Wales "we do not have sufficient competing understandings of our circumstances" (Davies, 1999). The monist culture of the Wales Labour Party and the growing concentration of the media in Wales are not the ideal conditions for the birth of the National Assembly, with its promise of a more pluralist politics.

These tensions are even more acute in New Labour, the modern Janus, which is genuinely committed to devolving power in principle but, in practice, wants to retain as much control as possible. This ambivalence seems to pervade everything the government touches, a point highlighted in Anthony Barnett's open letter to the leaders of New Labour:

> Wales can have an assembly but not the leader it wants. We have a human rights act, but not a commission to make it work for everyone. We can get rid of hereditary peers, but can't have a democratic second chamber. We will have a freedom of information act, but only after the spine has been filleted out.... You drain your policies of their politics, their principles and their spirit (Barnett, 1999).

The paradox of New Labour is that it is committed to devolving power in the *country* at the same time as it is concentrating power in the *party*, one sign of which is that no Minister is allowed to speak in public without first clearing the line with Alastair Campbell, the Prime Minister's press secretary. Critics of New Labour within the party have been contained to date by the personal popularity of Tony Blair and by the fact that his government had a remarkable 15% lead in the polls at mid-term, a unique political achievement which also owed something to the phenomenal unpopularity of the Conservative opposition. However, this opinion poll lead was not enough to save the Labour Party from some disastrous election results in 1999, a mystery which is solved by the fact that core Labour supporters were not bothering to vote. The notion that low turnout reflected content-ment was shown to be a nonsensical conceit by a landmark ICM poll in September 1999. Among other things the poll showed that barely half of those who voted Labour in 1997 thought the party was keeping its promises; more than one in three thought that Tony Blair had become 'too arrogant' since winning power; and almost half accused him of caring too little about Labour's traditional working class supporters and of paying too much attention to the party's rich donors (Kellner, 1999).

By mid-term, then, there were danger signs amid the cheer. Even sympathetic political columnists had begun to note how perceptions were changing: instead of appearing purposeful the government looked overbearing, instead of confident, vainglorious and instead of hubris it was "time for a touch of humility" (Stephens, 1999).

Other than not voting at all, traditional working class supporters may have no choice except to vote Labour in England, but this is certainly not true in Scotland and Wales, where the nationalist parties present themselves as the heirs to Labourism. In Wales it is not yet clear if "the most traditional Labour tribe of all" is in the process of changing its singular political allegiance. What is clear, though, is that this 'tribe' is beginning to experiment with its vote in growing numbers, a new and healthy development in Welsh politics because it means that the Labour Party must win votes on merit and not through force of habit. But time alone will tell if Wales is on the cusp of a post-Labour era or whether the Labour Party, suitably chastened and reformed, will reclaim its lost heartlands in future elections to the National Assembly. All we can say for the moment is that what began as a campaign to bring democratic devolution to Wales ended in a campaign for greater democracy in the Labour Party.

ONE: THE CONTEXT

1. The Fall and Rise
of Devolution

As a theoretical proposition the United Kingdom would probably win few converts because it seems such a fragile concoction. Imagine the reaction to a political scientist who proposed to create a country from the following design: three and a half nations, multiple religions, a number of languages, two separate legal systems and the whole thing ruled by a highly centralised government in a city in the south of the largest nation. That the UK – or the United Kingdom of Great Britain and Northern Ireland to be precise – has preserved its territorial integrity since the Irish Free State was established in 1921 is perhaps more remarkable than we think. The fact that this territorial integrity is so often taken for granted, that it should even appear 'natural' to so many people, speaks volumes for what has been achieved. It could easily have been so different, especially as many *multi-national* states around the world have shown themselves to be anything but united. In the course of the twentieth century alone this idiosyncratic multi-national state survived a whole series of potentially fatal crises, including two world wars, the inter-war Depression, relative economic decline and the accelerated closure of coal mines and steel mills, industries which were once considered synonymous with Scotland and Wales. With the luxury of hindsight we can say that some things clearly work better in practice than in theory.

For a political system which prides itself on having preserved its territorial integrity amidst such momentous social and economic change, it seems strange that UK governments could be so easily unsettled when territorial questions (especially national questions) have appeared on the mainstream political agenda. In part this reflects an avowedly 'modern' *Weltanschauung*: that territorial attachments are cultural residues of a pre-modern or pre-capitalist age, primordial attributes which, in the fullness of time, would be dissolved by the gastric juices of modernisation. In the 'first industrial nation' of all places it was supposed that modern political activity would be organised around functional issues like class rather than territorial issues like regions and stateless nations (Morgan, 1985).

This modernist perspective had its adherents on the left as well as the right, and it became all the more powerful and pervasive for that.

On the other hand, perhaps it was because territorial questions were the exception rather than the rule in the UK (in contrast to countries like Canada and Belgium, for example, where territorial considerations are an ever present part of the political equation) that UK governments have seemed so ill at ease with these 'pre-modern' issues. But politicians were not alone in thinking that territorial politics were a thing of the past. The subject of territorial politics in universities in the UK was very much the Cinderella of the political science discipline and the subject did not really begin to develop until the mid-1970s, stimulated as it was by the advent of devolution as a live political issue. Prior to the seventies politicians had demonstrated their confidence in the territorial integrity of the UK in the most convincing way possible: they rarely discussed the matter. According to one of the pioneers of territorial political studies in the UK a "search of *Hansard* from 1921 reveals very few debates about the Union for half a century" (Rose, 1982).

It was during this period, when the territorial integrity of the UK was most taken-for-granted, that we see the beginnings of a profound centralisation of the governance structures of the country, most notably in the realm of government itself but also in many other key institutions as well, like the labour movement, the nationalised industries and of course private sector corporations, all of which were concentrating their headquarters in and around London, the political capital of the UK. What we have here is a particularly compelling example of how the spatial concentration of political power induces other institutions to cluster their own command and control functions in a similar fashion, with the result that London becomes the hub of strategic decision-making in political life, corporate affairs, the mass media and cultural taste. Our understanding of this process – the process through which a spatial hierarchy is constructed – is most developed in the context of the economy, where large firms habitually locate their high-skill and high-status functions in and around London, while assigning their low-skill and low-status production functions to the peripheral regions of the UK (Massey, 1995).

But this spatial hierarchy is also at work in the public sector too, albeit in a more muted form, and the consequent polarisation of decision-making functions constitutes one of the most intractable features of the North-South divide in the UK today. Even the representative institutions of peripheral Britain (the Labour Party and the trade unions) have been as committed to this spatial hierarchy as the most capitalistic firms, proving that the centralisation of command and control was widely considered to be an exemplar of good organisational practice. How else are we to understand the fact that the Labour Party, like the trades unions on which it modelled itself, was totally opposed to devolving power to the regions in its own organisation. Centralism recommended itself to the labour movement for many reasons, not least because it seemed the surest way to nurture its embryonic power and also seemed the best antidote to parochialism. But there were alternative organisational models even in these early years of the labour movement. Alone among the large unions the miners, significantly the most powerful and class conscious of all the unions, organised themselves in a genuinely federal way because the Miners' Federation of Great Britain was a confederation of reasonably autonomous bodies up until the National Union of Mineworkers was formed in 1945 (McKibbin, 1974). The Miners' Federation may have been the exception to the rule in the formative years of the labour movement, but it is worth noting all the same because it shows that it was possible to secure many of its aims without surrendering all decision-making capacity to a centralised and remote head office.

If centralisation marched under the flag of modernisation, this became inextricably associated with a particular territorial expression of the UK, the post-1921 territorial settlement, in which successive governments often behaved as if the UK were a conventional unitary state, with power concentrated at a single centre in keeping with the sovereignty of Parliament. In unitary states all areas are supposed to be treated uniformly and all institutions are directly under the control of the centre (Rokkan and Urwin, 1982). This picture certainly resonates with some aspects of the UK policy, like the way political power is concentrated in London and the trend in central-local government relations, which have "tilted too far towards centralism" (House of Lords, 1996). In territorial terms, however, the UK was far from being a unitary state because Scotland, Wales and Northern Ireland have received distinctive treatment in recognition of their national status; though administrative devolution, by definition, was never allowed to compromise the powers and sovereignty of Parliament. For much of the time then, centralism implied Unionism (the defence of the UK's territorial integrity) and the latter seemed to require centralism (the centralisation of political power at Westminster).

Dominant as it was, this highly centralised model of the Unionist state was challenged on at least four occasions in the twentieth century: the Home Rule movement which lost momentum after the First World War; the short-lived experiment in national and regional planning in the 1960s; the rise and fall of Celtic devolution in the 1970s; and the advent of democratic devolution in 1997, the implications of which remain as clear as mud. Bracketing these very different experiences together may seem a travesty to historians, but it is a useful way to remind ourselves that the rationale for devolution has come in many shapes and sizes over the last hundred years. The rationale for devolving power to the nations and regions of the UK has involved one or more of the following: a *political* rationale (devolution as a step towards a deeper, more pluralistic democracy); an *administrative* rationale (devolution as a means to more efficient, locally-attuned policy-making); an *economic* rationale (devolution as a stimulant to regional development); and a *cultural* rationale (devolution as a means of protecting and promoting civic or ethnic identities).

What further complicates the matter is that the demand for devolution has been advanced by some very different political forces, like *regionalists*, who wish to create a more devolved or federal system within the UK, and *nationalists*, who view devolution as a staging post on the road to independence from the UK. To compound matters even more, nationalism in Scotland and Wales is not confined to the official Nationalist parties, since the Labour Party is a conduit for a diffuse civic-minded nationalism. In Wales, at least, the dividing line between these two forms of nationalism is becoming more difficult to discern as civic nationalism within the Wales Labour Party becomes more assertive and political nationalism in Plaid Cymru becomes less intransigent about the question of independence. When dealing with the complex trinity of devolution, regionalism and nationalism we have to be wary of labels, since they may not be a good guide as to what's really going on inside an organisation, especially one as catholic as a political party.

The occasions when devolution appeared on the UK's mainstream political agenda may have been few and far between, but they remain the only moments when a serious debate ever occurred in the UK with respect to the territorial balance of power in the Union. Today, as we grapple with the intended and unintended consequences of democratic devolution, it may be instructive to recall three earlier (and ultimately unsuccessful) occasions when devolution briefly raised its insignia, suggesting an alternative trajectory to the centralised model of the Unionist state.

Home Rule: A Pre-Modern Cause

E.P. Thompson once spoke of the need to rescue ideas and voices which had been sidelined and traduced by what he felicitously called "the enormous condescension of posterity". A case in point might be those 'lost voices' before and after the First World War who subscribed to the cause of Home Rule All Round, the name given to devolution at the time. As its name suggests, Home Rule All Round involved separate parliaments for Ireland, Scotland, Wales and England in addition to the 'Imperial' parliament at Westminster, in other words devolution in a federal context. One of the weaknesses of the Home Rule All Round movement – if 'movement' is not too strong a word for it – was the fact that it included not just principled federalists but more questionable supporters who hoped to use the issue to dilute, or even scupper, Irish Home Rule. Although federalists hoped that the momentum of the Irish Question would help them to secure Home Rule All Round, this hope was shattered in 1921, when the Stormont system and the Free State came into being without any associated benefits for Scotland and Wales.

While it was fashionable to draw analogies between Ireland and Wales prior to 1921, the similarities paled alongside the differences. Comparing the two countries it was said that:

> The ideal of Wales was to be recognised as a part of the British political and social structure: the ideal of Ireland was to be severed from it. The object of the one was equality: the aim of the other was exclusion. Home Rule in Wales, unlike Home Rule in Ireland, was indeed 'killed by kindness'. Wales was too much in contact with English influences (Morgan, 1970).

In Wales the Home Rule issue was one of the great Liberal causes, along with the disestablishment of the Church of England, education, land reform and temperance, the causes which fuelled the growth of Welsh nationalism after the 1868 election, when Liberalism became the dominant political creed. One of the most conspicuous demands for Home Rule at this time came from Cymru Fydd (The Wales To Be), a Liberal-led movement which was founded by the émigré Welsh in London in 1886 and which spread through Liberal circles in Wales in the 1890s. Shorn of a mass following Cymru Fydd eventually collapsed in 1896 when, at a critical meeting in south Wales, the demand for Home Rule was vehemently opposed by what Lloyd George contemptuously called "the Newport Englishmen" (Morgan, 1982).

The cause of Home Rule All Round was revived before and after the First World War, when it recommended itself as a means of reducing the burden of the 'Imperial Parliament' at Westminster, since the latter was encumbered with the domestic affairs of the Union, the external affairs of the Empire and, after 1918, the additional task of post-war reconstruction. The high point of federalist hopes came in 1919, when Lloyd George set up a conference, under the auspices of the Speaker of the House of Commons, to consider the prospects for devolution in the Union. Published in 1920 the Speaker's Report excited little interest and, in retrospect, the Speaker himself thought that "the driving force of necessity was absent" (Davies, 1994). Having found such little support for the issue, especially in England, Lloyd George declined to act on the Report, thereby killing (or perhaps just burying) a great Liberal cause.

It is not difficult to understand why the Liberal campaign for Home Rule ended in failure, since Liberalism itself was on the wane in the early 1920s. What is more difficult to explain, however, is why Home Rule did not fare better in the hands of the Labour Party, whose fortunes were on the rise. Up until the 1920s there was a strong current in the Labour Party, among both leaders and led, which favoured Home Rule All Round. Keir Hardie, who became the first socialist MP in the UK when he was elected for Merthyr and Aberdare in 1900, saw no contradiction between socialism and national identity, he therefore promoted the Red Dragon of Wales alongside the Red Flag (Hardie, 1912). But the most robust pro-devolution statement appeared in *Welsh Outlook* in June 1918, when Arthur Henderson, the powerful secretary of the Labour Party, said:

> A local parliament such as the Labour Party hopes to see established in Wales will encourage Welshmen and women to stake an interest in their own affairs and to seek speedy and safe solutions of the economic and social problems that Wales, like every other community, must handle. Wales in this respect is a microcosm; it is hardly possible to conceive an area in which a scheme of parliamentary self-government could be established with better chances of success. All the problems that embarrass statesmen

and challenge the imagination of reformers are to be seen in Wales reduced to manageable proportions.

Similar pro-devolution sentiments could be found among the rank and file in Wales. The high point of the Home Rule current within the labour movement in Wales was a congress, held in Cardiff on 27 July 1918, which unanimously supported "Federal Home Rule for the four nations" of the Union. Thomas Richards, the General Secretary of the South Wales Miners' Federation, set the tone with his opening remarks:

> We are present to discuss the question of relieving Parliament of obligations of vital importance to the people of this country. Local affairs could be dealt with better, more cheaply and more expeditiously by the people of a locality. The lifeblood of many districts is being drained by parliamentary procedure. Wales is especially progressive, and we are handicapped by the existing state of things. We have visions of better things after the war – better housing, better light, better surroundings, more care for the children. We need a more expeditious method of attaining these things (quoted in Griffiths, 1980).

Although this was the high water mark for Home Rule inside the labour movement in Wales, pro-devolution sentiments continued to be expressed years later. In 1923, for example, a prominent organiser was calling for devolution within the Labour Party, in the form of a Welsh Council, as a prelude to devolution in the country (Harris, 1923).

The decline of Home Rule within the Labour Party is usually explained by reference to the inter-war Depression, and it is certainly true that constitutional issues seemed a rather exotic menu in the context of mass unemployment. The only problem with this explanation is that it fails to appreciate how devolution was quietly being strangled within the labour movement *before* the Depression. We need only remind ourselves that Arthur Henderson, the party secretary between 1911-34, had little sympathy for devolution despite his *public* posturing on the issue. Time and again Henderson had vehemently opposed requests for a modicum of Welsh autonomy within the Labour Party. In fact when Henderson was designing a new organisation for the party in 1919 he even tried to remove Wales from the map. The classic account of these formative years describes how Henderson and his union-dominated Executive approached the issue of party organisation:

They were very conscious of creating a party to suit what they took to be contemporary conditions: a party that would be able to exploit modern social and economic forces. This meant to the Labour Party, as it did to the great unions, central control over a national organisation. It meant, furthermore, casting aside traditional and declining props of political power (McKibbin, 1974).

Regions and nations, in this functionalist perspective, were deemed to be traditional rather than modern entities, hence Henderson's organisational scheme was quite consciously written:

to follow what he understood to be the main lines of British economic development. Thus he drafted Wales out of existence, implanted it in England on the reasonably plausible grounds that north Wales was now part of Lancashire and Cheshire ...while south Wales was so closely linked with southern England as to make it impossible to disentangle the two. This was an analysis that did not recognise sentiments of nationality (McKibbin, 1974).

Although the National Executive forced Henderson to restore Wales to the party map, which he duly did by giving it the grand title of District H, this was not a defeat for the centralists; on the contrary "so far as devolution was concerned Henderson had won the battle, not that it required much winning" (McKibbin, 1974).

What this illustrates is that Labour Party leaders like Henderson, and the trade union notables who dominated the party's Executive, were deeply suspicious of anything that raised regional or national concerns, hence their sustained opposition to devolution in the party and the unions. If these leaders were so viscerally opposed to devolution in their own organisations, and their fight against federalising the party made this perfectly clear, it is unlikely that they were going to champion it in the country at large. In other words devolution was killed off long before the Depression arrived in the 1920s: the spectre of mass unemployment allowed it to be quietly buried without ceremony. The Labour Party Executive looked upon regional and national identities not merely as unfortunate relics of a bygone era, but as a threat to the modern party it was trying to fashion in the New Social Order. For both the Labour Party and the trade unions, then effectively one and the same thing, modernisation was synonymous with centralisation.

Going for Growth: The Great Planning Fiasco

Four decades on, the issue of devolution returned to the mainstream political agenda, this time in the context of a new economic strategy for the UK as a whole. By the early 1960s politicians and policy-makers alike had begun to fret about the UK's low rate of economic growth, a problem which had been obscured by post-war reconstruction at home and the temporary absence of war-damaged competitors abroad. The lurch towards indicative planning, as opposed to the *physical* planning of the 1939-49 period, began in the twilight years of the Tory government in the early 1960s. In an effort to escape the debilitating stop-go cycle of demand management the Tories became receptive to the idea of *indicative* planning, a system which appeared to be successful in countries, like France, which had better economic growth rates than the UK. What finally persuaded the Tories to embrace planning was the fact the Federation of British Industries, the forerunner to today's CBI, had already endorsed the idea in 1960 as a means of achieving faster economic growth. It was against this background that the Tories established the first peacetime planning institution, the National Economic Development Council (NEDC), which was created in 1962 along with its own secretariat, the National Economic Development Office (NEDO).

In brief, the regional dimension of the economy had suddenly acquired a new-found significance: if the under-employed resources of the poorer regions could be mobilised by surplus investment from congested regions then the UK economy might be able to grow at a higher and more sustainable rate. In other words a regionally balanced economy would be less prone to inflationary pressures in the core and to rising unemployment in the periphery, hence the regional dimension became one of the conditions favourable to faster growth (NEDC, 1962).

With the advent of a Labour government in 1964 the new planning experiment was embraced with greater alacrity, one sign of which was the burgeoning of planning institutions. Within two years an enormous planning apparatus had materialised and, to underline its commitment, a wholly new planning ministry was created within central government in the form of the Department of Economic Affairs (DEA). To complement the work of the DEA at the centre, a system of Regional Economic Planning Councils and Regional Economic Planning Boards was established in eight English planning regions and in Scotland and Wales as well: the Councils were made up of appointees from both sides of industry, local government, universities and the like, while the Boards consisted of regionally-based civil servants. Each regional apparatus was charged with preparing a regional economic plan for its own region and these plans were supposed to feed into a National Plan which was championed by the DEA, ostensibly a counterweight to the Treasury in central government.

On the face of it this looked like the belated regionalisation of an over-centralised state as well as a more regionally-attuned approach to policy-making. In practice, however, there was less to this institutional innovation than met the eye. Indeed, the planning experiment was effectively over before the ink was dry on the plans: the commitment to growth, along with the targets of the National Plan, were killed by the deflationary package of July 1966, a clear sign that the old order (the Treasury) had triumphed over the new (the DEA). Overly endowed with responsibilities the DEA was signally short of powers, and this fatal disjunction lay at the root of its failure, a flaw which stymied the Planning Councils and the Planning Boards in the regions as well. A comprehensive survey of the planning experiment was driven to conclude:

> From their inception, neither the government nor the administration intended that Councils and Boards should exercise autonomous powers, independently of the centre, to deal with problems as they arose in the region. Still less was it intended that Councils and Boards should formulate and then implement plans for future economic and social development. While local authorities retained their traditional statutory responsibilities for land-use planning, for housing, for transportation and for urban planning, Councils and Boards could not make or carry out regional plans without the active support and collaboration of those local authorities.... The existing constraints in the political and administrative system meant that the advent of regional planning was more apparent than real (Wright and Young, 1975).

The shock of the new regional planning machinery made less of an impression in Wales because it was simply absorbed – critics would say suffocated – by the newly created Welsh Office. The Planning Board largely consisted of Welsh Office civil servants and, of the 25 members appointed to the Welsh Economic Council, all but four were over the age of forty-five. Relevant expertise did not seem to be necessary for being a member of the Council because one member was openly mystified by his selection and another attributed his appointment to a personal friendship with James Griffiths, the first Secretary of State for Wales (Osmond, 1974).

Perhaps the most serious drawback of Welsh Office control of the planning machinery was that published reports became that much more cautious and conservative because they would be read as semi-official publications. This fear was sadly borne out by the story of *Wales: The Way Ahead*, the only economic plan that has ever seen the light of day in Wales (Welsh Office, 1967).

One of the key issues to be addressed in the economic plan was the projected number of jobs in Wales by the target date of 1971. A hazardous exercise at the best of times this task was rendered more difficult by the pit closure programme of the 1960s and a forthcoming shake-out in the steel industry. As it happened Professor Ted Nevin, a member of the Welsh Economic Council, was then engaged in an input-output study of the Welsh economy at University College, Aberystwyth. When the Welsh Office asked him to bring forward the results the Aberystwyth team delivered the goods: they estimated that the number of male jobs in Wales in 1971 would be 59,000 fewer than in 1966. A shortfall of this magnitude would have overwhelmed the regional policy budget, hence the Welsh Office rejected it in favour of its own estimated shortfall of 15,000 jobs, a figure more appropriate to its resources and more acceptable to its political masters (though for the record the shortfall turned out to be 57,000).

Further controversy dogged the new economic plan. When the final draft of *Wales: The Way Ahead* was discussed by the Welsh Economic Council in April 1967 it received a disastrous reception. Eirene White, the chair of the Council and a Welsh Office Minister, hastily adjourned the meeting to allow her to consult with the Secretary of State for Wales, Cledwyn Hughes. The next morning the Council was told that *Wales: The Way Ahead* was merely a background to a plan that would appear later, an outrageous lie which provoked Professor Nevin's resignation. In the event *Wales: The Way Ahead* was published as a White Paper in July 1967 and shortly afterwards Cledwyn Hughes went on record to say "I have never known a document to be so severely criticised before it has even been published" (Osmond, 1974).

In retrospect we can see the planning experiment for what it was, a fiasco. Even at the time there was something unreal about the whole exercise of economic devolution. At the centre a new planning ministry had been created in the shape of the DEA, but the Prime Minister and George Brown, the DEA Minister, had radically different ideas about the status of the new ministry and the latter, for all its youthful enthusiasm, was no match for the seasoned mandarins of the Treasury. In the regions economic devolution was largely welcomed as a first step towards regional economic planning, though this transpired to be not the beginning but the end. Although the DEA was abolished in 1969, the regional planning machinery limped on until the Councils were abolished by the first Thatcher government in 1979, leaving only the Planning Boards to survive in the regions, albeit under the new name of inter-departmental regional boards, a skeleton on which a new regional administration would develop in the English regions in the 1990s.

The ignominious collapse of the economic planning experiment seems to have had two longer term consequences: firstly it underlined the need for institutions which were more democratic than the Councils and, secondly, it encouraged more people in the Labour Party "to question the efficacy of centralised policies" (Jones and Keating, 1985).

Celtic Devolution: The National Question Returns

The advent of Celtic devolution in the UK in the 1970s was a direct, though delayed, response to the growing challenge from nationalist parties in Scotland and Wales in the 1960s. As we'll see in more detail in chapter three, the electoral success of Plaid Cymru induced particular alarm in the Labour government, as Richard Crossman noted in his diary:

> more Welsh nationalist success in Rhondda and absolute success in Carmarthen. I was reminded of how Ted Heath had said... that nationalism is the biggest single factor in our politics today (Crossman, 1976).

Shocked by this unexpected challenge in a Labour heartland the immediate aim of the Wilson government was to try to remove the national question from the political agenda and this was successfully achieved by establishing a Royal Commission on the Constitution to address the problem of 'distant government'. What we did not know until recently, however, was just how far the Labour government was prepared to go to resolve the national question, an issue which had not surfaced (in Westminster politics at least) since the days of Home Rule All Round. Thanks to Cabinet papers released under the 30-year rule we now know that Home Rule for Scotland and Wales was being considered as an option to counter the rise of nationalism. A memo from the Cabinet Secretary, Sir Burke Trend, said that other options should be considered first however, the preferred option being to "bash the nationalists and sweeten the unitary system" by dispersing more government jobs from London, by more administrative devolution to the Welsh Office and by creating a Council for Wales, a forerunner of the National Assembly of today (Settle, 1999).

If Westminster and Whitehall forgot about devolution until the Royal Commission reported in 1973, the internal debate within the Labour Party reached a new level of intensity as the Welsh and the Scots prepared their submissions to the Commission. At this time the two Celtic nations took a very different stance on devolution: the Wales Labour Party was very much in favour of an elected Assembly – or Council as it was called then – while the Scottish Labour Party was opposed. In the original evidence it planned to submit to the Commission the Wales Labour Party (WLP) came out in favour of a robust vision of devolution: namely a directly elected body with legislative and taxation powers (WLP, 1969). This draft provoked a storm of protest from Labour's headquarters in London and from those Welsh Labour MPs who opposed devolution and who could just about tolerate an *indirectly* elected Assembly. Under enormous pressure from centralists in London and from anti-devolutionists in Wales the WLP Executive struck a compromise: in return for Labour HQ accepting the principle of a directly elected Welsh Assembly, it would drop its demands for legislative and taxation powers (Osmond, 1977). The WLP's published evidence to the Commission was thus far removed from what it originally planned. In its published evidence, drafted by Labour HQ, the WLP renounced legislative powers on the grounds that these would "reduce the effectiveness of Welsh MPs and the influence of Wales in the UK, and would jeopardise the unity of the country as a whole" (WLP, 1970).

Having watered down its devolution proposals because of the deal with Labour HQ, and also to make it easier for the sceptical Scottish Labour Party to follow suit, the WLP found itself hopelessly out-manoeuvred. In the space of a few months in 1974 the Scottish Labour Party did a complete U-turn on devolution: having been totally opposed to an Assembly, Scottish Labour suddenly came out in favour of an Assembly with full legislative powers, a move designed to counter the growing nationalist threat (Osmond, 1977). We need to remember this episode because it reveals that the government's eventual proposals (for a legislative Assembly in Scotland and an executive one in Wales) had less to do with technical arguments, like the different Scottish legal system, as with *realpolitik*.

When the Royal Commission eventually reported, in 1973, it acknowledged that adverse economic problems in Scotland and Wales had fuelled the growth of nationalism. But it also found other sources of discontent:

> The concern for democracy seems to be particularly strong in Wales. This strength of feeling shows itself in the widespread demand for an elected Welsh Assembly, and in the vigorous criticism of appointed and *ad hoc* bodies. Such bodies have proliferated in Wales perhaps only a little more than elsewhere in Britain, but they appear to attract far more resentment (Kilbrandon, 1973).

The Royal Commission actually produced two reports: the majority report favoured elected legislative Assemblies in Scotland and Wales, while a minority report wanted to extend such political rights to the UK as a whole. Time and again the majority report reiterated that nothing should be done to impair the economic and political unity of the UK, the mantra of the Treasury's evidence. It also said that its central dilemma was the need for central government to maintain responsibility for inter-regional balance within the UK, while allowing Scotland and Wales a measure of economic discretion in the field of economic development.

Although the Royal Commission reported in 1973, the question of Celtic devolution only became a burning issue after the October 1974 election, when the SNP emerged with eleven seats in Scotland and Plaid Cymru won three seats in Wales. Devolution had 'suddenly' become a potentially explosive issue in Westminster politics: a minority Labour government could ill-afford to ignore fourteen nationalist votes, not to mention the pro-devolution MPs from Scotland and Wales.

Torn and sullen the Labour government reluctantly brought forward its devolution proposals, though James Callaghan, the newly installed Prime Minister, freely conceded that he had no enthusiasm for devolution, hence he wanted as few functions as possible stripped from Westminster and Whitehall (Morgan, 1997). As the devolution legislation limped through the Commons it provoked a growing chorus of criticism, not least from centralist-minded Labour MPs in Scotland and Wales and from the hitherto quiescent ranks of English regionalism, notably the Northern group of Labour MPs who feared that Celtic devolution would disadvantage their region.

The strident voice of English regionalism fortified centralist Welsh Labour MPs like Neil Kinnock and Leo Abse, the most articulate opponents of devolution. Once the centralists secured the concession of a referendum from the government they set about attacking devolution with a vengeance. In Wales the campaign against the Assembly used the spectre of an English-speaking majority becoming beholden to a Welsh-speaking minority if the electorate supported the 'nationalist' cause. But it also drew on the centralist tradition of socialism, arguing that devolution would fragment working class unity, an argument deployed to great effect by Neil Kinnock and originally inspired, as we'll see later, by Aneurin Bevan. Trading on new fears and old convictions the campaign against the Assembly seemed to grow in self-confidence.

By contrast the campaign for a Welsh Assembly had something of a funereal quality to it, sponsored as it was by a Labour government which was becoming ever more unpopular in the wake of the 'winter of discontent'. Come the referendum, on 1 March 1979, the results were as conclusive as they were disastrous for the cause of *devolution*: on a turnout of 58.3% just 11.8% of the total electorate voted for the Assembly, while 46.5% voted against, a majority of more than 4 to 1 against (Foulkes et al, 1993). Although the Scots registered a tiny majority in favour of an Assembly, it was not enough to pass the hurdle of 40% of the electorate, hence the government recoiled from devolution. The defeat of Celtic devolution was more than a little local setback: by inviting a motion of no confidence, in which the SNP voted with the Tories, it triggered the end of the Labour government.

Celtic devolution had been defeated within the Labour Party long before 1979 by a combination of British centralists and English regionalists: the former feared for the integrity of the UK, the latter feared fear itself. Resurrecting devolution from the ashes of 1979 seemed unthinkable, but then the unthinkable occurred in the form of Thatcherism.

Democratic Devolution and the New Labour Janus

Perhaps it is a comment on the changing nature of the Labour Party that devolution should have been seen as a 'pre-modern' cause at the beginning of the twentieth century but as a quintessentially 'modern' cause at the end of it. On the other hand perhaps this epiphany simply reflects the ever more palpable shortcomings of a centralised state which had few great achievements to show for itself, certainly not enough to justify the concentration of political power in Westminster and Whitehall. As in so many other things, New Labour's attitude to devolution was shaped by a long and chastening apprenticeship under the Tories and in particular by Thatcherism, which fuelled a further concentration of power. Inadvertently the Tories did much to prepare the ground for New Labour's rise to power: most important of all in this respect was the overriding sense of a rotting political corpse. A series of scandals, culminating in the highly damaging 'Cash-for-Questions' affair, resulted in the Tories becoming indelibly associated in the public mind with 'sleaze', a fatal image which was comparable to Labour's earlier association with 'the winter of discontent'. The most compelling indictments of Tory rule, and certainly the best insights into the arcane workings of government, will be found in the sober pages of the Scott report on the Arms-for Iraq affair, the Nolan report on Standards in Public Life and the Phillips report on the BSE crisis. It is no coincidence that it was during the early 1990s that the public standing of politicians fell to an all time low, well below all other professional groups save one, namely government ministers (Nolan, 1995).

But on the devolution front there were more particular ways in which the Tories prepared the ground for New Labour. Although successive Tory governments were ideologically opposed to devolving power to the nations and regions of the UK, a modest amount of administrative devolution nevertheless occurred. By far the most important institutional innovation under the Tories was the creation of integrated regional offices in the English regions in 1994, a sensible move which brought together civil servants in the regions from four hitherto separate departments (Mawson and Spencer, 1997).

Modest as it was, the formation of Government Offices for the Regions (GORs) created a more *visible* regional tier of government in England, where the process of administrative devolution was in its infancy compared to the Celtic nations. Two factors above all others persuaded the Tories to reform the 'regional state' in England. In the first place it was patently clear by the early 1990s that a crisis was looming in the English regions: the proliferation of uncoordinated regeneration programmes and a bewildering array of competing agencies created cacophony when 'partnership' was the name of the game, especially for unlocking funds from London and Brussels. Secondly, however, it was only when business added its voice to the demands for more and better coordination that the government decide to act. This new business attitude was summarised by the Director General of the CBI, Howard Davies, who said:

> There is one message I consistently get from pretty well all my regional members. That is a general dissatisfaction with the balance of power between the centre and the regions. And my perception is that things are getting worse. Or, at least, people are becoming more vociferous. The way they see it, Whitehall is a long way from the issues that affect business in the provinces. It has no real link with the regions and does not know what their concerns are.... Regional businesses have definitely welcomed having a single point of call for government in their region. But, curiously, rather than appease the enthusiasm for regional auton- omy, and make them think the government really does care about the world beyond the M25, the integrated regional offices seem to have had the opposite effect. It's woken them up to what they have been missing. This is perhaps not surprising. History suggests that reform is a slippery slope. The most dangerous time for a centralised regime is when it begins to unbend (Davies, 1995).

Although the GORs were meant to be the end, not the beginning, of the process so far as the Tories were concerned, there was the small matter of the 'slippery slope' or the unintended consequences of reform. The GORs, though widely welcomed, were criticised for the fact that they were accountable upwards, to Whitehall, but not down- wards, to the regions in which they operated; this added to the 'democratic deficit' of unelected and unaccountable bodies, the prob- lem of quangos which we examine in chapter two. In other words the Tories had inadvertently created a new agenda for regional devolu- tion in England, an important shift because it enabled New Labour to argue that, far from creating a new regional tier of bureaucracy in England, its own proposals were merely designed to make "the *exist- ing* one more accountable, coherent and democratic" as it was modestly put in *A Choice for England*, the party's consultation paper for English regional government (Labour Party, 1995).

Both before and after it came to office in 1997 New Labour was wont to present its devolution programme in a decidedly modest light, fearing it might otherwise be identified with 'big government' or accused of running ahead of the electorate, at least in England, where there was little or no manifest demand because the sense of regional identity was (and is) generally weak.

Labour's position on English devolution underwent a radical change two years prior to the 1997 election: this was a triumph for the more sceptical approach championed by Jack Straw, the Shadow Home Secretary, who chaired the all-important committee of Labour MPs which produced *A Choice for England*, in July 1995. Significantly, this was the first time the party's devolution programme for the English regions had been seriously reviewed since the death of John Smith, a noted devolutionist who was committed to settling Labour's 'unfinished business' but who left no detailed legacy. In the interregnum between Smith's death and Straw's revisionism, the party spoke often and earnestly about its commitment to regional government in England as a complement to its plans for Scotland and Wales. Indeed, in his personal manifesto for the party leadership, in 1994, Tony Blair had said that Labour should "make the case for regional government in England". In January 1995 the party was still committed to elected assemblies in each English region as the best answer to the thorny 'West Lothian Question'. For sceptics, like Straw, this was a case of the tail wagging the dog: Labour was treating England (the largest nation in the Union and a nation which evinced little support for regional government) as an appendage to its policy for Scotland, where there was strong support for a parliament.

The mood in the Labour Shadow Cabinet shifted decisively in favour of the sceptics during the course of 1995, a year which began with an emotionally-charged attack on the party's devolution programme by John Major, who said that Labour's policy was "one of the most dangerous propositions ever put to the British nation". The Prime Minister may have been innumerate, but the attack nevertheless unnerved the party, as did subsequent Tory charges that regional government in England was "unwanted, unworkable and would add another layer of bureaucracy to local government" Having begun the year with a top-down, one-size-fits-all policy for the English regions, a hangover from the John Smith era, the party ended the year with a bottom-up, devolution-on-demand policy which bore the imprimatur of New Labour. Masquerading as a consultative paper, *A Choice for England* was a canny policy statement which could be read in many ways. For example it was able to placate English regionalists by holding out the promise of elected assemblies and also satisfy sceptics because of the 'triple safeguard', three hurdles which made assemblies less rather than more likely.

Even so, some prominent English regionalists were furious with New Labour's revisionism. Sir Jeremy Beecham, the chairman of the Association of Metropolitan Authorities, wrote to Straw to protest at the watered down policy on English regional assemblies, saying:

> I have to say that the present proposals are likely to cause a storm of protest in the party, and indeed beyond, in a number of regions. It may be true, as the leader remarked, that support for regionalism is strongest among the afficionados. But then a radical party, to some degree at least, seeks to set an agenda and not merely respond to an existing agenda or someone else's agenda... How much power is to remain in Whitehall and its regional outposts and how much is to be exercised in the regions and by the regions? It is here that in my view the paper falls short of the hopes of many of us who have campaigned for over 20 years for a measure of regional government conducted on accountable lines (quoted in McGregor, 1995).

Straw publicly maintained that directly-elected regional assemblies were still part of New Labour's revised devolution policy, even to the point of saying that regions with the strongest identity, like the north, north-west and the south-west, "will be able to steam ahead" (Straw, 1995). The revised policy for England was based on a step-by-step approach. The first step, to be applied in every English region, would see the creation of *regional chambers* made up of elected councillors nominated from local authorities in the region, the functions of which were strategic coordination and democratic oversight. The second step, which was said to be optional, "would lead in the future to the establishment of directly elected regional assemblies in those regions in which public demand for these is evident" (Labour Party, 1995). Regions wishing to take the second step were obliged to meet a 'triple safeguard'. First, the plan for a regional assembly would have to be drawn up and approved by the regional chamber to demonstrate it had the support of most local authorities in the region; second, it would have to be approved by Parliament; third, it would have to gain the consent of local people, perhaps through a referendum. In reality, however, two additional preconditions had to be met, namely no new public expenditure was to be incurred and a basically unitary system of local government, both designed to allay fears about extra bureaucracy and extra spending. The fact that sceptics found more to celebrate here than supporters speaks volumes.

Having settled on a phased, demand-driven approach to regional assemblies the final component of New Labour's devolution programme for England was the proposal to create a Regional Development Agency (RDA) in each English region, to some extent modelled on the Welsh Development Agency. Whereas the sceptical Jack Straw had been the driving force behind the shift to regional chambers, the RDA proposal came out of a regional policy inquiry sponsored by the Deputy Leader, John Prescott, a strong supporter of devolution. In May 1996 it was reported that Tony Blair himself was forced to promise an early implementation of the RDA proposal to pre-empt a rebellion of English MPs against the party's proposals for a Scottish Parliament. Angered by the watering down of regional assemblies, the 40-strong Northern group of MPs, second only to the Scottish MPs in the Parliamentary Labour Party, were only persuaded to drop its plan to (once again) disrupt the devolution legislation by this enhanced commitment to RDAs. John McWilliams, a Northern MP, summed up the sentiment in this deprived region when he said: "All we ever wanted was fair treatment if devolution was on for Scotland" (Mawson, 1997).

The election of a Labour government in May 1997 promised a new era of democratic devolution in the UK as part of a wider programme of constitutional reform. Among other things this programme included a Parliament for Scotland; Assemblies for Wales, Northern Ireland and London; Regional Chambers along with Regional Development Agencies for the eight English regions; reform of the House of Lords; and the incorporation of the European Convention on Human Rights. Friends and foes alike agreed that this programme of constitutional reform was the 'big idea' of the Labour government, the thing that most clearly differentiated Labour from the Tories.

But there were significant differences on devolution *within* Labour as well. Indeed, the post-1997 experience in office, especially after the problems in Wales and Scotland, accentuated these differences to the point where two clearly defined factions could be discerned: the 'devo-sceptics' led by Jack Straw and the 'devo-enthusiasts' led by John Prescott, with the most important figure, Tony Blair, instinctively closer to the sceptics. The strongest card in the hand of the sceptics is the apparent lack of demand for directly elected regional assemblies in England, one reason why English regionalism is described as 'the dog that never barked'.

Two years into office the balance of power was clearly moving in the direction of the sceptics: the most palpable sign of this new balance of power came in the ministerial reshuffle in July 1999, when Richard Caborn, Minister for the Regions in Prescott's department and a doughty campaigner for regional government, was replaced by Hilary Armstrong, who believes regional government is a 'diversion'. Furthermore, following Labour's poor showing in the Welsh Assembly elections, there is a growing fear that regional assemblies might become alternative power bases, with Labour unable to command majorities if a system of proportional representation were used. These fears help to explain why, during the summer of 1999, Downing Street began to signal that 'elected assemblies are off the agenda' (Hetherington, 1999).

If the divisions over devolution are being accentuated, they are also becoming more complex. What is also now at issue is the form which devolution should take in England. For example, the Prime Minister seems to have more enthusiasm for New Labour's local government reforms (particularly elected mayors and cabinet-style executive committees), thus raising the question as to whether the devolution of power to cities is a surrogate for regional assemblies in England. Some local government experts have suggested that elected mayors in the big cities would look on regional assemblies as a threat to their urban empires (Travers, 1999). For those who are sceptical of regional assemblies, like Blair and Straw, focusing their decentralisation moves on cities seems an altogether less threatening model of devolution. Having said that, however, there is nothing mutually exclusive about elected city mayors *and* elected regional assemblies.

The hardening of New Labour's attitude to constitutional reform was not confined to English regional assemblies. By the summer of 1999 it was palpably clear that New Labour was losing the moral high ground it had captured in such an imaginative way by promising to modernise the UK's archaic political structures through constitutional change, by promising to restore public trust in the political process and by promising to deliver on its promises. The corrupting attitude of office shows itself in different ways, like the endorsement of undemocratic voting methods for the Labour leader of the Welsh Assembly, the self-serving proposals for reforming the House of Lords and, most damaging of all perhaps, the way in which credibility was so cynically sacrificed for the sake of control in the long promised Freedom of Information (FoI) Bill. FoI is no ordinary measure: information can empower the ruled, but it can embarrass the rulers. It is, in other words, the litmus test of how a government sees itself and the electorate; indeed it is second to none in conveying the true essence of a government, an infallible index of its commitment to an open and transparent political system. Tony Blair showed himself to be fully aware of the unique status of FoI in a speech to the Campaign for Freedom of Information in March 1996, when he said:

> It is not some isolated constitutional reform we are proposing with a freedom of information act. It is absolutely fundamental to how we see politics developing in this country. We want to end the obsessive and unnecessary secrecy which surrounds government activity and make government information available to the public unless there are good reasons not to do so.... A freedom of information act would entitle the public to information and would leave it to government to justify why it shouldn't be released. It would also signal a culture change that would make a dramatic difference to the way Britain is governed. The very fact of its introduction will signal a new relationship between government and people: a relationship which sees the public as legitimate stakeholders in the running of the country and sees election to serve the public as being given on trust (Blair, 1996).

A White Paper in 1997, *Your Right To Know*, had maintained the reforming spirit of Blair's inspirational speech to FoI campaigners. Eighteen months later this reforming spirit had totally disappeared from the draft FoI Bill. What had happened, in the meantime, was that the relevant sub-committee (CRPFOI in Whitehall jargon) had been hi-jacked by a small number of ministers who were opposed to more freedom of information, in particular Jack Straw, Peter Mandelson and Jack Cunningham (Hencke, 1999). Once responsibility for the FoI Bill was transferred to Jack Straw at the Home Office the reforming spirit was jettisoned, leaving the draft Bill with so many exemptions that it was rendered weaker than the voluntary code on 'open government' introduced by the Major government. In effect the draft Bill amounted to an assertion that 'Whitehall knows best', an astonishing stance in the wake of the Arms-to-Iraq and the BSE scandals, neither of which would have been prevented under Straw's proposals. Apart from its sweeping exemptions the draft Bill diluted the powers of the information commissioner and imposed no burden on government to prove, when introducing a ban, that disclosure would cause harm, substantial or otherwise. At bottom the draft Bill was offering to release information at the discretion of government ministers, when the mood of the country was for enforceable rights of access to information. When Straw presented the draft Bill to the public administration committee of the House of Commons (on the very day, ironically, that the public inquiry into the BSE crisis resumed) it was greeted with universal hostility. Under the title of 'Mr Straw's Secret Society' the normally sober *Financial Times* ran a scathing editorial comment, saying:

> In a display of illiberal sophistry of which his Conservative predecessor Michael Howard might have been proud, Mr Straw argued that his draft freedom of information bill would usher in a new era of open government. That is patent nonsense... Mr Blair often laments the ingrained public cynicism towards elected politicians. Yet on this issue his government shows contempt for the people. Doubtless they will draw the right conclusion (*Financial Times*, 23 June, 1999).

Although Straw was forced to offer a number of concessions to aggrieved MPs, the legislation still fell far short of the reforming spirit of the 1997 White Paper and Tony Blair's FoI speech in 1996. No matter, with or without the concessions, the damage had been done.

More than anything else the FoI reversal leaves the distinct impression of a Labour government which has been corrupted by what Harold Laski once called "the facts of office". But it is not quite as simple as that. In office New Labour has shown itself to be a modern Janus: while it is formally committed to devolving power, as evidenced by democratic devolution in the Celtic nations and London, it is at the same time pathologically obsessed with control. Be it the party, the government, the media, local authorities or indeed the devolved administrations themselves, New Labour seems congenitally bent on exercising control and manipulating outcomes to such an extent that its commitment to devolution, so clear in principle, seems more equivocal in practice.

The Blair government can take credit for things that would never have occurred under the Tories, in particular the New Deal, the minimum wage, the social chapter of the Maastricht treaty and, however imperfect, constitutional change as well. Although it is foolish to liken the Labour government to its discredited Tory predecessor, it is not at all fanciful to imagine New Labour becoming tarnished with the same charges that ultimately scuppered the sleaze-infected Tories. For example: the 1999 annual report of the commissioner for public appointments revealed that over the previous year the government appointed five times as many Labour activists to public bodies as Tory ones, and issued a warning that it was totally "unacceptable" for ministers to be sent lists of people to be appointed to quangos without any independent vetting of their skills. Charges of 'cronyism' have been frequently levelled at a number of Labour ministers, not least about Lord Irvine's former chambers (11 King's Bench Walk, where Tony Blair once worked) getting government contracts and senior government posts. Lord Neill's committee on standards in public life has heard evidence about the government's growing ranks of publicly-funded spin-doctors and special advisers, which together numbered 69 in June 1999, with 22 of them in Downing Street alone, up from just 8 in the John Major era.

The fact that there may be perfectly legitimate reasons for all these things is beside the point; what matters is that, taken together, they begin to create the *perception* that New Labour may be no better than the Tories, and perceptions are difficult to dislodge from the public mind, as the Tories know to their cost.

With the advent of democratic devolution New Labour's Janus character will be tested to the full because, whatever their limitations, the devolved administrations in Edinburgh, Cardiff, Belfast and London have their own popular mandates, hence they are not likely to accept the view that 'Whitehall knows best'. Democratic devolution has the potential to transform the UK into a more pluralist country, and perhaps even a federalised country. If the UK is to retain its integrity as a multi-national state then new political skills, indeed a new form of territorial statecraft, will be required from the devolved administrations *and* from central government, not an easy task for either side. The Labour Party now has a special role to play in preserving the territorial integrity of the UK because it is the only party with a significant presence in England, Scotland and Wales, the only party with a truly multi-national constituency in other words. Aided and abetted by its philosophy of centralism this is what Labour has done so successfully in the past of course, but whether it can do so in the future depends on how quickly it invents a new philosophy for itself, a philosophy more attuned to the era of democratic devolution.

2. Quangoland: The Unelected State

The arcane world of the quango (a merciful abbreviation of what is otherwise known as a quasi-autonomous non-governmental organisation) was exposed to an unprecedented amount of public scrutiny after 1979 because successive Conservative governments were thought to have politicised a system which had hitherto prided itself on being above party politics. Such was the stigma that they acquired during these years that it is difficult even now to have a dispassionate debate about quangos, especially in Wales, where the problems seemed to be more pervasive and more debilitating than elsewhere in the UK. That Wales had a higher density of quangos than the English regions was a corollary of devolution: being a nation rather than a region, and increasingly conscious of the fact, Wales had benefited from a process of *administrative* devolution which spawned a wide array of bodies to cater for Welsh national aspirations. If administrative devolution satisfied mainstream national sentiment concerning the institutional deficit in Wales, it did nothing to allay fears about a burgeoning democratic deficit within these newly devolved institutions. Although the democratic deficit pre-dated Thatcherism, the problem assumed more prominence after 1979 for three reasons: first, the number of quangos in Wales more than doubled during the Thatcher era; secondly, the Tories were thought to be abusing the quango appointments process; and, thirdly, a series of scandals left the impression that Welsh quangos were out of control. Without these baleful experiences, which signalled that there was something palpably rotten in the body politic in Wales, the cause of democratic devolution may not have won so many new converts between 1979 and 1997. Perversely, then, the Tories made a significant contribution to the pro-devolution mood in Wales when they set about reinventing government under Mrs Thatcher.

Reinventing Government, Conservative-Style

The Conservatives came to power in 1979 with two objectives uppermost in their minds: to reduce public expenditure as a proportion of national income and to roll back the frontiers of the state. While they manifestly failed to meet the first target they were more successful than they ever dared hope with the second. Indeed, if there was one consistent theme running through the policies of successive Conservative governments after 1979 it was a strong ideological aversion to the public sector. This aversion had a number of roots: the deeply-held notion that the public sector was inimical to the 'enterprise culture', a pathological antipathy to trades unions generally and public sector unions in particular, and the fact that the public sector was an easy target in the battle to contain public expenditure. For all these reasons the Tory governments subjected the public sector (the nationalised industries, the civil service, the public services and local government) to the chill winds of market forces. To prosecute these pro-market reforms, however, they were forced to invent new modes of governance to regulate economy and society and these provoked new questions about public accountability.

The Conservatives' ideological aversion to the public sector was most evident in the high premium attached to privatisation. With the possible exception of New Zealand no country has gone so far as the UK in disposing of public sector assets, though cash-strapped governments all over the world have sought to mimic this cash-generating strategy. Although the privatisation programme was justified in terms of consumer benefits, the results were a good deal more mixed than the Tories would have us believe: indeed, the National Consumer Council claims that consumer interests in the utility sector, for example, were subordinated to those of business users and shareholders (NCC, 1993). In governance terms, however, the main effect of the privatisation programme was to create a clutch of new quangos (like Oftel, Ofwat and Ofgas) to regulate the newly privatised companies. While there are major advantages in having a clear and robust regulatory regime for these privatised utilities, the UK lags way behind the US in making the deliberations between regulator and regulated open to public scrutiny.

Apart from redefining the relationship between government and industry, the Tory agenda for reinventing government also involved a radical shake-up in the structure and management of central *government* itself. Following a report from the Efficiency Unit in 1988 the government created Executive Agencies to improve the delivery of services to the public, to raise the quality of advice to Ministers and to achieve better value for money generally. The great merit of these Agencies, according to the government, was that they embodied clear lines of accountability to Ministers. Indeed, during the second reading of the Civil Service (Management Functions) Bill in 1992, the Chancellor of the Duchy of Lancaster, William Waldegrave, said that Executive Agencies were a major advance on the traditional quango model because quangos did not have 'any clear line of accountability to anybody' (Waldegrave, 1992). This was a damning admission for a government that relied so heavily on the traditional quango model of governance.

In principle the creation of Agencies did not have to compromise accountability but, in practice, they did so in two ways. First, direct accountability to Parliament suffered when parliamentary questions about the Agencies' work were blocked and MPs were sent replies not from the relevant Minister but from the chief executive of the Agency in question. Pressure from MPs forced the government to abandon this outrageous practice. Second, the division of labour between Agencies and Ministers, designed to separate the delivery of services from the policy-making 'core role' of their parent departments, could be a recipe for passing the buck: the classic case being Michael Howard, the Home Secretary, who had a habit of attributing successes to the 'policy' side (i.e. himself) and failures to the 'delivery' side (e.g. the chief executive of the Prison Service).

If Executive Agencies were designed to make the civil service more business-like in structure and ethos, Market Testing effectively amounted to privatisation. Market Testing, in which the costs of carrying out functions within government were compared with the costs of contracting out those functions to the private sector, was made mandatory in 1984 and took a terrible toll on the morale of civil servants, many of whom felt it was a glorified form of asset-stripping. Ostensibly designed to improve standards these reforms begged some large questions. Was it appropriate, for example, for the public sector to ape the performance targets of the private sector? In particular, was it appropriate for the newly created Executive Agencies to be driven by considerations of profit and loss? That these were not abstract concerns was made apparent in the early days of the Child Support Agency: one of its internal memos to staff in the Wales and Merseyside division set a new tone for the civil service, saying "the name of the game is maximising yield – don't waste a lot of time on the non-profitable stuff" (Morgan and Roberts, 1993).

The agenda for reinventing government also embraced the design and delivery of public services, like health, education, training, policing and urban renewal for example, those services which had the greatest impact on the quality of everyday life. Two common threads ran through these public service reforms. The first involved the separation of the *purchaser* function from the *provider* function in order to foster a 'contract culture' in each public service, part of an audacious strategy to create quasi-markets throughout the public sector. The second common thread was the reduction or outright removal of local government involvement in the new management arrangements, thus adding to the centralisation of power, another hallmark of these reforms. Although the reforms were presented as an extension of individual choice, this claim jarred with a radically different experience: in the NHS, for example, the real choices were made not by patients but by doctors and health authorities; while the notion of 'parental choice' in education turned out to be a grotesque reversal of the real situation, where schools not parents did the choosing. However spurious, this notion of patients and parents as consumers of public services was central to the Thatcherite goal of introducing a new, market-based definition of accountability in the public sector.

The Market versus the Ballot Box

Collectively, the Conservative reforms had created a new governance system to manage the delivery of public services and public policies. What was also apparent was that, in building this new system, successive governments had prosecuted a sustained and systematic offensive against the institution of local government, so much so that some experts spoke of an impending crisis of public accountability in the UK (Stewart, 1992). Stung by such criticisms, the Conservatives felt obliged to defend their reforms in a more vigorous manner. For example, John Patten claimed that the public service reforms augured nothing less than "a new constitutional settlement". The Citizen's Charter, he claimed, embodied this new settlement because it gave the citizen:

> real rather than paper rights, through encouraging participation and taking an active part in the way things are run locally, with the active citizen rather than the municipal citizen in charge, and pushing as much power as possible to the community (Patten, 1993).

This interpretation is difficult to square with reality. While many of the reforms did indeed involve a degree of devolution to the 'community', it was not citizens who were empowered so much as self-governing trusts in the health service and governing boards in the case of grant-maintained schools, boards on which there was no parental majority. The distinction was not lost on Joe Rogaly, the trenchant political columnist, who referred to the public service reform programme as "a mandarin's confidence trick". Rogaly made the telling point that "if elected local governments devolved responsibility to autonomous school boards, or if the boards themselves were elected, that would be decentralisation; what we actually have is the opposite" (Rogaly, 1993).

This called for a more robust defence. Fittingly, this was supplied by William Waldegrave, whose brief included the Citizen's Charter. Speaking to the Public Finance Foundation in London, Waldegrave went for the intellectual high ground:

> The key point in this argument is not whether those who run our public services are elected, but whether they are producer-responsive or consumer-responsive. Services are not necessarily made to respond to the public by giving citizens a democratic voice ...in their make-up. They can be made responsive by giving the public choices.... Far from presiding over a democratic deficit in the management of our public services, this government has launched a public service reform programme that helped create a democratic gain (Waldegrave, 1993).

This is the heart of the matter. The clear implication of Waldegrave's argument is that the traditional democratic mechanism of accountability (the ballot box) had been made redundant by the advent of new market-based mechanisms of accountability as embodied in the Citizen's Charter. But there are problems with this conception. It extols the market over the ballot box, as though these were mutually exclusive mechanisms for securing accountability. Equally objectionable it reduces the *multi-faceted citizen* to a *one-dimensional consumer*: the implication being that individuals have little need to burden themselves with the weight of political governance because they can exercise more economic choice. In short, this was a brazen attempt to substitute consumerism for citizenship.

While consumer rights are indeed very important, and while the Citizen's Charter was a step in the right direction, market-based mechanisms are not a substitute for the ballot box and this is what lay behind the burgeoning criticism of the 'contract culture'. John

Stewart, who did much to keep the issue of public accountability alive, expressed the problem very clearly:

> In 1888 responsibility for the administration of counties was taken away from the magistrates, a lay appointed elite, and given to elected councils. A new magistracy is being created in the sense that non-elected elites are assuming responsibility for a large part of local governance. They are found on the boards of health authorities and hospital trusts, Training and Enterprise Councils, the Boards of Governors of grant-maintained schools, the governing bodies of colleges of further education and Housing Action Trusts. There is no sense in which those appointed can be regarded as locally accountable. Indeed, the membership of these bodies is largely unknown locally. Nor are they necessarily subject to the same requirements for open meetings, access to information and external scrutiny that local authorities are subject to (Stewart, 1992).

Whatever the problems with local government in the 1980s there was at least a transparent and well-known mechanism, in the shape of the ballot box, for holding local elites locally accountable for their actions. But with the transfer of so many local government functions to non-elected quangos, and with central government assuming more control over the remaining functions, especially finance, there was growing confusion as to who was ultimately accountable for the delivery of public services. The weakness of public accountability was not confined to quangoland. Central government's (mis)use of the Standard Spending Assessment system to control local government spending, a task for which it was not designed, was a recipe for passing the buck between the two levels of government. While central government wanted to exercise more control over local expenditure, it clearly did not want to be held accountable for the problems of local service delivery. All of this was too much for the Audit Commission, which went so far as to say that the new reforms, by confusing the issue of accountability, were compromising the drive for economy, efficiency and effectiveness in the delivery of public services (Audit Commission, 1993). When some 80% of local authority income came from central government grants, many people wondered if it was not time for local government to change its name to local *administration*.

Mounting fears about efficacy and democracy at the local level were not confined to the government's political critics. Professor

Norman Lewis, for example, who was in sympathy with the public service reform programme, echoed many of the concerns raised by John Stewart. In a thoughtful essay on how to reinvent government in the UK he said:

> There is a need to redefine the public sector to make it more effi-cient, more responsive, more democratic and more innovative. This cannot be done through quangos and bodies dominated by patronage. It needs strategic vision at both the national and the local level. If local government is to lose its traditional role in rela-tion to service delivery it must be re-empowered in terms of genuine strategic autonomy. Central government needs the expe-rience of local communities to enrich policy-making in a way that can never be matched by quangos. Local government needs reform but it needs, at the strategic level, to be strengthened so that it can engage in dialogue and partnerships with its citizens and the business and voluntary community. Either the govern-ment is serious about handing back more power to ordinary people or it is not (Lewis, 1993).

Lewis made a persuasive case for a more decentralised system of government based on a new agreement about the functions and competences of central, regional and local government. Like other observers he had come to the conclusion that the UK political system had become "heavily over-centralised", a fatal weakness when we recognise that this system was responsible for "a crop of policy fail-ures in recent times that, in all probability, cannot be matched". In this perspective, then, a more effective *and* more democratic system of government would require a large dose of devolution. Whatever the shortcomings of the ballot box, he argued, "at least elected politicians have a long-term commitment to their communities and have to live in them, a consideration which does not ordinarily apply to business groupings or unelected quangos" (Lewis, 1993).

The Patronage State in Conservative Britain

The dwindling status of elected local government under the Conser-vatives was a stark contrast to the burgeoning influence of unelected quangos in the 1980s and early 1990s. Indeed, as we can see in Table 2.1, functions worth over £31 billion were transferred from local government to quangos and central government under successive Conservative governments.

Table 2.1   The Transfer of Public Spending from Local Authorities to Quangos & Central Government

A. Public spending on functions formerly carried out by elected local government (figures 1993-94 unless otherwise stated):

Roads (London)	£130m
UDCs	£463m
London Regional Transport	£722m
Higher Education	£737m
Grant maintained schools	£912m
Further Education	£2,700m
CTCs	£50m
HAT	£87m
Urban Regeneration Agency	£181m
TOTAL	**£5,982m**

B. Public Spending on functions transferred to local authorities:

Community Care	£1,050m

C. Net transfer of directly controlled services:

(A minus B)	£4932m

D. Public spending on services for which councils used to have a formal say

Health District HSAs	£11,652m
Family HSAs	£6,379m
NHS Trusts	£5,979m
TOTAL	**£26,210m**

E. The net overall transfer of public spending to *the unelected* state

TOTAL	**£31,142m**

Source: House of Commons Library

Because there is no universally accepted definition of a 'quango' successive governments have tended to understate their growth, perhaps not surprisingly since they are a byword for patronage. Officialdom eschews the term altogether, preferring the more anodyne 'Non-Departmental Public Body', of which there are three main types: Executive bodies: which between them carry out a wide array of operational and regulatory functions, scientific and cultural activities and certain commercial activities; Advisory bodies: which usually consist of a group of experts who advise the government in specialised fields; Tribunals: which perform judicial or semi-judicial functions.

Although quangos have been with us for many years, some of them older than the twentieth century, what was new about Conservative Britain was the scale and composition of this patronage state. Despite the pledge to reduce the numbers, powers and costs of quangos when they came to office in 1979, Conservative governments presided over the golden age of the quango. Admittedly, the official 'quango count' paints a rather different picture: the annual government publication, Public Bodies, shows that the number of NDPBs declined from 2,167 in 1979 to 1,345 in 1994 (a key date in the history of quangoland because it was the year the government set up the Nolan Committee to examine standards in public life). But this official picture, based on a very narrow definition of 'quangos', greatly understates the phenomenon. Using a less restrictive and more rigorous definition a Democratic Audit study unearthed a total of 6,424 executive and advisory quangos which together spent £60.4 billion in 1994-95, a 45% increase in spending in real terms over the previous 17 years. In other words the total quango budget had grown to such an extent that it accounted for one-third of all central government expenditure, while the people who ran the quangos were described as an "untouchable" elite (Hall and Weir, 1996).

Table 2.2   Summary of Public Appointments at 1st September 1994

Executive Bodies	3,850
NHS Bodies	5,015
Advisory Bodies	10,065
Tribunals	21,973
Boards of Visitors	1,782
Nationalized Industries	104
Public Corporations	87
TOTAL	**42,876**

If the scale of the patronage state changed under the Tories, so too did its political composition. All governments tend to favour their own supporters when they make key appointments, though pre-Thatcher governments tended to leaven their quango appointments with a smattering of the 'great and the good' whatever their political persuasions. What was deemed to be new, and disturbing, about the Thatcher era was the tendency to appoint people who were perceived to be 'one of us'. There was certainly plenty of scope to indulge this habit because (as Table 2.2 shows) over 42,000 appointments were made by Ministers, of which perhaps 10,000 were renewed annually.

By the early 1990s the writing was on the wall: the quango appointments process had become highly politicised. This view was confirmed by the reckless confession of Baroness Denton, then a Trade and Industry Minister, who said of the 800 odd public appointments she had made, "I can't remember knowingly appoint-ing a Labour supporter" (Cohen, 1993). A more systematic survey of the top 40 quangos conducted by the *Financial Times* found that appointees were not at all representative of the people for whom they provided public services, and the survey concluded by saying:

> If there is a new elite running Britain's public services... it appears the best qualifications to join are to be a businessman with Conservative leanings (Willman and Court, 1993).

The notion that businessmen with Conservative leanings were being targeted for top quango jobs was reinforced by other surveys. For example, in its own survey of the largest 38 quangos *The Observer* claimed to have "uncovered a picture of party patronage reminiscent of the rotton boroughs of the eighteenth century". Of these the paper found that at least 14 had chairmen who were "involved with busi-nesses that contibute to Tory coffers or have been party activists" (McGhie and Lewis, 1993). Such views were not confined to critics of the Conservative government: the Tory MP Nicholas Winterton told the BBC in no uncertain terms that "patronage today is more widespread than it has ever been in the history of our country" (Winterton, 1993).

Although the Nolan Committee admitted that the perception of bias had become widespread, it said the evidence was "circumstantial and inconclusive" because the issue of political bias "shades into a debate on the type of skills and personal qualities which are sought in the appointments system" (Nolan, 1995). Ironically, the lack of open-ness and transparency in the appointments process had prevented the Nolan Committee from reaching a conclusive judgement on bias. However, the Committee was sufficiently concerned – about percep-tions of bias, about the lack of balance on quango boards and about the lack of scrutiny of Ministers for example – to call for some long-overdue reforms, most notably an independent Public Appointments Commissioner with powers "to regulate, monitor and report on the public appointments process" (Nolan, 1995).

The Nolan Committee had been set up in 1994 to examine 'current concerns' about standards in public life, especially though not exclusively in relation to quangos. Nowhere in the UK were these 'concerns' more evident than in Wales, which had more than its fair share of quango-related scandals.

Quangoland: The Patronage State in Wales

Wales is a useful 'laboratory' in which to study the inner workings of governance because, in the course of the 1990s, it began to transform itself from a patronage state, based on unelected quangos, into a democratic state with a directly-elected Assembly. In this section we present a picture of quangoland in crisis, the pre-Nolan period when the system of governance in Wales was being called into question like never before. At the apex of the pre-Assembly political system in Wales stood the Welsh Office, a peculiar institution which never seemed to know if it was primarily the eyes and ears of Whitehall in Wales or the voice of Wales in Whitehall. As we'll see later, the Welsh Office's work was mainly of a policy nature, with local authorities and quangos doing the actual service delivery work. The main quangos, the executive NDPBs, were held to be necessary because they afforded specialised expertise which would not otherwise be available to the Welsh Office. Quangos thus functioned as specialised delivery arms of the Welsh Office and the latter was responsible for regulating their activities. But how were quangos actually regulated? According to the Welsh Office the regulatory system for NDPBs operated at a number of levels:

> NDPBs were established within a clear policy context, usually following legislation, providing their basic remit
>
> NDPBs framed their corporate plans in accordance with current policy and these were submitted annually to the Welsh Office in draft form for approval
>
> NDPBs were not intended to be subject to day-to-day direction, but to conform to current policy instead
>
> In the majority of cases the Chairs and Boards were appointed by the Secretary of State, who regularly met individual chairmen (there were no women)

The Welsh Office had regular meetings with NDPB chief executives and finance officers

Every 5 years each executive NDPB was subject to a Financial Management and Policy Review, which among other things reexamined the need for the NDPB (Welsh Office, 1993).

The great paradox of quangos in Wales, according to a parliamentary inquiry, was that "many NDPBs feel subject to unnecessary and intrusive restrictions at the same time that there is a public perception that they are inadequately supervised" (Welsh Affairs Committee, 1993). But this paradox is easily explained: aside from the quango-related scandals, the public perception was also shaped by the excessive secrecy which surrounded quango operations in Wales, and where there is secrecy people think the worst. Many quangos did themselves no favours in this respect, using commercial confidentiality as a pretext to absolve themselves of publishing their corporate plans for example, a practice deemed to be totally unacceptable (Welsh Affairs Committee, 1993).

A more robust regulatory regime became a necessity given the explosive growth of quangos in Wales: even the official figures showed that the number of quangos had doubled in Wales, from 40 in 1979 to 80 in 1991, a narrow definition which excluded bodies like TECs for example. Indeed, a 1995 survey, based on a broader definition, found nearly 350 quangos in Wales and accused the government of "seeking to conceal the scope of quango government by employing a very narrow definition of quangos" (CWD, 1995). However, even if we use the narrower official definition the vital statistics of quangoland in Wales in 1991 were still impressive:

The Secretary of State for Wales was responsible for making some 1400 appointments to 80 quangos.

Only 18% of all appointments were women.

In total these quangos employed 57,311 people.

The combined budget of the 80 quangos was £1.8 billion.

With the advent of new quangos after 1991, like the further and higher education funding councils and the NHS trusts, the combined quango budget in Wales increased to £2.3 billion, more than a third of all Welsh Office expenditure in 1993/94 and roughly equal to the entire local government revenue budget in Wales (Morgan and Roberts, 1993). Quangoland had become big business, and there were few areas of Welsh life that were untouched by these unelected bodies.

Controversies in Quangoland

As a small nation of just 2.8 million people Wales is something of a political village: rival politicians tend to be on better terms with each other than they care to admit, the key power brokers in politics and business are well known and, because information travels fast through a series of intersecting 'old boy' networks, it is difficult to keep secrets. In this village-like atmosphere the process of appointing people to positions of influence assumes a greater significance than it might in a more anonymous metropolitan environment, especially when the appointees are close to or active in the Conservative party, a minority party in Wales. With just 6 of the 38 parliamentary seats in the 1992 general election, and a position in local government border- ing on extinction, the Conservatives were thought to be extending their influence through the unelected state despite having been defeated at the ballot box in Wales. For a minority party to be control- ling the Welsh Office, and a growing network of power and patron- age, was perceived to be both unjust and unacceptable. This is the context in which we have to understand the controversies around Tory appointments in Wales in the early 1990s.

The appointments process began with a 'little list' of some 2000 people in the Welsh Office who had been put forward, or who had volunteered themselves, for public service. On the odd occasion when this subject saw the light of day, David Hunt, a former Welsh Secretary, said he would have been happier with a longer list of some 4000 names. While agreeing that the most transparent system of making appointments was through public advertisement, he said this route was only considered "where there are no immediate obvious candidates". But how did he, an MP for a Merseyside constituency, know the obvious candidates? When pressed on this matter Hunt confessed that he was "very much in the hands of those locally who know individuals and know their calibre" (Welsh Affairs Committee, 1993).

A rare shaft of light was shed on this process when Tony Lewis, a celebrity cricketer and a Welsh Conservative, was appointed to the chair of the Wales Tourist Board. In a session of the Welsh Affairs Committee on 23 November 1992 the following exchange took place between Tony Lewis and Gareth Wardell MP about the former's appointment:

> *Gareth Wardell MP*: You did not have an interview at all?
> *Tony Lewis*: Nothing at all
> *Wardell*: You had a letter just confirming your appointment as Chairman of the Board?
> *Lewis*: No, I had a telephone call to ask if I would accept tourism then I think I had the form and then I think the official letter came.
> *Wardell*: But in fact no interview, no situation where you were asked detailed questions by a panel of people, nothing like that?
> *Lewis*: No.
> *Wardell*: Just a straight forward telephone call asking you whether you would like the job and then in fact a letter confirming your appointment?
> *Lewis*: Yes.

The go-between for this less than demanding selection process was Sir Wyn Roberts, a Minister of State at the Welsh Office and one of the 'local hands' on whom David Hunt was so inordinately dependent in making public appointments. This suggests that the selection process may have been just as demanding for the other public appointments which caused so much controversy at the time. Let us recall some of the most prominent cases:

> In 1991 Jeff Sainsbury, a Tory councillor on Cardiff City Council and a close friend of David Hunt, was appointed to the Board of the high profile Cardiff Bay Development Corporation. The vacancy had been caused by the death of one of the Council's original nominees, but Hunt rejected the Council's new nominee.

> In July 1992 David Hunt appointed Ian Grist, a former Welsh Office Minister who had lost his seat in 1992, as the new Chief Executive of South Glamorgan Health Authority

> In August 1992 Mr Sainsbury's wife, Jan, was appointed Chair of South Glamorgan Family Health Services Association

> In October 1992 Carolyn Jones, the constituency secretary to Welsh Office Minister Gwilym Jones, was appointed to the Board of South Glamorgan Health Authority

> Mr O.J. Williams, a serial Conservative parliamentary candidate, was appointed to the East Dyfed Health Authority

In 1992 Phil Pedley, a former Tory councillor in the Wirral constituency of David Hunt, was made Deputy Chair of Tai Cymru/Housing for Wales

Sir Donald Walters, President of the National Union of Conservative Associations, was appointed as Chair of the Llandough Hospital Trust on top of his positions as Chair of the Welsh Development Agency and member of the Development Board for Rural Wales

Michael Griffith, who described himself as a "crusty old Tory", was appointed to the Chair of the Countryside Council for Wales, the Chair of Glanclwyd Hospital Trust and to the Higher Education Funding Council for Wales

Dr Gwyn Jones, an ardent admirer of Mrs Thatcher, was appointed Chair of the Welsh Development Agency until he was forced to resign in 1993; he was also appointed Chair of the Broadcasting Council for Wales and a BBC National Governor for Wales

Sir Geoffrey Inkin, a former Conservative parliamentary candidate, was appointed to the Chairs of the Land Authority for Wales and the Cardiff Bay Development Corporation (Morgan and Roberts, 1993).

Clearly, certain people held multiple offices, hence the likes of Sir Donald Walters, Sir Geoffrey Inkin and Dr Gwyn Jones were often described as the 'quango kings' or the "inner circle that runs Wales" (Jones, 1993). Pampered and privileged, these people were able to exercise their own powers of patronage, with devastating results in the case of the Welsh Development Agency (WDA).

The Crisis of the WDA

If the appointments process was one reason why quangos became stigmatised in Wales in the early 1990s, another reason was ineffective regulation. These two factors (political appointments and weak regulation) produced an explosive mixture at the WDA, where the most damaging scandals occurred. Founded in 1976 to promote economic development and environmental improvement, tasks which were second to none, the WDA rapidly became the flagship quango in Wales with a budget in excess of £170 million in the early 1990s. But this flagship was badly holed in December 1992, when a parliamentary inquiry uncovered a series of malpractices which spoke volumes for the lack of probity at the very top of the Agency. Among the most serious problems were:

> The loss of £1.4 million through the use of an inappropriate redundancy payments scheme and no disciplinary action was taken against the Executive Director responsible for this irregularity

> The irregular expenditure of £33,000 on a car scheme for senior executives which subsidised their private motoring costs

> An excessive £228,000 early retirement package for a senior executive (Mike Price), with a gagging clause which prevented him from speaking about the Agency or its then Chairman, Dr Gwyn Jones

> The appointment of Mr Neil Smith, an alleged fraudster, to the position of Marketing Director without checking his references, which caused enormous public embarrassment to the Agency

> Conflicts of interest and irregularities surrounding the payment of a rural conversion grant from the Agency to its own Chairman, Dr Gwyn Jones

> The failure to identify £308,000 in payments to consultancy firms for Operation Wizard, a project which examined the possible privatisation of Agency activities (Committee of Public Accounts, 1993).

Some of these malpractices occurred under the Chairmanship of Dr Gwyn Jones, who was appointed to the post in October 1988 by Peter Walker, then Secretary of State for Wales. The most astonishing thing about this appointment – to a job which was arguably the most influential in Wales after the Secretary of State – is that neither Walker nor the Welsh Office thought it necessary to seek a single reference for the candidate. This was one of the many improprieties exposed by the Committee, which concluded its inquiry by saying that "the standards of the Agency have been well below what this Committee and Parliament have a right to expect" (Committee of Public Accounts, 1993). This was also an indictment of the Welsh Office, and its lax regulation, which only added to the belief that quangos in Wales were "out of control" (Perry, 1993).

Most people in Wales are still at a loss to understand why things went so badly awry at the WDA, precipitating the worst crisis in the

Agency's history. The answers are to be sought in political patronage, which allowed Walker to appoint at whim, and weak supervision on the part of the Welsh Office.

Peter Walker met Gwyn Jones at a fund-raising event for the Conservative party at a time when the latter was thought to be looking for a Westminster seat. As a self-proclaimed 'man of action' Walker was suitably impressed by Jones and perhaps saw in him a reflection of himself, albeit in his younger days. What especially impressed Walker was Jones' image as a successful entrepreneur from the high-tech computer industry, the ideal type to inject a bit of private sector dynamism into a ponderous public sector agency. However, the decision to install Gwyn Jones in the top quango job provoked some disquiet among senior Welsh Office civil servants, so much so that Richard Lloyd Jones, the Permanent Secretary, made desperate last minute calls to third parties to ask 'who is Dr Gwyn Jones?', an outsider who had risen without trace in quangoland. In the absence of a simple character reference, the Welsh Office found itself knowing little or nothing about the person who, in a matter of hours, would be appointed to head the WDA. The little information he was able to garner left the Permanent Secretary less than ecstatic, not least because Jones' image as a dynamic and successful entrepreneur was said to be wide of the mark. These last minute anxieties among the civil servants counted for nothing, however, since Peter Walker had made up his mind: in pre-Assembly Wales the Secretary of State was king.

If Welsh Secretaries had plenty of scope to indulge in patronage, so too did the 'quango kings', though in a more modest way. Of all the 'quango kings' Jones was the most powerful because he alone had won the ultimate accolade, the imprimatur of Mrs Thatcher: in a rare visit to the Valleys, in March 1990, the Prime Minister was at pains to demonstrate her personal admiration for the handsome young man at her side, telling the local media "what a wonderful chap you have at the WDA" (Morgan, 1993). Politicians and civil servants at the Welsh Office quickly got the message: Gwyn Jones was beyond reproach.

The Agency's external performance at this time, especially with respect to inward investment, was moving in the right direction and this reinforced the message that Jones was untouchable. Internally, however, the WDA was imploding. Impatient with public service protocols, the Jones management style evolved into a cult of the personality: indeed the Chairman's office was transformed into a narcissistic shrine, adorned as it was with pictures and newspaper stories of Dr Jones doing the business. To get on in the Agency one had to get on with the Chairman and this management style spawned some very questionable appointments, many of them close associates of Dr Jones. Perhaps the final word on the Jones era ought to go to the independent inquiry which the Agency itself instigated in the wake of the crisis, which concluded by saying:

> It is something of a paradox that a period of outward success and fine results should have been accompanied by declining staff morale. We have received too many comments about low morale, poor communications upwards and downwards within the WDA and poor leadership to dismiss them as mere random moans from those who could not stand the heat or resented the changes made to the prevailing culture. We have to conclude that good staff management was sacrificed to the attainment of results. This may not matter in the short run but the price gets paid later as disaffection grows and eventually erupts into damaging leaks of truth and half-truths and into adverse publicity. An organisation cannot prosper if its morale remains at a low ebb for any length of time. We have also been told that staff generally lacked confidence in the Executive Group (Caines, 1993).

Being hauled before the Public Accounts Committee, and named as one of the bodies responsible for the decline in standards, is the greatest ignominy for a public body in the UK, and this must count as the WDA's darkest hour. The notion that malpractice was mitigated by the Agency's 'outward success' doesn't bear scrutiny because low staff morale finally took its toll in the aftermath of the Jones era: some of the better, and untarnished, managers jumped ship and the Agency's record in winning inward investment became less impressive. In other words there is a connection between accountability and performance: far from being a luxury we can ill-afford, public accountability is an essential ingredient in the recipe for well-motivated and successful organisations, and this is the most salutary lesson of the WDA's crisis in the early 1990s (Morgan, 1997).

If the crisis exposed irregularities in the Agency it also revealed the shortcomings of the Welsh Office, the WDA's regulatory watchdog. Although the Welsh Office was also named and shamed by the Public Accounts Committee, it managed to escape the opprobrium meted out to the WDA. Indeed, the then Secretary of State for Wales, John

Redwood, brazenly absolved the Welsh Office of any culpability in the affair, a stance which was considered bizarre even by his own standards.

The Welsh Office: A Suitable Case for Treatment

The Welsh Office used to induce schizophrenia in devolutionists because, having campaigned for so long to get it established, they were loath to criticise it too much lest it fell into disrepute. There was also something schizophrenic about the Welsh Office itself because, as we have seen, it was never sure if it should be the eyes and ears of Whitehall in Wales or the voice of Wales in Whitehall. In reality, of course, it was a bit of both, though the voice was the weaker of the two roles. Founded in 1964 as a 'territorial department' of Whitehall, the Welsh Office acquired more and more devolved functions from London, to the point where it was employing 2,400 staff by the mid-1990s. As we shall see in the next chapter, the idea of a Welsh Office provoked deep divisions within the Wales Labour Party. More predictably, perhaps, it also triggered bitter conflicts with centrally-minded politicians and civil servants in Whitehall. Readers of the *Crossman Diaries* will remember that Dick Crossman in particular was viscerally opposed to the idea of a Welsh Office, an "idiotic creation", he thundered, and "the result of a silly election pledge" (Crossman, 1976). Despite opposition from Whitehall the Welsh Office created a momentum for more functions to be devolved from London to Cardiff. More to the point, it also reinforced the demand for "democratic institutions to supervise the new growing bureaucracy in Wales" (Rowlands, 1972). It was this new political momentum that provoked the former Secretary of State, George Thomas, and an ardent opponent of devolution, to say "Our greatest mistake was to have set up the Welsh Office" (Osmond, 1977).

Whatever criticisms are made of the performance of the Welsh Office we should always remember its historical significance because, more than anything else, it furnished an institutional framework in which a Welsh system of governance could develop. But the Scottish Office, which had been established as early as 1885, seemed a much more robust institution. A senior civil servant in the Welsh Office told us in confidence that there was a very different 'mindset' in the two territorial departments: where the Scottish Office tended to be proactive and developmental in its thinking, the Welsh Office was inclined to be reactive and more dependent on Whitehall. These differences were shaped by differential resources (the Welsh Office being more constrained with respect to budgets and personnel), political hierarchy (the Welsh Office being the lowlier department) and geographical proximity (which encouraged greater cultural homogeneity between Cardiff and London). For all these reasons the Welsh Office rarely if ever departed from the Whitehall script, except when it was required to give a Welsh gloss to policy which was designed in London (Rhodes, 1988).

Although the day-to-day work of the Welsh Office took the same course regardless of who was in power, the personality of the Secretary of State could make a difference as regards the substance of policy and the style of policy-making.

The Tory-led Welsh Office

The notion of the unelected state used to be confined to the quangos but, under successive Conservative governments, it began to be applied to the Welsh Office as well because the Tories were perceived to have no electoral mandate in Wales. This perception became widely held during the John Redwood era for the simple reason that his pronounced Thatcherite views were manifestly at odds with Welsh political values. In fact the Redwood appointment appeared to flout the unwritten convention that the Welsh Office was a sanctuary for Disraelian Tories, those 'one nation' Conservatives in the tradition of Disraeli, Macmillan and Heath who believed that government had a moral obligation to play an active role in promoting economic renewal and social justice, a tradition which was uncomfortably close to Labourism.

The Disraelian tradition at the Welsh Office, however, was confined to the years 1987-1992, when Peter Walker and David Hunt were the Welsh Secretaries. The image of a proactive and interventionist Welsh Office was carefully cultivated by Peter Walker, who projected his own self-image onto the Welsh Office. Walker claims that he accepted the Welsh job on condition that "I can do it my way", a condition which Mrs Thatcher accepted (Walker, 1991). For three years he pursued his own brand of Toryism, a joint venture between the public and private sectors which was far removed from the Thatcherite mantra of 'public bad, private good'. The best illustration of Walker's Toryism was the Valleys Initiative, a grand-sounding package to regenerate the Valleys communities. With little or no new money, and nothing like as successful as Walker's autobiography claims, the Valleys Initiative was a triumph of style over substance. Still, it made Walker more popular in Wales than Labour critics cared to admit. Although this Disraelian tradition was continued by David Hunt, he manifestly lacked the style and stature of his predecessor.

The Disraelian tradition was anathema to John Redwood, a committed member of Thatcher's praetorian guard. But the real significance of his appointment was that it brutally exposed the conceit that Welsh political values counted for something in the choice of a Welsh Secretary. Indeed, in the short history of the office no Secretary of State was less disposed to Welsh political culture, an amalgam of socialism and civic nationalism, than John Redwood. Although he had a reputation for being cerebral and competent, Redwood often gave the appearance of being an exotic specimen in an alien habitat, an impression reinforced by his tragi-comic rendition of the Welsh national anthem. All these things conspired to give Redwood the look of a governor-general who had been imposed on a people against their will. That he sat as the MP for prosperous Wokingham only served to heighten the contrast between Wales and its Secretary and underlined the galling fact that the third successive Welsh Secretary had no seat in Wales. Under these circumstances it is not difficult to understand why the Welsh Office itself was considered to be part of the unelected state in Wales.

John Redwood's sojourn at the Welsh Office affected the substance as well as the style of politics. Civil servants, local government officials and quangocrats were told in no uncertain terms that 'the market' should be the engine of economic renewal. Another big change was made on Europe: whereas previous Welsh Secretaries had encouraged bodies like the WDA to develop a European perspective, these signals were reversed by Redwood, a leading Eurosceptic. These examples illustrate the difficulty of securing continuity at the Welsh Office when policy-making was so dependent on the whims of a Secretary of State who was neither elected by nor accountable to the people of Wales.

In the summer of 1993 it was widely reported that Redwood had summoned the quango chairmen to London to remind them of their duties and he was said to have warned them "I do not want Quangoland to grow too fat on functions transferred from local government." In fact nothing of the sort occurred: the meeting took place, but Redwood issued his warning *not* to their faces but through a press release the following day. After reading Redwood's fictitious account of the meeting the quango chairmen deputed Sir Geoffrey Inkin to express their disapproval.

As the debate about a Welsh Assembly got underway in earnest John Redwood and William Hague, the last Tory Secretaries, used the Welsh Office to undermine support for the Assembly by playing up the virtues of local government, a strategy which resonated with local Labour politicians like Billy Murphy, for example, the leader of Rhondda Cynon Taff. More controversially, Redwood claimed that Welsh Office figures showed that Labour's proposed Assembly would cost some £100 million, a move that made the Welsh Office look like a branch of Conservative Central Office. But what ultimately gave the Tory-led Welsh Office the appearance of being in but not of Wales was the occasion when John Redwood, in an effort to champion public expenditure cuts, returned an estimated £112 million from Wales to the Treasury, resources which might have been invested in social or economic renewal. From a Welsh standpoint it seemed that here was a Secretary of State using the Welsh Office not to promote Wales, but to champion a political creed which was largely alien to the country. Inadvertently, John Redwood proved himself to be a powerful recruiting officer for the cause of democratic devolution in Wales.

The Labour-led Welsh Office

After an eighteen year absence Labour re-entered the Welsh Office in 1997 with a commitment to rid Wales of the unelected state. In opposition the Wales Labour Party had talked loosely of a 'bonfire of the quangos' and of a 'quango-free zone' in which the Assembly "would take over most of the work being done by the 1400 appointees now running the unelected bodies, with the rest of their duties going to local councils" (Sparrow, 1995). This was ill-considered because, even in opposition, the Ron Davies team never intended to abolish quangos across the board; instead the aim was to render them more accountable and, wherever possible, to reduce their numbers through merger. Although the Assembly would eventually assume responsibility for quangoland, the Labour-led Welsh Office had to deal with these problems in the meantime.

The first ten months in office saw mixed fortunes on the quango front. Labour's promise of a new era of open and meritocratic appointments bore fruit when Elan Closs Stephens, the newly appointed chair of S4C, became the first person to head a quango by replying to an advertisement. What spoiled the new era, though, was the revelation that the two top posts in the WDA had been filled without recourse to public advertisements, raising the spectre that "an old boys' network" was far from dead in Wales (Settle, 1998). The decision to appoint without advertisement was defended on the grounds that it provided some continuity amidst so much flux, a reference to the merger of three quangos to form a revamped WDA. The new era was still a reality, said Peter Hain, because the new board members of the WDA were to be appointed "in the same fair and open way as the chairwoman of S4C" (Settle, 1998).

Despite these teething problems the Labour-led Welsh Office could fairly claim to have made good progress in redressing the two worst features of quangoland, namely an appointments process which lacked transparency and a weak regulatory regime. Having under-regulated the WDA in the 1980s, the Tory Welsh Office had begun to over-regulate it in the Redwood era, with the result that compliance stymied innovation. A robust regulatory regime had to strike a judicious balance between controlling the quangos and encouraging them to innovate. There was little understanding of this issue in the Wales Labour Party, where regulation was largely seen in terms of the control function. Other sections of the party, including some Labour MPs, criticised the Welsh Office for not having 'a bonfire of the quangos', as though the specialised functions of the WDA, for example, could be run by 22 unitary authorities. Striking the right regulatory balance between control and innovation is essentially a moving target, and the new Welsh Office team could not be expected to have resolved the issue.

The personality of the Secretary of State, as we have seen, could make a difference to the style and substance of policy-making at the Welsh Office, and the Ron Davies era was no exception. Indeed, one of the very first acts of the Davies team was so totally out of character for the Welsh Office that it sent shock waves through the UK civil service and provoked political resentment from some members of the Cabinet as well. The occasion for this untypical Welsh Office behaviour was the abolition of the nursery voucher scheme, which was announced in Wales ahead of anywhere else in the UK, making Whitehall and Edinburgh look pedestrian. Although this was largely the work of Peter Hain, with his well-known eye for publicity, the 'premature' decision was publicly defended by Ron Davies and his

Permanent Secretary at the Welsh Office, Rachel Lomax. However controversial it was outside Wales, the early abolition of nursery vouchers did something for the self-confidence of Welsh Office civil servants, who had never been in the vanguard of anything before.

Across a wide range of topics (health, education, training, economic development and the environment for example) the policy-making process began to be more inclusive and more interactive as Welsh Office civil servants were now actively encouraged to engage with external organisations. For example, the secretary of the Welsh Local Government Association, Colin Jones, told us that the advent of a Labour-led Welsh Office signalled a totally different atmosphere, as if someone had attached a 'welcome' sign to the Welsh Office. This new atmosphere was personified by Ron Davies and Peter Hain, who were far more open and accessible than their Tory predecessors and a good deal more proactive as well. In fact the main criticism of the Labour-led Welsh Office was that it launched rather too many new initiatives and consultative exercises, with the result that civil servants were too over-stretched to follow through properly, while outside parties were over-burdened by the demands of constant consultation.

Whatever the problems of this new era of democratic devolution it was possible to discern a fresh culture of engagement and openness among both politicians and civil servants at the Welsh Office. For civil servants the new ethos was embodied above all in Rachel Lomax, whose openness set an example as to how the Assembly should conduct itself. Ron Davies, Peter Hain and Win Griffiths, the original Labour team at the Welsh Office, did the same on the political front. Perhaps the best testament to the Labour-led Welsh Office is that, within a year, quangoland had lost its capacity to excite the tabloid journalists.

3. Labourland:
The Party and the People

If the scandals of quangoland contributed to a new climate of opinion in Wales in the 1990s, so too did the trials and tribulations of the Labour Party. In fact one cannot possibly understand the epoch-making events of 1997-99, from the referendum campaign to the National Assembly elections, without some knowledge of the history of Labourland, the network of individuals and organisations affiliated to or supportive of the Wales Labour Party. Arguably, these momentous events were shaped less by the cut and thrust of the referendum campaign, short and febrile as it was, than by the deeper structures of feeling which pervaded the subterranean world of Welsh politics in the postwar period, like the schizophrenic attitude towards devolution inside the Wales Labour Party. For much of the twentieth century it was possible to confuse Welsh politics with the politics of the Labour Party in Wales, such was its dominance in the political life of the nation. Political scientists have coined the term 'one-partyism' to describe prolonged electoral dominance by one party (McAllister, 1981). The most obvious examples of one-partyism in the UK are the Ulster Unionist Party in Northern Ireland and the Labour Party in Wales. As we shall see, however, one-partyism carries costs as well as benefits for the dominant party because the bigger and more durable the electoral majority, the weaker the incentive to maintain an efficient party organisation.

It seems astonishing that this history of one-partyism in twentieth century Wales has not been written, especially when Wales is the most loyal electoral heartland of British Labourism. Sadly, the flowering of Labour historiography in Wales in the 1970s and 1980s stopped short of the Labour Party in Wales: the miners found their historians (Francis and Smith, 1980), so too did the quarreymen (Jones, 1986) and Wales has been well-served by panoramic histories (Morgan, 1981; Williams, 1985; Davies, 1993). Local histories not-withstanding, the fact that there is no serious history of the Labour Party in Wales is a truly remarkable intellectual lacuna and it suggests that a metropolitan provincialism might be lurking in the professional ranks of political historiography in the UK.

Although this chapter is mainly concerned with recent develop-ments in the Wales Labour Party we need to understand the strong historic appeal of Labourism, especially in the Valleys, hence we begin by examining the historical growth of one-partyism and how it rendered Wales an integral part of a wider British political identity. Having looked at 'British Labour' we turn to consider 'Local Labour' because the institution of local government has been a major fiefdom of one-partyism in Wales. The third main theme deals with the advent of 'Welsh Labour', where we chart the schizophrenia over devolution inside the Wales Labour Party. Finally we examine a dimension of Labourland that remains something of a mystery even to ardent supporters, namely the party machinery through which agendas are shaped and controlled.

Labourland: The Rise of One-Partyism

Wales has been a fertile breeding ground for one-partyism for well over a century, ever since the Liberals became the dominant party in Wales following the extension of the franchise. The Liberal ascen-dancy, which in electoral terms endured until 1922, was said to be more pronounced in Wales than in any other part of the UK (Morgan, 1981). Although the Labour ascendancy in Wales may be formally traced to the 1922 election, the post-Liberal era had set in years earlier, as the raw issues of coal and trade unionism displaced the nonconformist issues of land reform and religion. In a painfully condensed way we might say that the transition from Liberalism to Labourism, from one kind of one-partyism to another, was due to the burgeoning coal industry and the Klondike working conditions which it spawned. The notion that coal determined the level of prosperity and so much else besides was perhaps best captured in the statistical research of Brinley Thomas, who showed in graphic detail how things like the marriage rate and the growth of livestock in Wales were closely related to the selling price of coal (Thomas, 1962).

These statistical exercises greatly impressed the historian Gwyn Alf Williams, who used the population data to highlight the fact that Wales was out of step with the UK in having a declining net loss of people between 1871-1901, a trend which reflected the awesome labour requirements of the colliery districts of Glamorgan and Monmouth. Most remarkable of all was the decade 1901-11, when

Wales became the only country outside the USA to register a plus in the migration tables on account of the remarkable population flows into these southern colliery districts. This phenomenal coal-induced immigration into the valleys of south Wales amounted to nothing less than a social, linguistic and political revolution. It was a period of "boundless self-confidence" within the working class in Wales, and there is no better symbol of this mood than the revolutionary syndicalist statement of 1912, the *Miners' Next Step* (Williams, 1982).

If these were the social forces which damaged the Liberal hegemony in Wales the issue which finally destroyed it came in 1919, when the Lloyd George government refused to implement the Sankey Commission's recommendation to nationalise the mines: in the eyes of the miners Sankey killed the Liberals in Wales.

The "boundless self-confidence" which characterised the pre-war period was shattered by a post-war climacteric – the Depression – which lasted for much of the inter-war period: in these years nearly half a million people were forced to quit Wales, mostly from the crisis-ridden southern coalfield. For a small country to lose a fifth of its entire population in less than 20 years was calamitous; indeed, in terms of social disruption and identity crisis "the Depression plays the same role in Welsh history as the Famine in Irish" (Williams, 1982).

Political pluralism was one of the less obvious casualties of the Depression. If pre-war Edwardian Wales sustained a wide range of political views, the post-war Depression narrowed the range, especially in the south Wales valleys. The Depression may have strangled social confidence but it standardised political loyalty because, in the face of the life-threatening problems of unemployment, sickness and starvation, the only feasible solution seemed to be what was on offer from British Labourism, namely the use of central exchequer resources. With little or no capacity for self-renewal within Wales, the task of social and economic regeneration was manifestly a task for central government, hence winning power in London became the single most important act in the political repertoire of Labourism. In the most depressed areas of the UK (the 'Special Areas' as they were christened in the 'thirties) this single political act assumed a totemic significance. It is in this chilling collective experience of the Depression, when Wales had no indigenous resources, other than for survival, that we have to understand the majority appeal which British Labourism has had for the Welsh working class and why the latter has been so loyal to the Labour Party.

There was no better illustration of such loyalty than the 1931

71

General Election: while the Labour vote slumped in the UK as a whole, decimating its Westminster seats, its share of the vote in Wales actually increased and it returned 16 Labour MPs, thanks largely to the loyalty of the south Wales valleys. As one interested observer put it:

> In South Wales we were glad to note that we had fared better than any of the other old Labour strongholds – better than Scotland or the North East (Griffiths, 1978).

A history of one-partyism could be written in which the growth of Labour in Wales is portrayed as a linear and effortless political triumph up to 1945. But such a history would be blind to the challenges, some of them finely balanced, which the Labour Party faced in securing its political hegemony. Posterity might forget these challenges, but party activists knew that the Communist Party was considered to be a real contender in certain places and at certain points, even if its political presence was nothing like as influential as its industrial presence. But the key challenges came in Rhondda East in a series of elections, when a right wing Labour candidate eventually beat off the very best the CP had to offer, namely Arthur Horner in 1931 and 1933 and Harry Pollitt in 1945, when the CP lost by less than a thousand votes.

In his last political memoir Labour's Jim Griffiths said with characteristic honesty that the CP was a genuine threat right up to 1945, not least because of its strong base in the grassroots of the miners' union and its highly effective local leaders, Arthur Horner and Will Paynter in particular. Fortunately for the Labour Party, he said:

> their top leaders were absorbed in union work and, throughout the careers of Horner and Paynter, politics was a secondary consideration. One wonders what might have happened if Horner had used his influence and devoted his gifts and talents mainly to the organisation of the Communist Party. I think it might have presented a major challenge to the Labour Party in South Wales (Griffiths, 1978).

The localised political contests with the CP, fraught as they were, actually confirmed the majority appeal of British Labourism, all the more significant since these contests were fought in areas which considered themselves to be in the vanguard of the industrial class struggle, proving that workers could quite easily support the CP in industrial matters whilst backing the Labour Party in parliamentary politics.

Although most Labour leaders seemed surprised by the scale of their historic election victory in 1945, the result was entirely predictable in Wales, where Labour's share of the vote rose to 58.5%, compared to 48% for the UK as a whole (Morgan, 1981). From a Welsh standpoint the Attlee government's most important contributions were twofold: jobs and welfare. The most active regional policy of the twentieth century was prosecuted immediately after 1945 to ensure that the full employment enjoyed during a war economy did not evaporate with the peace. On the welfare front there was a good deal of pride throughout Wales in the fact that two local MPs – Aneurin Bevan and Jim Griffiths, respectively the Ministers for National Health and National Insurance – were centrally involved in creating the welfare state, the most important reform for raising the quality of working class life in the twentieth century. Whatever the shortcomings of the Attlee government, its contribution to jobs and welfare seemed to confirm the belief at the heart of British Labourism, that winning power in London was a political act second to none.

The so-called 'age of affluence' was the first of two long periods of Tory rule in the post-war period, 1951 and 1979, when Labour seemed fated never to return to office. But long periods of one-party government tend to corrupt and exhaust the office holders, and the revival of Labourism in 1964 owed as much to Tory exhaustion as to the merits of the Labour Party. Even so, the following election of 1966 marked a unique political occasion in Wales: with a 60.6% share of the vote, and 32 of the 36 Welsh MPs, this was British Labour's greatest triumph in Wales. Neither before nor after did Labour poll so well, hence 1966 can rightly be seen as the high-water mark of one-partyism in Wales. At this point Labour could rightly claim to be the 'national party of Wales' since it had won rural seats which in England, and even Scotland, would have been expected to return Conservatives or Liberals. This capacity to win across the political spectrum, from miners and steelworkers in the urbanised south to hill farmers in the rural north, owed much to the broadly based intake of Welsh MPs in 1966, eleven of whom were Welsh-speakers (Osmond, 1977). In retrospect there was a great paradox about Labour's finest hour in Wales because:

the more Labour won the more it had to represent and the more it had to lose. Labour became the Welsh political establishment more clearly than ever before precisely at a moment when the intractability of Welsh economic problems was becoming more evident. It was also a time when a new generation of Welsh youth was becoming fired by an acute sense of linguistic and cultural crisis. Labour had invoked Welshness as an issue and had therefore unwittingly contributed to what was to become the most widespread and fundamental re-definition of Welshness that had taken place for generations. Labour had set itself up to represent and administer a Wales that was already in many of its most vital parts moving away from it (Stead, 1995).

The Labour Party had little time to savour its greatest ever triumph in Wales. Within months Plaid Cymru had secured its first Westminster seat at a by-election in Carmarthen, narrowly beating one of Labour's most nationalist-minded candidates. Even more unnerving for party and government were the by-elections in Rhondda West in 1967 and Caerphilly in 1968 – Labourist heartlands if ever there were – when astronomical Labour majorities were substantially reduced by huge swings to Plaid Cymru. In the wake of these hitherto unthinkable results a miners' official told Jim Griffiths, the patron-saint of Welsh Labourism, "all your seats are marginal now" (Morgan, 1981).

Although apocalyptic scenarios about Labour's imminent demise in Wales failed to materialise, the growth of one-partyism had reached its limits. In the following decade Labour lost most of its seats in 'Welsh Wales' and consequently looked less like the national party of Wales. If generational and cultural factors played their part in Labour's fall from grace, so too did burgeoning economic problems. Indeed, the relative decline of the UK economy had begun to claim cities and regions in England which added to the competition for scarce public funds. Relative decline, in other words, compromised the core idea of British Labourism: that winning power in London would automatically allow a Labour government to channel resources to its heartlands throughout the UK.

Modest as it was, the nationalists' success in the valleys in the 1960s and 1970s was based not on their separatist agenda but on the bread and butter issues of social and economic regeneration – this was the message from Rhondda West in 1967 and Caerphilly in 1968. The key ingredients for a strong nationalist challenge in Wales are the same now as they were then, namely an embittered electorate and a Labour government. Back in 1973, just two years before he died, Jim Griffiths said that Plaid was "the biggest challenge to Labour in Wales" and he attributed their appeal to three factors: (i) a convenient vehicle for the Welsh protest vote under Labour governments (ii) growing fears about language, culture and identity in Wales and (iii) the revolt against 'remoteness', which he feared would swell the ranks of Plaid Cymru if Labour failed to promote a measure of self-government for Wales (Griffiths, 1978).

Although the 1997 election gave Labour its best share of the Welsh vote in General Elections since 1966, with 54.7% against a mere 9.9% for Plaid Cymru, suggesting that one-partyism was far from dead, the much closer Assembly and European elections seemed to confirm Griffiths' fears, as we'll see in chapter seven.

The growth of one-partyism paradoxically obscured Labour's decline as an effective political organisation in Wales, the hallmarks of which are declining individual membership (hence the decision to cease publishing the figures since 1963), low levels of participation among party members and a more sceptical trade union movement which is less able and willing to pay the bills. Party membership seemed to be weakest in those areas where Labour enjoyed its biggest electoral majorities, which is not surprising because the bigger the majority the weaker the incentive to maintain an efficient party organisation (McAllister, 1981). Having been the political establishment in Wales the Labour Party is regularly criticised for the fact that its heartland areas, the Valleys, have some of the worst conditions in Europe despite some 70 years of one-party rule. The explanation for this, according to one critic, is because:

> Episodes of corruption have punctuated a permanent complacency founded on unassailable majorities. Domination of constituency politics has been matched by a strangle-hold on local authorities which has only recently been challenged in South Wales by some Plaid Cymru successes in the Labour heartlands. The security of tenure of the town halls enjoyed by the Labour Party has created a conservative and reactionary political culture which has presided over the decline of our working-class communities (Adamson, 1996).

At the end of the 1990s Welsh political affiliations were becoming more difficult to predict than at any time in the post-war period. In terms of Westminster politics the historic attachment to British Labourism remained, though the high point of one-partyism was probably gone. Within Wales, however, one-partyism was being assailed in local politics and in the new national politics of the Assembly and Labour's municipal record shaped popular attitudes in both contests.

Municipal Labour: A Little Local Difficulty

It was in the world of local government that Labour's political hegemony was first established, so it is not surprising that one-partyism should be most pronounced at this local level. For the best part of the twentieth century the Labour Party has dominated town halls and county halls throughout Wales and, in most authorities in the Valleys, it has held unbroken office the whole time. Although Labour-led local authorities have earned some notoriety in recent years it is easy to forget that these authorities were all that stood between life and death in Wales during the Depression. Appalling standards of public health, due to a noxious cocktail of poor diet, sub-standard housing and general poverty, marked Wales out from the rest of the UK in the inter-war period, and these problems fell largely on local authorities. In contrast to the penny-pinching response in Welsh rural districts, Labour-led local authorities in south Wales maintained a high level of expenditure on health, housing and education – often exceeding the permitted spending levels – and they did so because "social duty came before concern for the financial protection of ratepayers" (Morgan, 1981).

For much of the post-war period, too, Labour-led local authorities played a full and active role in extending the services of the welfare state, particularly in education. With seemingly impregnable electoral majorities local Labour parties became the key brokers of power and patronage in their communities. Because of the weak business culture in Wales the corporate community spawned few civic or political leaders, hence the personnel of local Labour establishments have come from the trade unions, the public sector and the professions. As local government budgets mushroomed after 1945 the leader of the council became a local notable of some considerable influence, none more so than the former railway worker Lord Heycock, leader of Glamorgan County Council, the biggest local Labour fiefdom of them all until it fell victim to the 1974 local government reorganisation.

Large and durable electoral majorities give the governing party a near permanent monopoly of power and these one-party states are clearly more open to abuse than pluralistic systems, where rival parties help to keep the governing party on its toes. Aside from this problem of one-partyism, which is particularly acute in the Valleys, Labour-led local authorities in Wales have had to contend with three problems which are common to all authorities throughout the UK – the problems of centralisation, calibre and credibility.

A creeping *centralisation* has characterised central-local government relations since the inter-war period as successive governments have sought to contain and control local government finance. This trend reached ludicrous proportions under the Tories, when central 'capping' controls effectively removed local spending decisions from the locality and the balance between central and local finance was so skewed that barely more than 20% of local authority expenditure was funded from local tax, compared to at least 40% in France, Germany and the US (House of Lords, 1996). In addition, the transfer of local government functions to central government and quangos has devalued the status of the institution of local government.

Concerns about declining councillor *calibre* have been expressed more or less continuously for the past 50 years, but this problem is compounded by the devalued status of local government, an institution which now manifestly lacks real power, thus making it even less attractive to high-calibre men and women.

The third systemic problem concerns *credibility*, or rather the lack of it when UK local government elections have a low turn out of some 40%, one of the lowest in Europe. Furthermore, participation in local decision-making often starts and ends at the polling booth, at least for those who bother to vote.

Some of these problems have been exacerbated in Wales by the tradition of one-partyism, as the Welsh Office frankly acknowledged in 1998 when it launched its White Paper on the modernisation of local government in Wales:

> Local government derives its power and legitimacy from its local democratic mandate. But a quarter of wards were uncontested in Wales in the 1995 local elections. And one fifth of Welsh councillors were returned unopposed.... This is a culture which can deny a council the capacity to lead its local community effectively, and which can open the door to instances of corruption and wrongdoing. And we have evidence of this in Wales. Many councils are dominated by a single party with no effective opposition to promote debate within the council chamber. Uncontested seats

and single party domination can give rise to concerns that party structures and processes might take over from council structures and processes, and undermine effective monitoring. Reflecting this culture of inwardness among councils, and the monolithic nature of many of our councils, there is too often within communities a culture of apathy and cynicism about local democracy (Welsh Office, 1998).

It is difficult to recall a government being so candid about the problems of local government, especially when its own party controls so much of it. But the frankness served a purpose: the Labour government was determined to modernise the structures and practices of local government, some of which were residues of the nineteenth century. A census of Welsh councillors conducted by the Local Government Management Board found them to be totally unrepresentative of the population at large: the local political elite was a gerontocracy, since fewer than one in five were women, less than half were employed, they were more likely to be over 70 than under 45 years of age, only a handful were drawn from ethnic minorities and, of the total, 57.5% were Labour, 8.5% were Plaid, 7.5% were Liberal Democrat, 3.7% were Conservative and the remainder were so-called Independent.

On top of these enduring problems local government also suffered from turf wars between county and district councils, the two-tier system which was abolished in Wales in 1996 in favour of a single tier of 22 unitary authorities. Although this single-tier system makes local government more transparent, in theory at least, Welsh councils had their fair share of controversy both before and after 1996. The spectre of patronage was not confined to quangoland. In 1993, for example, Labour councillors in Brecknock district council were charged with acting like 'feudal barons' in the allocation of council houses, and this was just one of a number of councils criticised by the Ombudsman for allocating houses on "a quite arbitrary basis which gave undesirable scope for abuse" (Jacobs, 1993).

The Sorry Saga of Rhondda Cynon Taff

Ironically, the most widely reported problems in local government in Wales occurred *after* the more transparent single-tier system came into effect in 1996; there again, the new system made it easier to detect the problems. Of all the 22 newly formed unitary authorities none has so far experienced the traumatic problems of Rhondda Cynon Taff (RCT), the second largest council in Wales after Cardiff, covering some of the most deprived areas in the UK. The amalgamation of four authorities – Rhondda, Cynon Valley and Taff Ely District Councils along with a significant part of Mid-Glamorgan County Council – was clearly not made in heaven. Quite apart from the myriad organisational problems that had to be addressed, the political atmosphere *within* the Labour Group left a lot to be desired, to say nothing of relations between Labour and Plaid, the main opposition party. Secret deals were struck within the Labour Group between Rhondda and Taff Ely councillors to share the spoils of committee posts, leaving Cynon Valley members with nothing except animosity. Political considerations, rather than administrative logic, persuaded RCT to adopt the organisational model of Mid-Glamorgan county council because this model had thirteen departments, each of which needed a committee, giving a total of 26 posts for patronage purposes when deputy chairs were included. No other local authority in Wales had so many departments and this was one reason, among many others, why RCT failed to achieve the expected economies of unitary authority status.

Within two years RCT's problems began to leak out, starting with housing, where the council was severely criticised by an independent consultant for operating a points system which was hopelessly biased in favour of Rhondda, the home base of Bill Murphy, the Labour leader. Although RCT has the worst housing problems in Wales, it failed to spend £900,000 of its grants allowance in 1997 and only a fraction of the budget for slum clearance was spent. The underspend was the result of "poor efficiency levels" and, having noted that the top management response had been "conspicuous by its absence", the consultant said that staff would have to abandon their "tribalistic and insular culture and offer a service for all RCT" (Thomson, 1998). Other problems in 1998/99 included:

Depleted balances: RCT began life with £26 million in balances, money needed for emergency situations, but these had fallen to dangerously low levels by the end of 1998/99, and well below the recommended minimum level of £5 million. These high balances were depleted because chronic budget overspends were financed out of this emergency fund, a symptom of very poor financial management

DSO Losses: Soaring losses in the council's Direct Service

Organisation were initially estimated to be £3.5 million for 1998/99, but this sum was later revised to £5 million, triggering the threat of major redundancies. At bottom these losses stem from weak management, which led to such things as high absenteeism, wrong orders, poor invoicing and materials which could not be accounted for, giving the DSO the worst record in Wales

Nant-y-Gwyddon Tip: the cost of reducing pollution at this politically-sensitive refuse tip was estimated to cost a minimum of £900,000, while the cost of closing the tip was estimated at anything up to £9 million

Welsh Office: RCT faced unprecedented warnings that the Welsh Office could take over the management of the council unless order was restored

Management: underlying all these other problems was the simple fact that RCT management – officers and politicians – were not up to the job and, as the new chief executive put it, a new management culture would need to subscribe to a 'must do' rather than the traditional 'can't do' philosophy (RCT, 1999).

Some of these problems, along with some very serious criticisms, formed the brunt of a District Auditor's management letter on 30 March 1999, but this was considered too sensitive to publish ahead of the local elections on 6 May, so it was released later that month instead. In other words, voters were not aware of how bad the situation really was when they went to the polls.

To avoid direct control by the Welsh Office, RCT agreed to a 'Joint Improvement Strategy and Action Plan' to reverse the dire financial plight of its Direct Service Organisations, thus giving the council more time to negotiate a solution with the General and Municipal Workers' Union. (Alun Michael was keen to mollify the G&M union at this delicate point because he wanted their votes in the race for the Labour leadership). Faced with the prospect of up to 200 redundancies in the summer of 1999, RCT council workers organised the first large-scale protest at the National Assembly.

RCT may have inherited problems – socially deprived communities and a gargantuan organisational challenge not the least of them – but this does not explain, still less justify, basic managerial incompetence, political tribalism and crass patronage. RCT had some good stories to tell (like care for the elderly and a recently improved education service for example), but these islands of good practice were overwhelmed in the public mind by a sea of mediocrity. In addition to poor services and escalating losses in its DSOs, the council compounded its poor public image by self-indulgent spending on new chains of office, regalia and mayorial costs when it faced cuts of £50 million in its first three years. In themselves these were small items of expenditure, but they spoke volumes for the Labour Group's perverse and insular priorities and these 'small' things were clearly not forgotten on 6 May, election day.

RCT may have had the worst problems adjusting to the new world of unitary authority status, but it was not alone. Towards the end of 1998 it was reported that 14 councils were making illegal losses on their direct labour departments, all of them Labour-led apart from Plaid-run Gwynedd. More damaging still was the catalogue of alleged fraud at four Labour-led councils, Vale of Glamorgan, Cardiff, Merthyr and, above all, at Blaenau Gwent, where half the entire membership, including the leader, was arrested for alleged financial irregularities (Settle, 1998). It was a rich coincidence that on the very day the Assembly opened for business the former leader of Blaenau Gwent, Bernard Assinder, was in court pleading guilty to fraud, provoking calls for the Assembly to launch "a radical crackdown on town hall mismanagement" (*Western Mail*, 1999).

Although these problems usually involved a small number of politicians, indeed a tiny fraction of Labour's total complement, they nevertheless devalued the whole of local government in the public mind. It was to redress this popular perception that the government launched its radical agenda for local government modernisation, in which the two key aims were to raise the quality of local services and to encourage more democratic local decision-making. Huge variations in service quality are apparent in Wales, attributable not to genuine local diversity but to significantly different levels of council efficiency.

New models of local government are now beginning to emerge in Wales, with the traditional committee system giving way to a cabinet system, a shift which promises to make local decision-making more transparent and accountable the more the monitoring and executive roles are separated. If councils are serious about increasing participation, however, more accessible and decentralised structures will need to be introduced, like neighbourhood committees and citizen juries for example, to give local people a role in the running of their services.

How well councils respond to this twin challenge – of better service provision and more democratic decision-making – will determine whether the relationship they have with the Assembly will be more or less cooperative. This relationship may not be as cosy as some people assume because a partnership will be predicated on performance and those councils who fail to perform may find that the Assembly is a more demanding interlocutor than the Welsh Office. Although local government was always more open to public scrutiny than the quangos, it still left much to be desired in terms of democracy, transparency and high-quality service provision. In the years ahead Labour-led councils will have to prove that one-partyism, to the extent that it survives, is not inconsistent with the new challenges facing local government. The advent of democratic devolution is therefore an opportunity and a threat to local authorities in Wales, particularly to Labour-led local authorities.

One Party, Two Traditions: Centralism vs Devolution

One of the distinguishing features of the Labour Party is that it is the only party with a major presence in 'the periphery' which is committed to the maintenance of the British state, the issue which most conspicuously sets it apart from its nationalist rivals, the SNP in Scotland and Plaid Cymru in Wales. To the extent that it has championed the national claims of Scotland and Wales, as it did until the 1920s, the Labour Party has always sought to realise these claims in and through the British state, and the likes of Keir Hardie saw no inherent contradiction between devolution and the maintenance of a British state. Such equanimity did not last. In the years after 1945 Welsh Labourism became increasingly schizophrenic, torn between *centralism*, the dominant tradition since the Depression, and *devolution*, the flag of those who wanted the claims of Wales as a nation to be recognised in the structures of party and government. The conflict between these two political traditions has been a constant if subdued theme in the subterranean world of Welsh politics, occasionally surfacing to provoke a crisis for a party which was adept at dealing with class-based issues but easily unsettled by national or territorial questions. One such crisis, as we have seen, was the 1979 referendum, when the centralists won the day with arguments which were first deployed by the political generation of the Depression, Bevan and Griffiths in particular.

In the pantheon of Welsh Labourism the centralist tradition takes its inspiration from Aneurin Bevan, even though his credentials render him a more ambiguous role model than is commonly thought.

Certainly the conventional understanding of Bevan is that he was first and foremost a *British* socialist who had little or no time for things Welsh. Perhaps the main evidence for this view of Bevan as an incorrigible centralist is the devastating attack he delivered on the newly created institution of the Welsh Day debate in Parliament on 17 October 1944. It is worth dwelling on this historic occasion because Bevan is often misquoted, giving the impression that the speech was more centralist-minded than it actually was. At a key point Bevan said:

> My colleagues, all of them members of the Miners' Federation of Great Britain, have no special Welsh solution for the Welsh coal industry which is not a solution for the whole of the mining industry of Great Britain. There is no Welsh coal problem (Bevan, 1944).

Some leading writers on Welsh political history have seized on this passage as evidence of Bevan's centralism, but for some obscure reason they omit the reference to coal in the final sentence (Osmond, 1977; Smith, 1997). Far from being a minor pedantic point, the omission gives a totally different meaning to the speech, reducing both the complexity and the ambiguity of Bevan's position. Indeed in the very same speech Bevan is at pains to emphasise that:

> Wales has a special place, a special individuality, a special culture and special claims, and I do not think that this is the place where any of them can properly be considered. There may be an argument – I think there is an argument – for considerable devolution of government, but there is no need for a special day in Parliament and this Debate has demonstrated it completely (Bevan, 1944).

To the extent that this speech was informed by a coherent philosophy, which is unlikely, it was a plea for things to be considered 'in their proper place', that is for centralism *and* devolution where they were appropriate. In economic matters, like coal, steel and agriculture for example, he favoured a British approach on the grounds that only central government had the power to temper the market. On the other hand, in matters of language, art, culture and education he welcomed a distinctively Welsh approach. This thinking was developed at greater length three years later when he argued that "distinctive cultures, values and institutions should flourish, so as to

endorsed a demand, expressed the previous year by the Executive, for a directly-elected Welsh Council as the top tier of a reformed local government system (Osmond, 1977). This commitment to democratic devolution coincided with, and actually owed a good deal to, a more assertive and imaginative Labour Party organisation in Wales, probably the first and last occasion when this Welsh party apparatus showed it could think and act for itself. Unfortunately, this new, pro-devolution current within the party apparatus was first stymied (by Welsh Labour MPs opposed to devolution) and then destroyed (by the 1979 referendum), a result which showed that the party apparatus had been too self-referential in its commitment to devolution: in other words it focused too much on securing committee and conference votes and too little on winning the hearts and minds of voters at large.

Understandably, no section of the Labour Party in Wales had any appetite for raising the cause of devolution after the ignominy of the 1979 referendum defeat. But this shattering experience was tempered in 1987 by something even more shattering, namely Labour's third successive election defeat. By now it was clear, even to those who had viscerally opposed devolution, that the governance question was back on the agenda, not least because of the over-centralisation of power in Whitehall, the emasculation of local government, the growth of unelected quangos and a Welsh Office regime which seemed imperious and unaccountable, all of which was part of the democratic deficit in Wales.

Resurrecting its earlier policy, the Executive of the Wales Labour Party used the medium of local government reform to advance the cause of democratic devolution. This was the *smuggler's road* to constitutional change: an elected Wales-wide body was, quite consciously, smuggled into being via the provisions for local government reform in Wales, a stark contrast to Scotland, where an elected parliament was openly demanded as an expression of national identity. At its 1990 annual conference the WLP received the results of a two year consultation exercise, in which over 80 organisations had expressed their views on reforming the structures of local and regional government in Wales. As a result of this exercise conference committed itself to the following proposals:

A single-tier of most purpose local authorities

An elected body for Wales to deal with the functions of the Welsh Office and its nominated bodies

> Instead of a referendum there should be a manifesto commitment to local government reorganisation

> The pace of reform in Wales should parallel progress towards regional government in England (WLP, 1990).

A further sign of the new climate came early in 1990 when Neil Kinnock, then Labour Party Leader and the most famous opponent of devolution in the 1970s, said that "in the decade ahead we are going to see the national boundaries of Europe diminish in importance while regional and local identities grow in significance" (Kinnock, 1990). By the time of the 1992 election Labour was once again committed to a directly-elected Wales-wide body and some former opponents of devolution had reversed their position in the light of the centralisation of power under Thatcherism (Anderson, 1992).

By predicating the pace of constitutional change in Wales on progress in England, however, devolutionists queried the WLP's real commitment to a directly-elected institution at a time when their counterparts in Scotland were energetically building a pro-devolution coalition in the form of a Constitutional Convention. Faced with demands for a similar cross-party vehicle in Wales the WLP suddenly found itself in a dilemma: should it lend its weight to a cross-party movement as in Scotland or should it go it alone? There was never a shadow of doubt as to what the WLP Executive would do. It would go it alone because this seemed like the least-cost option on two counts: first, it meant that the WLP did not have to share control with other organisations; and second, going it alone seemed the surest way to preserve party unity in Wales because centralist-minded Labour MPs would never entertain joint action with nationalists.

The decision to settle the constitutional issue *within* the party, rather than through cross-party collaboration, meant that the WLP was acting in time-honoured fashion, almost as though it were programmed to act in this way. This was its response in the 1950s, when it resolutely opposed the cross-party Parliament for Wales Campaign. It was also the response when it faced a more recent cross-party challenge from the Campaign for a Welsh Assembly (CWA), which was launched in 1987. Modelled on the Campaign for a Scottish Assembly, which had been formed in 1980, the CWA was undoubtedly the most significant coalition for democratic devolution, the nearest Wales ever came to having a cross-party Constitutional

Convention. Chaired by Jon Owen Jones for the first four years, until he stepped down to become a Labour MP, the CWA attracted significant support from the grassroots of the WLP. Indeed, the organisation of the CWA seemed to shade into the WLP itself because constituency parties and local authorities decided to affiliate in growing numbers. In the light of later events it is significant that the area where the CWA faced the greatest hostility was Rhondda, where the local Labour MP, Allan Rogers, warned the Campaign to stay off his patch.

The architects of the CWA had carefully chosen the name 'Assembly' rather than 'Parliament' so as not to alienate the WLP Executive, a sensitivity that would not be reciprocated. Right from the outset, in fact, the WLP Executive tried repeatedly to strangle the CWA and sought to prohibit party members from having anything to do with such dangerous liaisons. The Labour Executive stepped up its offensive against the CWA when the latter decided to change its name to the Parliament for Wales Campaign in 1993 and sought legislative and financial powers (Andrews, 1999).

Matters came to a head when the Campaign organised a well-attended Democracy Conference in Llandrindod Wells in March 1994, when party affiliation counted for less than a commitment to democratic devolution. The WLP Executive spared no effort to prevent MPs and party members from attending; in fact it even organised a rival conference on the same weekend in Newport, which proved an embarrassing failure. Nevertheless, such was the pressure that prominent devolutionists in the party, like Rhodri Morgan and Wayne David, eventually withdrew from the Llandrindod conference. In the event only three Labour MPs defied the party ban – Paul Flynn, Peter Hain and Jon Owen Jones – all of whom were summoned before the Executive and reprimanded for liaising with outside bodies and for defying the injunction to keep the devolution debate inside the party. The WLP Executive maintained that Wales should never follow the Scots for the simple reason that the nationalists were strong in Scotland but weak in Wales, a mantra which justified their go-it-alone strategy. In other words there is no mystery as to why a cross-party Constitutional Convention did not emerge in Wales as it did in Scotland and the answer is twofold: the 'exclusivist' politics of the WLP and the weakness of Welsh civil society (Jones and Lewis, 1998).

The contest between centralism and devolution had put the Wales Labour Party under strain on a number of occasions in the past but now, in what was to be the key encounter of the twentieth century, the contest would produce the most paradoxical result of all: the party's policy would triumph, but the party itself would end up in disarray. To understand this paradox we need to understand how the party works.

How Labour Works: The Party Machine in Wales

The contest between centralism and devolution can be traced through the changing structures of the Labour Party in Wales, where even the party's name has been a hotly contested issue. Although Wales was one of the original electoral heartlands of the British Labour Party it was not until 1947 that a unified Welsh party organisation was created through an amalgamation of the regional councils of the north and the south. In fact the South Wales Regional Council of Labour (which comprised constituency Labour parties, trades unions, trades councils, women's sections and other affiliated bodies) was itself only created in 1937, and then largely at the instigation of the South Wales Miners' Federation to counter the surging influence of the Communist Party in the union and in the valleys generally (McAllister, 1981). Without this external threat it is by no means certain that a regional council would have emerged when it did since the party's National Executive Committee (NEC) had been less than enthusiastic about regional organisation. Knowing full well that centralism infused the party's corridors of power, Jim Griffiths rightly considered it a major achievement when the Welsh Regional Council of Labour was finally established in 1947.

The Welsh Council of Labour, as it was commonly called, effectively operated like a regional branch-office and this is certainly how it was perceived by the party's three most powerful institutions, the Parliamentary Labour Party (PLP), Conference and the NEC. To understand how the party works, either in Britain or in Wales, is no easy matter because things are sometimes other than what they seem. While the NEC represents the different sections of the party, according to the constitution the Executive is "subject to the control and directions of the Party Conference, the Administrative Authority of the Party". Conference may be the sovereign body of the party in theory, but in practice its formal powers have been tempered by the block votes of the trade unions on the one hand and the de facto independence of the PLP on the other.

Political scientists long ago noted how the British Labour Party privileges some forms of representation over others: for example one finds functional representation in the trade union section of the NEC and social representation in the women's section, but "many other aspects of democracy – concerning 'real' members, territorial representation and equal weighting of each individual vote – have been ignored" (Kavanagh, 1982). It seems little short of remarkable that an electoral heartland like Wales, or any other nation and region for that matter, should have no representation on the ruling NEC, a testament perhaps to the party's impervious attitude to territorial questions.

Despite occasional mutterings of protest from the rank and file the Welsh Council of Labour accepted its branch-office status and its first secretary, Cliff Prothero, an ex-miner, was not one to rock the boat. With the growth of national consciousness in the 1960s, and the unnerving nationalist upsurge in particular, the Welsh Council of Labour became more assertive after 1965, when Emrys Jones became the Council's new secretary. Unlike his predecessor Jones thought that the Council should involve itself in policy matters as well as the more prosaic organisational issues, hence during his tenure the Labour Party in Wales launched a whole series of study groups into different aspects of Welsh life, including the Council's views on constitutional change in preparation for the Commission on the Constitution (Osmond, 1977). In other words a more exacting political environment, combined with new and more committed personnel in the Welsh Council, made the party organisation in Wales a genuinely innovative body for the first time in its history. Not surprisingly, perhaps, it was during this period that the relationship between the Welsh parliamentary party and the party organisation in Wales became estranged like never before, as the former felt challenged and threatened by the latter's pro-devolution stance.

The relationship between MPs and the party organisation in Wales was always rather tenuous since MPs divided their activities between Westminster and their constituencies, with the result that the annual conference of the Welsh Council of Labour never attracted more than a tiny minority of Labour MPs, except when devolution became high politics in the mid-1970s. Thereafter, however, the annual conference grew in both numbers and stature as the Labour Party Leader began to find it a useful platform for addressing the party in Wales. It was at the annual conference in Llandudno in 1975 that the Council officially changed its name to 'Labour Party in Wales', even though some delegates preferred 'Welsh Labour Party'. The new name was consciously meant to signal the primacy of the party over the country, though in more recent years the term 'Wales Labour Party' has crept into use. The sensitivity surrounding the party's nomenclature in Wales is not as trivial as it might seem; on the contrary it suggests that the days are long gone when the party hierarchy could ride roughshod over national sentiment.

Much the same could be said of the trade unions, which have never played less than a crucial role in the politics of the Labour Party in Wales. Since the early part of the twentieth century trade unionists have made demands for a Wales-wide organisation to coordinate the disparate activities of the Welsh labour movement, but these demands foundered on a lethal mixture of local parochialism and central hostility from the London headquarters (Griffiths, 1980). But just as the party organisation in Wales came to see the benefits of better country-wide organisation, so too did the trades unions in Wales. Indeed, the creation of the Wales TUC in 1973 was itself a triumph for the cause of devolution because, formed as it was in the face of stiff opposition from the British TUC, it would not have happened were it not for a determined alliance between the TGWU and the NUM in Wales. Fittingly, the first chairman of the Wales TUC was the inspirational Dai Francis, the Welsh miners leader and a committed devolutionist. Significantly, the draft constitution of the Wales TUC provided for the Executive of the Labour Party in Wales to be represented on its General Council, but the inaugural conference voted against the new body having any formal links with the Labour Party in Wales or any other party, a sign that Welsh politics had become more fluid by the 1970s (Osmond, 1977).

With the retirement of the energetic Emrys Jones, and the referendum defeat in 1979, the party organisation in Wales reverted to type and became a pedestrian branch-office once again. Before devolution was resurrected in the 1990s the most controversial issue concerned the appointment of a new secretary, a conflict which revealed the fragmented nature of power in the British Labour Party. At the behest of Neil Kinnock, the Leader, the NEC had taken the unprecedented step of over-turning a sub-committee decision in favour of Anita Gale, who many people considered not up to the job. But, having appealed against the decision with the support of her union, Gale eventually secured the job in 1984 after winning over an arbitration panel. What this seemingly trivial issue revealed was that neither the party Leader nor the NEC could prevent the appointment of a regional secretary; that power, in other words, was more diffuse than was commonly thought. One senior party insider said that opponents of Anita Gale consoled themselves with the thought that Wales was "a safe and sleepy political backwater, so it didn't matter about the calibre of the party's staff". When Ms Gale retired in 1999, the last seven years of her office would go down as the most momentous in the party's history, so much so that the words 'safe' and 'sleepy' would not immediately spring to mind.

As the party developed its proposals for the Assembly in the 1990s it became clear that the twists and turns on policy were partly attributable to the diffuse pattern of power in the Wales Labour Party and, in particular, to the fact that there was no formally recognised head of the party in Wales. The absence of a recognised party leader meant that rival centres of power and authority could co-exist until the issue was finally resolved by the annual conference of the Wales Labour Party, the key decision-making body in Wales. Apart from the annual conference, however, there were other centres of power and authority during the devolution saga of the 1990s, namely the General Secretary of the Wales Labour Party, the Secretary of State or the Shadow Secretary, the Chair of the WLP Executive, the Chair of the Welsh PLP and, not least, the Chair of the WLP Policy Commission, of which Ken Hopkins was the sole occupant.

Although the annual conference of the WLP is the highest authority in Wales, the day-to-day affairs of the party are managed by the General Secretary in association with the WLP Executive. As General Secretary Anita Gale liked to stress, while she *reported* to the party Executive in Wales, she was *accountable* only to the NEC in London. If there was a potential conflict of interest between the WLP and its General Secretary this rarely occurred in practice because Anita Gale would always work in close conjunction with the Executive, or rather with an *inner circle* on the Executive.

Of all the institutions in Labourland none carries as much power to shape the course of events in the party as the Executive, a body which is as much a mystery to political scientists as it is to the general public in Wales. Composed of all the various sections of the party in Wales – constituency parties, trade unions, MPs, MEPs and affiliated bodies and the like – the Executive is not the most open and communicative of bodies, which makes it all the more surprising that it has never been properly studied. Drawing on his unique experience as a former member of the Executive and ex-employee of the Wales Labour Party, Andrew Davies offered a rare glimpse of the way it works when he told us that:

The Wales Labour Party Executive is a very compliant body, dominated by the trade unions, and it's through them that Anita Gale gets her way. There's a big turnover in the constituency section of the Executive, so talented people tend not to stay too long. The trade union section on the other hand has the lowest turnover, so these are the most permanent elements on the Executive.

This alliance helps to explain how the party managed its internal politics during the most difficult years, from the formation of the Policy Commission in 1992 to the Assembly elections in 1999. Essentially what we have is the General Secretary working hand in glove with an inner circle of the most trusted members of the Executive, in particular with Terry Thomas (the political organiser of the GMBW and the Chair of the Executive in 1997) and Ken Hopkins (the Secretary of Rhondda Labour Party and the Chair of the Policy Commission). This alliance was underwritten by long-standing personal ties and political loyalties, and the fact that Terry Thomas was one of the arbitrators who helped Anita Gale secure her job in 1984 would have cemented the alliance.

Throughout the 1990s the Executive was determined to maintain complete ownership of the party's Assembly proposals and the inner circle became deeply suspicious of initiatives which ran counter to the party line or which threatened party unity as it understood these terms. From the standpoint of the inner circle the main threats to its ownership came from two directions: from a new pressure group within the party called Welsh Labour Action and, more surprisingly, from Ron Davies. Set up in 1992 to lobby for a robust Assembly, Welsh Labour Action was threatened with disciplinary action by an Executive which questioned its very right to exist inside the party.

What seems much more difficult to understand, however, is why Ron Davies, the Shadow Secretary of State, should have been perceived as a threat at the very highest levels of the party in Wales. For one thing Davies was considered an 'outsider' by the party machine in both Cardiff and London, an impression which deepened as he pushed the party beyond its comfort zone and into territory which the inner circle considered potentially damaging to the party, like proportional representation for example. As Shadow Secretary of State he may have been the most senior Labour figure in Wales, but this counted for little inside a party machine where there were multiple centres of authority and rival factions, some of which were less than impressed with his criticisms of Labour-controlled local authorities and his growing popularity among nationalists.

In their different ways Ron Davies and Welsh Labour Action had much in common: both were 'outsiders' in terms of the party machine, both wanted to push the party beyond its instincts on devolution and both wished to create a more democratic, more pluralist party in Wales in which Welshness was an asset to be nurtured in the name of a modern civic nationalism rather than an attribute to be jettisoned in favour of a desiccated notion of Britishness.

Ostensibly about the Assembly, these struggles were also about introducing democratic devolution into the Labour Party, which had become more centralised during the 1990s. In a self-proclaimed "war-cry for total modernisation" in the party a key advisor at Labour headquarters in London went so far as to say that: "Labour must replace competing existing structures with a single chain of command leading directly to the leader of the party" (Gould, 1998).

Against this paean to centralisation a more devolved model for modernising the party would begin to emerge in Wales in the wake of the internal battles of the 1990s and a radical overhaul of the Executive, to render it more accountable to ordinary party members, would figure prominently on the reform agenda. Having unleashed the forces of democratic devolution in Wales it would have been truly bizarre had these forces touched everything except the Wales Labour Party.

Two: The Campaign

4. Unfinished Business: Labour's Devolution Policy

The news was hardly encouraging. Having been dispatched to Wales to test public attitudes to devolution, Philip Gould (the party's polling expert) felt obliged to send a sombre memo back to Millbank Tower, the Labour Party's London headquarters. On the basis of focus group meetings which he had convened just four months ahead of the referendum, Gould, a shrewd polling expert, was disturbed by what he had found. For someone who knew little of Wales, Gould proved to be remarkably prescient in his assessment of the situation. The referendum, he wrote to his Millbank colleagues, was going to be problematical for a number of reasons:

> It could be close, and the no vote could win. The most recent poll shows a lead of 10% with a large number of undecideds. These focus groups show the yes vote only just ahead of the no vote (49% to 45%).
>
> Awareness is so low that the eventual vote is very hard to call.
>
> The arguments against are quite widely and deeply held. More no arguments were spontaneously listed in the groups than yes arguments.
>
> There is a lot of emotional resistance to the Assembly. People in Wales feel vulnerable and uncertain both on a personal and national level. They do not want things to start going wrong and are suspicious and nervous of change.
>
> I am not sure that I trust the polls. If anywhere was to suffer from a 'spiral of silence' it is Wales, which has an electorate that combines such a lack of confidence with a public desire to please and a subtle and convoluted approach to political issues (Gould, 1997).

Why should the Assembly, a key part of Labour's programme of constitutional reform, elicit such 'emotional resistance' from some of the party's very own supporters? The answer to this question is to be found not so much in the cut and thrust of the referendum campaign as in the deeper structures of feeling, the political schizophrenia in particular, which pervaded the Wales Labour Party (WLP) for most of the post-war period. Indeed, in this chapter we shall argue that the trials and tribulations of Labour's devolution policy in Wales, both before and after the debacle of 1979, owed much to the unresolved schizophrenic tension between two political traditions – centralism and devolution – which had co-evolved in the Welsh labour movement.

From John Smith to the 1997 White Paper:

Labour had fought the 1992 election with a nominal commitment to devolution. The then Leader of the Party – Neil Kinnock – showed no real enthusiasm for the devolution project, a coolness shared by Barry Jones, then Shadow Secretary of State. Indeed, according to one highly placed Labour source, while "Jones dutifully did a tour of local Labour parties in Wales to explain the Party's devolution proposals, in doing so he managed to undermine the whole idea".

This reluctance to promote the devolution issue is understandable to any student of Labour politics. The strong urge to maintain Party unity, so easily dismissed by many outside of the movement as a 'gag' on argument and debate, is deeply rooted in the Labour tradition of solidarity and collective action. Producing a policy for devolution that would command a workable consensus inside the Party has always eluded the Party leadership. Small wonder, then, that in the 1992 election, there was no real appetite for campaigning on an issue that was likely to 'distract' the Party from the 'real business' of winning the election and putting Labour back into power after thirteen long years in opposition.

But Labour's defeat in 1992 helped revive the devolution issue. Three events in that year combined to draw attention again to Labour's 'unfinished business'. Firstly, shortly after the General Election, the Wales TUC at its Annual Conference passed a resolution calling for the setting up of a 'Welsh Constitutional Convention' (along the lines of the one already operating in Scotland) and even drew up a framework document out of which such a Convention might emerge. This initiative trigged alarm inside the Wales Labour Party Executive, reflecting "its nervous attitude towards cross-party collaboration on any issue, and least of all Welsh devolution"

(Osmond, 1995). Secondly, in June 1992 the Executive responded by establishing its own 'Constitutional Policy Commission', charged with the task of updating key areas of Party policy ready for the next General Election and, in particular, "to re-examine policy in relation to the creation of a directly elected Welsh Assembly".

Thirdly, John Smith, the newly elected labour Leader, appointed Ron Davies as the new Shadow Secretary of State for Wales. In Davies' own account of the meeting when the post was offered, Smith spoke of the need to get on with completing Labour's 'unfinished business' and asked him (Davies) to "develop the same policies for Wales as we have for our planned Scottish Parliament". Davies needed no persuading. He had talked earlier about how strongly he had been affected by Labour's defeat in June 1992 and of how "any lingering doubts" he might have had about the need for a Welsh Assembly were "dispelled" by the prospect of a largely Labour-voting Wales forced to face a further five years of Thatcher rule from Westminster. Nor could anyone else doubt the strength of Davies' conviction following a speech he made in Treorchy in November 1992, when he argued for an elected Welsh Parliament and more powerful local government in Wales. This speech, described by one commentator as "the most radical speech about Wales by a Labour politician for a generation", set Davies on a course that was to result in a referendum in favour of the setting up of a National Assembly for Wales.

The course, as might have been predicted, was never going to be a smooth one. Davies had to produce proposals that would keep both local government and the PLP happy. The concerns of the former were fuelled by impending government plans to introduce unitary authorities in Wales; the latter, by their interest in not allowing any talk of an Assembly to undermine Party unity. Davies began to try to build consensus by releasing a paper, *No Devolution – No Deal*, which he succeeded in getting all sections of the Party to support.

As Davies took his first steps towards trying to build a coalition of support for the Assembly in Wales, Labour's Policy Commission submitted an interim report, *The Welsh Assembly: the Way Forward*, in 1993 to the Wales Labour Party Conference. It was clear the Commission was proceeding cautiously. Conference called for further detailed examination of the structures and powers of an Assembly and committed the Party to a "wide-ranging consultation process" on the issues involved. The Commission's caution was understandable in the context of Labour Party politics in Wales. There was no real support either in the Wales Labour Party or the Party's Executive for a Constitutional Convention. A Convention would have meant Labour, in the words of one source, "having to bring in Plaid and this would have caused mayhem in the Valleys". And a Convention – which would almost certainly have raised the issue of electoral reform – "would only have pushed the Party in Wales close to civil war". While this claim may have tended towards the hyperbolic, it served to underline the problems facing Davies in seeking to bring his Party with him on devolution.

The following year (1994) saw a number of significant developments. The sudden death of John Smith – a keen devolutionist – inevitably raised the question of how enthusiastic his successor might be for the devolution project in Wales. When Blair sought Davies' support in his leadership bid, Davies offered it on three conditions: that Blair would bring in a bill banning fox hunting; support devolution; and continue with Smith's commitment to the principle of 'inclusiveness' as a building block for the Assembly (the 'i' word, as we shall see later, was to be the code for some form of proportional representation in elections to the Assembly). Although Davies got the reassurances he wanted, one of Blair's first acts on becoming Leader in July, was to appoint Dr Kim Howells as part of Jack Straw's new Shadow team at the Home Office, with special responsibility for 'constitutional reform'. Dr Howells was at that time a known anti-devolutionist and Davies was later to record that he saw the posting as an attempt by Blair to 'rein back' on the devolution commitment.

The emergence of the new Labour Leader coincided with the Policy Commission issuing a consultation paper, *Shaping the Vision*, which tentatively raised three questions: on tax-varying powers, the power of making primary legislation and whether the Assembly should embrace a new method of election. From here, in the Autumn, the Commission organised six "public consultation meetings" around Wales. These sessions were described as "little advertised... low-key affairs. They were held on weekdays rather than during the evenings or weekends – times which minimised participation" (Osmond, 1995).

While the Commission was touring Wales, Davies tried to push the Liberal-Democratic notion of a *Senedd*, as a device for building cross-party support for the devolution idea and suggested the body should have "significant financial and legislative autonomy". All this was carried in a front-page story in the *Western Mail* in November, on the eve of a visit by Blair to Cardiff. The story implied that Blair was generally supportive – and the following day Davies issued a press release claiming that "Tony Blair has put himself and the Party solidly behind a *Senedd* for Wales". Unfortunately, a few days later, Davies was forced to backtrack after Alistair Campbell, Blair's Press Officer, wrote to the *Western Mail* denying Blair had made any such commitment.

In December there were further problems for Davies. Llew Smith – in a warning to Davies – published a 'personal manifesto' with the uncompromising title, *The Welsh Assembly: Why it has No Place in Wales*, which restated the familiar 'devo-sceptic' line. This was followed by the Wales TUC's submission to the Policy Commission, which counselled caution on devolution portraying it as a troubling 'diversion' from the main project of returning a Labour Government.

TUC fears about 'diversions' seemed confirmed when John Major, in a series of speeches and interviews given around the turn of the New Year, said he would be putting Labour's devolution plans at the top of the agenda for next General Election. This declaration threw the national leadership on the defensive (perhaps remembering the success Major had enjoyed late in the 1992 campaign when he played the 'union card'). While there was little that could be done at this stage about Scotland – where commitments had already been made about tax and law making powers and on PR – there was pressure to soft-pedal on these matters in relation to Wales. It was as if Blair's team in London had started to view devolution as a political liability.

In Wales itself a difficult meeting of the Policy Commission took place in Transport House (Cardiff) in March. Davies was surprised to find Dr Howells present and suspected he had either "been put there by Blair... or by some connivance between Anita Gale and the Leader's office". Davies challenged Howell's right to be in attendance but was over-ruled by Gale. His suspicion that Howells was there to play some kind of 'watch-dog' role seemed confirmed when Howells lodged objections to the proposed size of the Assembly (100 members), its having full legislative powers and to any suggestion of the method of election containing a PR element. This took Davies by surprise, since shortly after Howells' appointment, Davies had outlined an Assembly proposal with 100 members and full legislative powers, a proposal which Davies later insisted Howells had supported. Howells' change of tack appeared to hint that the Party leadership was seeking to dampen down expectations about the Welsh Assembly.

The Commission next met at South Glamorgan County Hall in an atmosphere which several of those present described as "bloody" and "extremely unpleasant". Much of the meeting saw Davies and Rhodri Morgan ranged against Kim Howells and Terry Thomas, with Wayne David MEP trying to act as an 'intermediary'. Some time before the meeting Andrew Bold (the Commission's secretary) had written a report for the Commission which had been leaked to the *Western Mail*. Davies' account of what happened as soon as the meeting started makes interesting reading: "When I arrived I found myself facing what was basically a kangaroo court. Ken accused me of leaking the report, which was not true, but caused a row. I had gone along with a series of amendments to put to the report, but found a majority – built around Ken Hopkins, [the Commission Chair], Kim, Terry and a couple of TU representatives – stitched up against me. They successfully opposed all my amendments, and just wanted to endorse the document as it was – with no reference to electoral reform and no primary legislative power". What happened next, according to Davies, was to give him some room for manoeuvre in subsequent negotiations: "Over lunch – and by this time there were only 7 people left – I talked to Wayne and worked out a form of words acceptable to him along the lines of: there might be a case for primary legislative powers in certain areas, and agreeing that the Executive should resolve the question of the electoral system. As far as I was concerned this left the door open just far enough to allow me to come back to these issues later".

The "open door" Davies referred to proved difficult to pass through. A meeting of the Executive, called to discuss a draft of *Shaping the Vision*, resulted in Davies losing the argument to Thomas and Hopkins, in what was said to be a "very nasty" and "ill-tempered" confrontation. Davies had made a particular point at the meeting about the importance of the Assembly elections containing a PR element, arguing that the broader the political base of the Assembly, the greater its popular legitimacy, so making it harder for any Westminster government to try to weaken or scrap it. The argument was lost both inside the Commission and inside the Executive.

In May 1995 *Shaping the Vision* was approved at the Wales Labour Party Conference with little debate. The report claimed the Assembly would "assist the process of local government reorganisation" (then taking place in Wales), rejected the case for "general powers of primary legislation", said "measures should be taken to ensure... gender balance" and crucially came down in favour of the First Past the Post method of election. It now seemed that Labour's internal debate on devolution had been settled in favour of the 'minimalists', but there were many in the Party who saw the matter as being far from resolved.

Prominent among those unhappy about the minimalist package was Gareth Hughes, a leading figure in Davies' Caerphilly constituency and a member of the Policy Commission and the Party Executive. On 10th April Hughes had written to Anita Gale, arguing the Commission had been wrong to reject primary legislative powers for the proposed Assembly. In his letter he rejected the Commission's claim in its report that the case for such powers had not been established. He argued: "I attended half the public consultations and by far the main view to emerge was that [these powers] were... necessary... to make the Assembly a body that could meet the aspirations of the Welsh people". Hughes pointed out that in January the Commission heard the Wales PLP express a view in favour of primary powers, adding: "It was around these views that Andrew Bold was asked to write a draft document. I was dismayed that by the next meeting to discuss Andrew's draft, the Commission had moved to a new position that there was no case for primary legislation." Hughes made it clear that he – along with others – was not prepared to leave the matter here, indicating they would run an internal Labour Party campaign, to beef up the proposals for an Assembly.

The first reaction came with the formation of Wales Labour Action, a pressure group within the Labour Party, to campaign for a more radical and 'inclusive' approach to the business of Assembly making. Chaired by Gareth Hughes, the group won the backing of several CLPs, some trade unions and prominent Labour figures like Rhodri Morgan and the MEPs Eluned Morgan and David Morris. Predictably the Group came under fierce attack from the Party leadership in Wales, led by Anita Gale.

An appeal to Hughes and his colleagues to shut-up and close ranks was made by Peter Hain (Campaign Co-ordinator for the Labour frontbench) who argued: "Any kind of squabble about this now could blow the chances of getting a Welsh Assembly for another generation". Hughes, who seemed to imply that the draft had been watered down under pressure "from London", was also strongly censured by the Party's Executive, who struck two blows. The first (at its 18th September meeting), called for Gale to lead an investigation into the membership and objectives of Wales Labour Action. The second was to come later the following year: on 15th July 1996 the Executive voted to remove Hughes as an Executive representative on the Policy Commission reconvened to consider PR for the Assembly elections.

Like Hughes, Davies, too, was unwilling to accept the verdict of Conference. His tactic was to appeal directly to trade union leaders in Wales, telling them there was a need to reconvene the Policy Commission "to move things on" and in this got the key backing of George Wright (Regional Secretary of the Wales TGWU) and Derek Gregory (General Secretary of UNISON, the big public sector employees union).

Union support was crucial for Davies, since Union representatives dominated the Executive. At a September 1995 Executive meeting Davies was to claim, "I got my way". It was agreed to re-open the issue of voting reform and to consider giving the Assembly 'additional power' – specifically the power to reform the Quangos. For Davies these were vital steps forward. Voting reform allowed him to return again to his central theme of making the assembly 'inclusive'. The opportunity to revisit the issue of electoral reform was given to Davies by a clever piece of drafting in the final, approved version of *Shaping the Vision*. This referred to the first-past-the-post system as the 'preferred version' for electing Assembly members, giving Davies the opening he needed to return to the issue. And on the matter of 'additional powers', Davies was later to argue that "in practice, legislative power to deal with Quangos were, in effect, primary powers".

In 1996 the Wales Labour Party Conference was presented with a report which represented a major advance on *Shaping the Vision*. The report, *Preparing for a New Wales: A Report on the Structure and Workings of the Welsh Assembly*, included a call for an Assembly "which will operate on a more consensual basis and whose workings will be more open and accessible".

From here on events began to move in Davies' favour. By this time, according to Davies, "Blair was coming round to the idea of PR for the Assembly, to put us in line with Scotland", but he "was also interested in greater Lib-Lab co-operation" for reasons that went beyond any calculations about the best way of garnering broad support for Labour's devolution plans for Wales. At the same time, by Davies' own reckoning, "Ken [Hopkins] was becoming more amenable, realising that I was now likely to be Secretary of State in Blair's first government – and he also realised that Blair himself was now leaning towards PR" at least for Wales and Scotland, if not for Westminster.

Blair's apparent new-found enthusiasm for PR found expression in a major speech he made in Wales on 28th June on Labour's devolution proposals where he said: "It is vital that all of Wales feels included in the process of devolving power and feels represented in the Welsh Assembly". More significantly, earlier that month Davies had organised a meeting in Blair's office where Hopkins and Thomas were told by Blair that he wanted PR and "won them over by asking for their help in delivering it". Equally significantly – as a sign of the tensions within the leadership of the Labour Party in Wales – this meeting was to have taken place without Anita Gale being told. Having got wind of what was happening she was said to have been "furious" at her exclusion. As a result, when the meeting took place, she made sure that Andrew Bold, one of her team, was there.

One other important event took place in June – when Blair declared Labour's intention to legislate for devolution in Scotland and Wales through a referendum after the election. Blair's original position was that this measure was essential for Scotland, but not necessary in Wales. Davies talked him out of this, arguing that such an approach was "untenable". The decision to call for a referendum played badly with some Welsh Labour MPs. One, Paul Flynn (Newport West), came close to resigning the Party Whip over what he saw as a "betrayal" by the Party leadership. By Flynn's account: "We had agreed on a compromise to make sure a referendum on devolution would not be part of Labour's manifesto. Yet now, without a discussion with Welsh MPs, that policy has been shattered" (Flynn, 1999). Flynn added – prophetically as it turned out – "I was worried a vote on the issue of devolution would cause deep wounds in the Labour Party in Wales". Blair's announcement (made on 28th June) came only three days after Davies had spoken against holding a referendum, arguing a General Election victory would be mandate enough to set up an Assembly. Exactly what Davies did or did not know about Blair's calculations is still a source of some dispute. If backbench Welsh Labour MPs had not been consulted, it was also being suggested by some MPs that Davies himself was unaware of any plan for a referendum until three days before the launch of the new policy in Cardiff. What was apparent, however, was backbench anger at what was seen as an abrupt policy U-turn. Allan Rogers (Rhondda) declared himself "flabbergasted", telling the *Western Mail* he would campaign for a No vote if a PR pledge was included in the promised legislation. A similar line was taken by Llanelli MP, Denzil Davies, who stated that if the Welsh Assembly were to contain a PR element, then "I won't, with a heavy heart, be supporting a Welsh Assembly". Other opinions were mixed. Alan Williams (Swansea East) and Llew Smith (Blaenau Gwent) welcomed the referendum proposal, but only because it would allow people to vote Labour in the General Election – and then vote against an Assembly in a separate vote. Ann Clwyd (Cynon Valley) came out in support of a PR component, but objected to the idea of a referendum. In general, though, the new policy was accepted by the Party in Wales – and by the Welsh press – and the Policy Commission would be reconvened to look again at the PR issue. The Party's readiness to swallow the new deal was another powerful demonstration of its instinct for unity, its loyalty to Blair's leadership, as well as a keen appreciation of the imminence of a General Election it was poised to win. What made the new conformity all the more remarkable was that the weekend before, at the Party's annual conference in Swansea, no delegate or MP had mentioned the 'R' word except to belittle it. Prominent among the 'belittlers' was Alun Michael, who asked why a vote was needed for a manifesto pledge which proposed to make so few changes in how Wales would be governed.

Nevertheless, the decision to opt for a referendum gave Davies the opportunity to link the Assembly with PR, thus making it easier to secure the backing of the other pro-devolution parties in Wales. At Davies' request, Blair then wrote formally to the Welsh Executive asking them to re-open the PR issue, "which, of course, they did", and the appropriate resolution was moved by Terry Thomas, on behalf of the GMB. Davies was keen to move quickly on the issue: "I wanted this settled well in advance of a General Election, based on a decision of Conference... I didn't want it forced in at the Manifesto writing stage" when it could possibly have opened up old wounds.

On 15th July 1996 the Executive agreed to reconvene the Policy Commission, instructing it to report back in time to place a report before the 1997 Wales Labour Party Conference. The Commission set off on another round of consultations, taking in CBI Wales, the Wales TUC, the Welsh Parliamentary Labour Party, the Welsh Local Government Association, other parties and the Labour Party in Wales itself. In the course of a series of Commission meetings in September 1996, it was proposed to slim down the Assembly to 60 members, based on the now familiar 40:20 formula. Davies asked Hopkins to put this idea to Thomas, which he did with the result Thomas took the lead on the issue on the Commission, which in turn meant "the GMB had been brought into line".

The gathering momentum in favour of electoral reform found expression in the Commission's Report and its recommendation that the Assembly be elected according to "an element of proportionality" (specifically, the AMS system) was unanimously approved at the 1997 Party Conference. By endorsing the principle of PR, Labour was reinforcing its "commitment to a new, more open style of politics that will ensure that the Assembly enjoys the confidence of all the people it serves".

Flying Blind: Labour's Referendum Campaign

During the summer of 1996 some in Labour circles were beginning to think ahead about how to best manage the referendum campaign should Labour win the next election. The first portents were not encouraging. In July 1996 Andrew Davies (a former member of the Executive and a Party official) was approached by Peter Hain to take the post of 'Special Projects Officer' to do preparatory work for the campaign. Hain, sceptical of the ability of the Wales Labour Party to do the job, was keen to draw upon Davies' experience as an election campaigner. But his appointment was initially blocked by Anita Gale and nearly 10 months passed before Davies was finally confirmed in post, in April 1997.

The fight over Davies' position pre-figured some of the wider problems that were later to weaken Labour's referendum campaign. In the first place, the 10 month delay meant vital time was lost on doing the kind of preparatory work essential for effective campaigning. More important, perhaps, was how the dispute over Davies' appointment revealed, right from the outset, some of the lines of conflict and division between many of those who were going to form the core of Labour's referendum campaign team. Even if these tensions had been absent, Labour still faced a formidable campaign task. Despite the heady rhetoric around the Assembly which came out of the 1997 Wales Labour Party Conference, the issue was not one which had enthused the wider Party membership. For the most part the often rancorous debate which locked together Ron Davies, the Executive, the Policy Commission and Blair's office over the structure and functions of the Assembly had largely by-passed local Labour parties and the great majority of Labour's 25,000 members in Wales. Nor was it clear how actively Labour local authority leaders would work for a 'Yes' vote, and there was – crucially as it turned out – little appreciation of public sentiment. As Andrew Davies put it: "We were all to some extent flying blind. We had no idea, at the start, of what real popular feeling was about the Assembly".

Shortly after the return of the new Labour Government in May 1997, two steps were taken to push forward Labour's campaign. These meetings served to underline Labour's lack of a clear campaign strategy, the little time in which to formulate one and the deep-seated tensions within the campaign team.

Late in May there was a meeting, in Millbank, of Labour's 'National Referendum Co-ordinating Committee', chaired by Margaret McDonagh, then the Party's National Campaign Co-ordinator. There was an inauspicious start when it had to be pointed out to McDonagh that the Welsh referendum was to be held in 1997 – and not 1998 as she seemed to think. It was eventually agreed to do Focus Group research and in-depth polling to better gauge the 'national mood' in Wales, though it was not possible to immediately implement this idea because of budget constraints. In the end Wales was awarded the bulk of Labour's referendum budget, over Scotland, after Dave Hill (Labour's Chief Press Officer) made the point that in Labour election-speak: "Scotland is the majority seat and Wales is the key marginal". Hill also stressed that the referendum would be very different from the running of the recent General Election campaign, using the analogy of the 1975 referendum campaign on Britain's entry into Europe, "where Wilson needed to appeal for a 'Yes' vote over the head of the Labour Party". For this reason it was argued that it was vital that Blair be closely associated with the campaign in Wales. Finally, it was decided that Alan Barnard (a senior member of the Labour's Millbank team) would be the 'link' between Millbank and the campaign in Wales and would control the campaign budget.

In Wales the first meeting of a newly established 'Strategy Committee' took place at the end of May. The Committee – chaired by Ron Davies – was to meet at least weekly throughout the campaign. Its membership included Peter Hain, Andrew Davies, Nick Ainger (Davies' PPS), John Adams (appointed Secretary), Huw Roberts (Davies' Press Officer), Terry Thomas (Chair of the Welsh Executive), Alun Williams (the Welsh Executive's Treasurer), Marlene Thomas (a former Chair of the Welsh Executive), Harry Jones (Leader of the Welsh Local Government Association), Andrew Bold and Huw Lewis (Wales Labour Party officers) and Alan Barnard (since he came to exert a major influence, through his control of the campaign budget and because he was a Millbank 'import' he quickly earned the soubriquet of 'Governor-General').

On paper, it was a powerful team, but tensions within it became apparent from the start. Labour's General Election campaign had been essentially a national strategy with a 'Welsh spin'. But the referendum was to be entirely a 'Welsh affair', and there was a feeling in some quarters that the Labour Party machine in Wales – and especially its General Secretary, Anita Gale – 'was not up to the job'. Just who was felt to be 'up to it' was a moot point. Relations between Ron Davies and Peter Hain were said to be strained. Although Davies chaired the 'Strategy Committee', Hain claimed a mandate from Blair to deliver a 'Yes' vote. Hain was known to have close links with Millbank. There was a feeling in some Labour circles that while Millbank regarded Hain as 'one of us', they did not extend this trust to Davies (one telling example of the 'partisan' way in which Millbank distributed its favours came early in the campaign when Philip Gould – who had been given the job of running Labour's focus groups and overseeing the Party's private polling work – gave polling 'de-briefs' to Hain, but without informing Davies' office).

Davies' uneasy relationship with Hain was further fuelled by impatience with what was seen as the latter's 'media-junkieism' – Hain's well documented tendency to endlessly give 'private' briefings to the press. To add to these fault lines within the campaign team, there were numerous other points of tensions. There was also the problem of how to use Rhodri Morgan in the campaign. There had been wide-spread dismay in Welsh Labour circles at Blair's refusal to appoint him to Davies' team at the Welsh Office. Morgan was a popular, high profile figure in Wales and it was believed Davies wanted him to play a leading role in Labour's referendum campaign. Morgan, though, insists that he was never asked to play any formal part in Labour's campaign, but believed "there was something of a row" in Blair's office when it was pointed out that there was no Welsh speaker in the referendum team. This, according to one well placed Labour source, got an "abrupt response" from Alaistair Campbell, who dismissed the point by saying Morgan, had a "moral obligation" to play a full part in securing a 'Yes' vote.

The unwieldly size of the Strategy Committee led to the setting up of a smaller Task Force to spearhead the campaign, comprising: Ron Davies, Adams, Ainger, Barnard, Thomas and Gale. The move was not successful. Because Davies was often absent, the Task Force was never taken seriously. This, in turn, generated further tensions between Davies and Gale. There were also problems with Thomas, who felt the Executive was being side-lined in the campaign, resented Millbank's influence and, according to one source, "at one stage threatened to withdraw trade union funding and go public over what he saw as a Millbank take-over".

In the event, Thomas did neither, but his antipathy towards the 'Millbank Tendency' was shared by other Labour campaigners in Wales. There were constant complaints about Millbank's alleged 'lack of a grasp of politics in Wales'. Many were unhappy about what became dubbed as the 'control freak' aspect of the Millbank manage-ment style, based – it was said – on a 'mistrust of "outsiders"' and a 'dismissive' attitude towards ordinary Party workers.

Yet perhaps the biggest weakness evident in Labour's early campaign planning was, as one source put it, "the failure to educate and enthuse our activists", something compounded by the lack of preparatory work and lack of time once the campaign had been launched. Time constraints meant that what emerged was very much a 'top down' campaign, though there were those who believed that had the political will existed to do so, it would have been possible to mobilise Labour's grass-roots workers. Unfortunately one major initiative in this direction fell foul of intra-Labour Party politics. In June, Andrew Davies invited a group of party activists to Transport House to give them a SWOT analysis of the campaign to date, based on a summary of NOP poll findings and to ask them to 'evangelise' in the branches in their local constituencies. Those present at the meeting included Gareth Hughes (Chair of Wales Labour Action) and Kevin Brennan (political researcher for Rhodri Morgan). For various reasons the two had incurred the wrath of Anita Gale. Davies was 'severely reprimanded' for talking to them, (the two soon after moved on to play an active role in the Yes for Wales Campaign instead).

The problem of carving out a clear profile and message for Labour's campaign was first approached by the use of focus groups. Philip Gould was sent by Millbank to do the work, but as Andrew Davies noted: "Even someone as well connected as Gould was not fully trusted. Barnard said to me 'we'd like you to be there. We don't entirely trust him – he does tend to lead them'." This aside, the feed-back from the groups was to suggest that the signs of a 'Yes' vote were not encouraging.

Four focus groups were arranged. Two (one male, one female) met in Maesteg on 11th June; the other two on the following day in Wrex-ham. The groups were drawn from Labour voters aged 30 or over, an age thought to contain Labour's core vote. Gould came away from the Maesteg meetings extremely downcast. He was depressed by the groups' lack of basic knowledge about the Assembly and by the general absence of enthusiasm for the Assembly idea. Talking to Gould afterwards, Davies heard him keep repeating "They just don't want it – they just don't want it". The response in Wrexham, however, was more positive. In the memo which Gould sent to Barnard and McDonagh reporting on his findings, he – with remarkable foresight – noted that "awareness is so low that the eventual vote is very hard to call" and argued that if things were to be turned Labour's way, then the endorsement of Tony Blair was necessary. "If he takes the Assembly seriously, then so will the people of Wales... he will have to visit". If these conclusions were not entirely unexpected by Davies, he was taken aback by Gould's comments on the way to Wrexham. At one stage in the journey Gould observed: "You realise that none of this was part of the Project?" In other words, Gould was claiming that the issues around devolution for Wales had not been subjected to detailed scrutiny in Labour's Policy Review, with the clear implication that Blair was either 'lukewarm' about it or even not in favour of the *policy*.

Any 'coolness' Blair may have felt towards the 'project' was replicated by other groups inside the Labour movement in Wales. Labour's devolutionists had particular problems with the local government sector and with some members of the Welsh Parliamentary Labour Group. Labour had strengthened its already formidable grip on local government in Wales under successive Conservative Party administrations since 1979. Every attempt by different Conservative Governments to 'squeeze' local authorities in Wales (through a variety of fiscal measures and the stripping away of some of the core service functions of local councils) only served to increase the level of popular support for councils astute enough to present themselves as 'defenders of local communities' against the ravages of a Westminster Government that a majority in Wales had never voted for. In 1995 Welsh local government started on a difficult – and for many, unwanted – process of reorganisation into 22 unitary authorities. This 're-engineering' was taking place at the same time as Labour was wrestling with its plans for devolution. There were clearly some Leaders of Labour-controlled local authorities in Wales who saw no advantage in devolution. For them, the prospect of an Assembly was more of a *threat* than an opportunity to redress the 'democratic deficit' in Wales. Their calculation was essentially self interested: an Assembly would, so they argued (in private), inevitably want to encroach upon local Government territory.

There was also another problem, this time to do with the poor reputation of Labour local authorities in several parts of Wales, linked to notions of 'cronyism', 'inefficiency' and being resistant to new ideas. Andrew Davies was responsible for providing liaison between the campaign team and those local, Labour 'statelets'. Throughout, said Davies, "local government was a big, big problem for us". Soon after the May election, Davies met Harry Jones – Leader of both Newport Council and the Welsh Local Government Association. Jones was a keen devolutionist and gave Davies what help he could, though constrained by the fact that two of the most populous local authority areas in Wales (Cardiff and RCT) had opted out of the Association in a dispute over subscription fees. Davies himself produced a paper on the role local government could play in the campaign, via newsletters and endorsements. In the event, only Newport came out with a newsletter and only a handful of local parties mobilised their electoral machinery on behalf of the campaign.

Ron Davies was acutely aware of the significance of the local government sector. With Don Touhig, he worked hard to get every Labour Group to come out and publicly support the Assembly. While they were successful, much of the support so publicly given was largely token. Perhaps this was all Davies and Touhig could have hoped for. This much seems to have been hinted at in Andrew Davies' comment: "In some respects the strategy was to 'neutralise' them, rather than get their active involvement".

The Welsh Group of Labour MPs proved to be equally problematic. Some were to give Davies and his team problems during the House of Commons debates on the Referendum Bill. Alan Williams was to be especially outspoken. He was to savage Peter Hain's suggestion that a Yes vote was a loyalty vote, with the rejoinder, "blind loyalty is the aspiration of zealots and the demand of despots".

The Welsh PLP could not be accused of being high profile campaigners. Apart from a small group of outspoken anti-devolutionists (like Llew Smith), there were a number (among them Ted Rowlands and Denzil Davies) who could be described as 'willing to wound, but afraid to strike'. There were others (like Alun Michael and Paul Murphy) who were conspicuous by their absence. Early in the campaign (June 1997) Llew Smith publicly alleged that Ron Davies had made threats of expulsion from the party unless Smith dropped his devo-sceptic line. Davies refuted the charges saying, when interviewed by the BBC (24th June), "It's not in my nature to behave in this way". This denial did not convince everyone, particularly since it had been strongly rumoured that Huw Roberts (Davies' Special Advisor) had phoned Smith warning him and others of the consequences of taking an anti-devolution stance. In the end, in the interests of unity, the Party was not ready to formally discipline 'errant' MPs, which could also be taken as an indication that the devolutionists had only a weak hand to play in relation to the various groupings that form the Labour Party in Wales. Nevertheless, the majority of Welsh Labour MPs believed Smith should have been disciplined, *pour encourager les autres*.

The 'dissidents' created two other problems for Labour's referendum campaign. At least one of them (Smith) was rumoured to be helping the No Campaign by phoning in with advice about tactics and strategy. But arguably even more damaging was the input from devo-sceptics like Denzil Davies and Allan Rogers. Their nit-picking at details of the referendum regularly grabbed the attention of the Welsh media, keen, as always, to spot grit in the Labour machine.

A key part of Andrew Davies' role was to work with the other pro-devolution parties. This task, perhaps not surprisingly, was described by Davies as "by far the most enjoyable part of my job". The job, though, had a certain clandestine aspect to it, which maybe added to Davies' sense of excitement. In his first meetings with Plaid MPs he was told, by Hain, "not to tell anyone, in case it caused problems with Millbank and with some officers at Transport House". Since a successful campaign depended on building good relations with Plaid (who were nervous about a repeat of 1979) Davies went to great lengths to win their trust by showing them Labour briefing papers and poll results. Plaid workers, in turn, handed over their canvass returns to Labour in some areas. Where it proved impossible to bridge mistrust between Plaid and Labour at the purely *local* level, Davies chose instead to work through the local all-party Yes for Wales campaign groups. Ron Davies was especially supportive of this kind of cross party co-operation, seeing it as a concrete demonstration of his own commitment to developing a more 'inclusive' style of politics (though, ironically, it seemed easier for Davies to promote an inclusive political culture across the parties rather than in his own).

The publication of the White Paper, *A Voice for Wales*, on 27th July 1997, roughly marked the mid-way point in Labour's post-election devolution campaign. With the referendum election only 10 weeks away, Labour could hardly claim to have put in place an effective campaigning machine. The campaign team was scarred by internal tensions; many in the different factions in the Party in Wales were giving only grudging and passive support; the Party had failed to excite the mass of its own membership over the Assembly idea and the level of interest in and awareness of the issue among the wider public was low. And yet, if Labour's pro-devolution coalition was tightly stretched it was, nevertheless, still in place and that, in itself, represented a considerable achievement for Ron Davies and his closest allies.

From the publication of the White Paper to polling day (18th September) Labour ran a generally lack-lustre campaign. Over large tracts of Wales Labour's much vaunted election machine was scarcely visible. In many constituencies the only real signs of activity came from the Yes Campaign, which provided a refuge for those Labour members who often found their own local parties dormant. Typical of these local 'sleeping partners' in the devolution project was the Labour controlled Cardiff South and Penarth constituency. Maximising the Yes vote was of great symbolic importance in Cardiff, which was always going to house the new Assembly if the vote was won. Yet the constituency, with a leading Labour MP and where every ward was Labour controlled, barely stirred itself. Apart from the efforts of Yes Campaign workers – who mobilised staff at Splott Market and organised an eve-of-poll leaflet blitz – the pro-devolution campaign largely passed the area by.

The absence of any serious attempt by Labour to mobilise its core vote in many parts of Wales was the fatal weakness, since there was evidence that where the Party did canvass its traditional working class support, people were often willing to be persuaded. This was certainly noted by some Yes campaigners in the working class areas of Cardiff South and Cardiff West. Rhodri Morgan, for instance, observed that when canvassing was done in these areas, "there was no problem in turning people into Yes supporters". The same response was found on one council estate in Cardiff South, when Yes campaigners talked to local residents: "People wanted to know what it was all about. They were interested – but kept saying that they hadn't been given information. When we explained as best we could, we had a good response". Unfortunately, Labour did little of this kind of 'face-to-face' work. The Party hadn't the number of workers needed – or, more the point willing – to do systematic canvassing. Certainly many key Party activists didn't show the commitment to the referendum campaign they normally gave to general and local election campaigning. This failure to commit was one explanation for the poor turn-out of Labour supporters on voting day. According to a comprehensive survey of voting behaviour in the referendum "...over 40% of those who identified themselves as Labour supporters did not vote, a higher percentage than for the supporters of all other parties" (Jones and Trystan, 1999).

Labour was running against a No Campaign widely acknowledged by many of its own supporters to have been badly planned and shambolic. It was afraid to be too closely associated with the Conservative Party and was seriously under-funded having, in the words of the Neill Report "to rely for financial support essentially on a single wealthy donor". That the source of their bounty was Julian Hodge, a tax-exile living in Jersey, did not help their cause. If the No Campaign could not attract big-money sponsors, it was equally unsuccessful in trying to enlist high-profile public figures to support its cause. As a result, the public face of the No Campaign was represented by Hodge's son, Robert, who chaired the Campaign (but was a political novice), Matthew Gunther Bushell (their main publicist, whose previous – and dubious – claim to fame was an association with the discredited former Tory MP, Jonathan Aitken) and Carys Pugh and Betty Williams – two veteran Rhondda Labour dissidents who were to earn the rather cruel soubriquet of 'Stalin's grannies'.

How, then, did this ramshackle, poorly staffed and cash-starved outfit – opposed by nearly all of Wales' political, cultural and media elites – come so close to scuppering Labour's devolution project? The answers help provide some further insight into the problems that dogged Labour's own campaign. To begin with, there were those who thought Labour's main campaign slogan, 'Wales Deserves a Voice', played straight in to the hands of those depicting the Assembly as a mere 'talking shop'. One person who shared this view was Rhodri Morgan, who said: "I would have preferred slogan-playing on the theme of people in Wales having a greater *control* over their own affairs".

Nor did Labour – or the national Yes Campaign – effectively counter the core, negative arguments pushed by the No lobby. In 1979 the No's had won it by playing on fears about 'more bureaucracy', 'jobs for the boys', the spectre of 'separatism' and 'the waste of public money'. They presented much the same case in 1997. It was a repeat message which clearly resonated with a large slice of the Welsh electorate, but one Labour never really got to grips with. This fundamental failure of political communication can be attributed, in large part, to the failure of the pro-devolution parties and groupings in Wales to inform people about devolution and persuade them on the main issues. The contrast between Wales and Scotland in this respect was stark. In Scotland, as Kevin Williams shows, the Constitutional Convention established in 1989 collected together Labour and the Liberal Democrats and other minor political parties and various groups in Scottish society to build a consensus for constitutional change. By 1995 a consensus was in place; the Convention's discussions had been widely reported in the media and had become an integral part of the political agenda. In Wales, for reasons we've already seen, the idea of a Convention had been rejected by the Labour Party. As a result, Williams argues: "The overwhelming influence of the Labour machine in Wales and the weakness of Welsh civil society meant that the consequence of this decision was that devolution was not widely discussed in the public domain. As a result, prior to 1997, a significant proportion of people in Wales had little or no information on devolution" (Williams, 1999).

Some of the reasons advanced for the near-failure of the Yes Campaign, only served to underline Williams' thesis. It was argued that the death of Princess Diana three weeks before the vote had 'derailed' the campaign, when campaigning was suspended for a week. There was also the argument that it would have helped if there had been a longer gap between the vote in Scotland (the Scots polled a week before the Welsh), to allow the national media to spend more time in Wales, since the London-based papers dominate Wales' newspaper market. These claims have a whiff of desperation about them. If there had been a sustained and popular debate in Wales about the merits of devolution well in advance of 1997, the death of a Princess and the timing of the ballot would not have been of concern.

In the end, Labour narrowly got its Yes vote, even if the wave of support was largely whipped by others. Yet in some respects the campaign ended for Labour as it had begun – in recrimination and controversy. One senior Party figure in Wales, writing to Ron Davies shortly after D-Day, to make the point that Davies' success was all the more remarkable for having been achieved "...against a background of some Parliamentary colleagues publicly undermining [your] position and a lethargy amongst other MPs who were not prepared to work towards a successful conclusion". He went on: "there are those who hold office within the Party who should be ashamed of their inaction".

Davies' correspondent urged Labour to learn lessons from the campaign: "...we need to take seriously the state of the Wales Labour

Party. The Party needs a root and branch reform of its structures to parallel the constitutional changes we are shortly to embark on". This was not a lone voice. Concerns about the organisation and culture of the Party in Wales were being expressed elsewhere. On 22nd September the *Western Mail* ran the front page lead, 'Labour was on the brink of Civil War', citing several unnamed sources claiming a No vote would have triggered bitter recriminations and "blood-letting" inside the Party. While victory was enough to head-off full scale warfare, there were calls for disciplinary action to be taken against Labour MPs who had voted No in the referendum.

Though these calls were ignored, a more difficult issue to ignore surfaced in January 1998, over alleged 'irregularities' at some of the referendum counts. Embarrassingly, for Ron Davies, the first accusations came from Labour party officers in his own Caerphilly constituency. Some saw a 'conspiracy' behind the leaks from Davies' own backyard. Interviewed by the *Western Mail* Carwyn Jones – formerly Secretary of the Bridgend Yes campaign – believed the leaking of confidential internal Party documents "was done to damage Mr Davies' standing and could have been inspired by someone in the Labour Party hierarchy in London" (a view shared by David Sage, a Bridgend councillor, who said many Party members felt the row had been orchestrated to undermine Davies). This speculation was not, perhaps, too fanciful. Throughout the devolution campaign the London press had carried a number of derogatory references about Davies. These carried through to the day of the vote itself, when the *Financial Times* described Davies as looking "more like a bodyguard than a bosom buddy when Blair has been around" and how Davies had "struggled to keep up a statesmanlike appearance" implying Blair was keeping a discreet distance from his man in Wales. Earlier, other political diaries in the London press had routinely referred to Davies as a "bruiser" and "lack-lustre". In the week of the referendum vote *The Sunday Telegraph* damned him as a "strutting Welsh bantam in the Kinnock mould" and as "your actual South Walian oaf". Seeking to pin down the source of these briefings against Davies, *Wales on Sunday* looked no further than the usual suspect when they headlined a story, 'Has Mandy got it in for Ron?'

It is worth recording the vitriolic way in which the London press treated Ron Davies even *before* his fall from grace, a person who was perceived to have 'gone native' by forsaking Westminster for Wales. It was a measure of the growing divide between Wales and Westminster (the source of the malicious press stories) that these anti-

Davies sentiments hardly registered at all west of Offa's Dyke. Perhaps this had something to do with the fact that, whatever his weaknesses, Ron Davies was known to have committed everything to the cause of democratic devolution, and for that reason alone he will be remembered as the politician who designed and delivered the National Assembly for Wales.

However, the trials and tribulations of the Labour Party in Wales should not be allowed to obscure the historical significance of the referendum result on 19th September 1997, certainly one of the most dramatic occasions in Welsh politics (Andrews, 1999). The wafer-thin majority in favour of a Yes vote – 50.3% to 49.7% on a turnout of just 50% of the electorate – proved that voters were far from persuaded of the virtues of a Welsh Assembly; indeed, in many ways devolution was (and remains) a minority sport. On the other hand the closeness of the 1997 result conceals the fact that Wales registered an enormous swing of 30% in favour of an Assembly since the previous referendum in 1979, much greater than the 23% swing in Scotland.

All manner of interpretations have been put on the referendum result, and the conventional wisdom seems to be that the result was due to the west and the valleys voting Yes, with the areas adjacent to England voting No, along with maverick Pembrokeshire, which is known as the 'Little England Beyond Wales' (Osmond, 1999). On the surface the result seemed to confirm the continued salience of the 'Three Wales Model', which suggested that in two of the three regions of Wales the population considered itself significantly more 'Welsh' than 'British' with the reverse being true in the third region (Balsom, 1985). The three regions were: *Y Fro Gymraeg* (the Welsh-speaking heartland in north-west and west Wales), *Welsh Wales* (the former coalfield communities of the valleys) and finally *British Wales* (south-east and north-east Wales along with parts of Pembrokeshire).

Conventional wisdom often conceals as much as it reveals and this interpretation is no exception. What mattered most in the 1997 referendum was votes not the areas in which they were cast. Thanks to Paul O'Leary we are now beginning to appreciate that nearly 40% of the Yes vote was cast in so-called No counties. Although there is no question that support for the Assembly was profoundly uneven across Wales, the fact of the matter is that twice as many Yes votes were cast in Powys, for example, as in Merthyr, yet Powys is portrayed as a No voting county in area-based interpretations of the result. The significance of this analysis is that, in political terms at least, it reveals "a much less polarised Wales than reports have suggested hitherto" (O'Leary, 1998).

But the most systematic analysis of the referendum result suggests that *generational* change was perhaps the single most important dimension because those under 45 years of age were more likely to vote Yes by a margin of 3:2, while those over 45 voted No by a similar margin (Jones and Trystan, 1999). Younger voters appear to be more self-confident than their parents, less deferential to the powers that be and, compared to their elders, more receptive to the idea of an independent Wales (Beaufort Research, 1999).

The leading figures in the Wales Labour Party were ill-equipped to appreciate the new mood among younger voters, not least because youth was conspicuous by its absence in the upper echelons of the party. If young people were anything to go by, then a new Wales was struggling to free itself from the stultifying stereotypes of the Welsh, many of which were testaments to the past rather than models for the future. To win over this new Wales the Labour Party would have to rely on merit rather than habit, argument rather than tradition and it would have to show respect rather than contempt for members and voters alike. The test came sooner than expected, when the party was faced with the seemingly simple, but novel task of finding a leader in Wales.

5. A Question of Leadership

In all the turmoil and recriminations over the drawn out Labour leadership contest between Rhodri Morgan and Alun Michael, an earlier important episode in Welsh Labour's recent troubled history seems to have slipped from memory. Yet the first struggle for the Labour leadership, fought out by Morgan and Ron Davies from March-September 1998, was highly significant. In so many ways the arguments and controversies that marked this campaign pre-figured the bruising contest that was to follow between Morgan and Michael. The story of Labour's first leadership battle was to provide confirmation of the old dictum – that those who do not learn from history are condemned to repeat it.

The First Contest: "This is like North Korea"

Morgan wasted little time after the referendum vote in announcing his decision to run for the Assembly and the Labour leadership, issuing a statement in October 1997 about his intentions. Davies finally decided to run in March 1998, handing in his application papers for a place on Labour's list of approved Assembly candidates shortly before the deadline at mid-day on 30th March. Pressed on his late entry, Davies explained: "...if I had made a declaration before [the devolution legislation was through the Commons] the issue wouldn't have been the merits of the Bill, but Ron Davies' own personal intentions".

The day after Davies' announcement to seek election to the Assembly, Morgan said he was looking forward to a "friendly contest", though quickly antagonised the Davies camp by projecting himself as the 'unity candidate', claiming he was popularly seen as a Welsh rather than a Cardiff politician. The anger among Davies' backers was real, for them, the implication of Morgan's remarks was that their man was the *disunity* candidate. But though a contest was clearly in the offing, the Wales Labour Party had, as yet, no machinery in place for electing its first leader. *How* the rules of the contest were to be drawn up – and *who* was to do the drafting – were going to be crucial to the outcome. According to Anita Gale, the Party's

Annual Conference in May would be asked to set up a Task Force to address the issue.

Deciding on the rules of engagement was always going to be a major battleground. Morgan supporters were already pressing for the election to be settled by One Member One Vote (OMOV), so playing to his known support among Labour's grassroots membership. The Davies camp, aware of Morgan's areas of strength, clearly preferred a method that would keep grassroots participation to a minimum. The emerging argument first surfaced at the Party's Annual Conference, when Kevin Brennan (Chair of the Cardiff West CLP and Morgan's political researcher) warned the Party hierarchy against any attempts at "stitch-ups and backroom deals" in the leadership election. He went on: "The Party members in Wales are not sheep. The system of OMOV has to be adopted. We don't want cronyism" (*Western Mail*, 16th May 1998).

As we shall see, Brennan's fears about the Party leadership going for an electoral arrangement constructed to keep Morgan out, were fully justified. Indeed, within days of the Conference ending, there was speculation that the Task Force would opt for some kind of electoral college, a formula that would strongly favour Davies. But the issue raised the question of why Davies' supporters were apparently reluctant to back the OMOV option. While Morgan certainly had grassroots backing, on the face of it Davies' position seemed unassailable. He had led the Party through the successful referendum campaign. He was the grand architect and pilot of the referendum bill and enjoyed a high profile across Wales. However, as in the way of politics, he had made enemies en route. His enemies included the usual suspects (Labour's back-bench devo-sceptics). In addition he had offended different sections of the Party through his handling of the issue of the siting of the Assembly, and for his (privately expressed) opposition to 'twinning' (Labour's highly contentious 'twinning' policy – aimed at securing gender balance when it came to selecting Assembly candidates – had been effectively forced through at the 1998 Annual Conference without any real consultation with Party members).

The first really decisive moves in the struggle to shape the leadership election came early in August. The five person Task Force, at its meeting on 3rd August, was expected to propose a method of election (after a long meeting on the Friday before had failed to reach a conclusion) to be put to the WLP Executive at its session on 4th August. A senior Labour Party source was quoted as saying: "The meeting of the Task Force is going to see an almighty struggle. What sort of image this is presenting to the people of Wales I dread to think" (*Western Mail*, 3rd August). The same source also pointed out how the first meeting of the Task Force had been delayed for nearly 10 weeks until it had met on Friday but "is now expected to come to a decision in a great hurry". Rushed, or not, the two main options under consideration were clear. Either OMOV or an electoral college in which the total vote is divided between three sections made up of: ordinary members, affliated organisations (dominated by the unions); and MPs, MEPs and nominated Assembly candidates.

The Task Force's recommendation to go for an electoral college came as no real surprise to anyone with a knowledge of how Labour machine politics work in moments of potential crisis. Indeed, given the composition of the Task Force, probably the only surprise was that it actually needed more than one meeting to settle the issue. Equally underwhelming was the rapid endorsement of the proposals by the Party's executive, a group dominated by those very bodies – the trade unions – that were now given the decisive role to play in the workings of the electoral college.

If this part went smoothly, the reactions to the adoption of the electoral college method revealed, once again, how deeply divided the Party was over the issue – sources close to Davies' were quick to say he was "very pleased" by the decision. Davies himself went on record to say how delighted he was by what he described (somewhat cynically perhaps) as 'OMOV-plus'. Further support for the Task Force formula came from Ken Hopkins (a member of the Executive, a strong supporter of Davies and an implacable opponent of Morgan) who claimed the electoral college was "democratic and was the method used to elect Tony Blair as Labour leader". He also claimed OMOV was too expensive an option to run, arguing it would cost over £5000 to organise a postal ballot of Party members in Wales. In trying to defend the electoral college, Hopkins was being economical with the truth when suggesting that the Task Force had opted for the same method used to elect Blair. True, both contests involved an electoral college. But there were two hugely significant differences. In Blair's election all Party members had been given a vote and the unions balloted their members. Neither of these methods applied in the contest between Davies and Morgan. The calculation was simple: the use of genuine OMOV across all sections of the electoral college would put Morgan in with a good chance of winning.

In terms of narrow political self-interest it made no sense for

Davies to go head-to-head with Morgan in any debate (the one occasion Davies relented was an eve-of-poll television debate with Morgan). The electoral rules made him the firm favourite to win. In these circumstances, with everything to lose, why give Morgan – a much more assured debater than Davies – a chance to increase his exposure and gain ground?

The second obstacle facing Morgan was more difficult to identify, but which would play a major, though largely hidden role in the electoral process. Early in August Morgan had hinted that the officers and machinery of the Wales Labour Party might be quietly mobilised against him. He said: "I hope the contest will be fair and open [and] there will be complete neutrality of the Labour Party machinery" (6th August). Assurances were duly given by Anita Gale: "All candidates will be treated fairly and openly. There will be no favours to any particular candidate". From the point of view of Morgan's camp, this promise carried little weight. It was made after the Party's Executive – dominated by Davies' supporters – had endorsed an electoral system clearly designed to make it as easy as possible for Davies. There was also the strong feeling on Morgan's side that a party machinery controlled by people thought to be determined to block him at all costs, was not likely to be scrupulously even-handed in its treatment of the two candidates.

As the campaign edged closer to the September conference date, the wounds inside the Party over the electoral college deal continued to fester. At the end of August the Merthyr Tydfil and Rhymney CLP had called for a boycott of the leadership contest and launched its own OMOV campaign. Morgan Chambers, the CLP Chair, made clear the anger of local Party members that the OMOV principle had been set aside. Other CLPs were making similar noises. There were now clear signs that if Davies were to win, many in the Party were going to judge it as something of a deeply flawed victory.

Five days before the convening of the (19th) September special conference Davies had issued a 'triumphalist statement' claiming victory and urging the Party to unite behind him. Anticipating criticism of the electoral machinery that had delivered him the votes he needed, Davies stated: "The Labour Party set down the rules of this contest. The rules are the rules". This line immediately brought a stinging retort from John Marek, the Wrexham Labour MP. In counselling Davies to be "a little less triumphalist" in advance of the conference, Marek declared: "Ron cannot have it both ways. On the one hand he says that rules are rules, that he has won and everybody should unite behind him... he also says the Assembly must be an inclusive body, where everyone counts. If the rules had been inclusive, each member of the Labour Party in Wales would have had a vote. Instead, the rules allowed the Finance and General Purposes Committee of the TGWU to plump for Ron to give him 50,000 votes this Saturday. What sort of inclusivity is that as far as the ordinary Labour Party member or Trade Unionist is concerned?"

While claiming widespread support in all three sections of the electoral college, some in Davies' camp were privately surprised at the amount of grassroots support for Morgan – even going so far as to concede that on a full OMOV ballot, Morgan might well have won. This was certainly the view taken by Morgan's team. As one of his spokeswomen put it: "If we had had OMOV, Rhodri would have won by now".

Although, of course, it's not possible to predict what would have happened had there been an election by OMOV, we can pinpoint some of the peculiar anomalies of the Davies and Morgan contest. The first thing to note is the extent to which the electoral college voting system was a minority sport. Section One of the college was made up of 84 'Party Units', each with one vote. These 'units' were comprised of: 40 CLPs, 5 Euro-Party constituencies, 22 County Labour Parties and 17 Women's Councils. Their method of voting varied widely. In the case of some CLPs (e.g. Cardiff North, Wrexham) meetings were called giving every constituency member a chance to vote. In other CLPs (e.g. Swansea West) only members of their General Management Committees had a vote. Where ordinary CLP members had the chance to vote, they went by a decisive margin for Morgan (of the 2,061 votes cast in this way, Morgan picked up 1,185 (57.5%) votes and Davies 878 (42.5%)). The numbers attending the meetings of the other 'Party Unit' meetings is not clear, nor were the majorities in favour of either candidate. What is clear, however, is that this system of what might be called 'representative balloting', produced its own version of 'OMOV-plus'. In theory it would have been possible for a Party activist, with membership in each Party Unit, to have voted up to three times in this section. He – or she – could then have accumulated even more votes, by dint of membership of bodies in Sections Two and Three of the electoral college.

Section Two was made up of the 'affiliated bodies', but in effect dominated by the trade union vote which was, in turn, dominated by the four biggest trade unions in Wales. These – UNISON, TGWU, GMB, AEEU – were joined in this section by a clutch of smaller unions – the FBU, CWU, GMPU, RMT, ASLEF, UCATT, TSSA, NUM, ISTC, MSF, USDAW. Completing this section were a number of non-union bodies – SEA, SHA, Fabians, Labour Students, Co-operative Party – of which the latter (claiming 19,000 members in Wales), was by far the largest. Each organisation had a proportion of the vote depending on the size of its membership. In other words, the bigger the affiliated membership, the bigger the proportion of this section's 33.3% of the overall vote. To take the extremes, the vote of UNISON's 50,000 members in Wales counted for 6% of the total vote in this section, while the Fabians – with a membership of around 200 in Wales – could claim only a 0.1% share. No trade union balloted its members in this election, nor did most of the other affiliated groups. This section, as we shall see, came out in overwhelming favour of Davies.

Section Three of the electoral college had a constituency of around 200, comprising the 34 Welsh Labour MPs, 5 Labour MEPs and about 160 approved Assembly candidates. Each had one vote in a section, which like the other two, controlled a third of the college's total vote. How the membership of this section voted is of some interest. To vote, each member had to attend the 19th September Special Conference in Newport. Some had already declared their intentions before the conference met. By the eve-of-poll 18 MPs – including all of the 'payroll vote' had publicly backed Davies, along with 3 MEPs. How the 160 or so Labour approved Assembly candidates were likely to vote, was harder to read. All had been canvassed – usually by telephone – by both camps in the run-up to the conference vote. Many were in a difficult position, especially those who leaned towards Morgan. Knowing they were soon to be setting off on the trail of seat selection, there were those who thought their interests would be best served by going for the likely winner (i.e. Davies, who by the time the conference finally met, was widely thought to have it wrapped up). What is clear is that some of them thought it 'prudent' to indicate their support for Davies, on the calculation that being seen to identify with the winner might bring the benefit of patronage on their behalf later. What is equally clear is that some candidates were put under enormous pressure to back Davies. As one put it after the event: "I felt I was being bullied. They [Davies' team] had a pretty good idea of the seats I'd be looking for. The implication was obvious. If I didn't come out for Ron, things might be made difficult for me".

This digression, on the composition of the electoral college is important, since it demonstrates four key points. First, the quite byzantine structure of the Wales Labour Party, with its complex mix of 'Party Units', affiliated bodies and other groupings. This mosaic is often underpinned by a dense network of personal relationships and contacts, which provide links between different parts of the 'machine'. Second, those at the centre of these networks – whose names are often barely known to many ordinary Party members, let alone the wider public – can exert enormous influence on the decision-making process. This was apparent in the Davies-Morgan contest where, for the most part, the key 'power-brokers' were determined to block Morgan at any cost. Third, the role of Wales Labour Party officers (based in Transport House, Cardiff) and the Wales Labour Party Executive in settling the contest rules – and so the result of the contest itself. The role of the Executive is especially important here, since its membership is dominated by 'agents of influence' who are also major players in the most powerful trade unions in Wales. Finally, the operation of the college gave an extraordinary twist to the concept of OMOV. While the overwhelming majority of ordinary Party and trade union members was effectively excluded from participating in the contest, a small number of Party activists were (quite legitimately) using the rules to cast multiple votes. In the Wales Labour Party truly all members are equal, but some are a lot more equal than others.

Table 5.1 The First Labour Leadership Election

	Ron Davies	Rhodri Morgan
Party Units	52.17%	47.83%
Trade Unions/Affiliated Bodie	91.72	8.28
MPs, MEPs, Assembly Candidates	60.77	39.23

When the votes were finally announced, Davies had come first in each of the three sections (see Table 5.1). Morgan had run Davies close in Section One (doing particularly well in the CLP vote) and also did well in Section Three, polling nearly 40% among a group which had come under strong pressure to back Davies. It was only in the trade union dominated Section Two that Davies scored a resounding victory, polling over 90% of votes cast. As the size of Davies' majority in this section was read out, one journalist present was heard to exclaim: "This is like North Korea".

The declaration of the vote was followed by speeches from Morgan and then Davies (though even at the moment of climax, there was to be no shared platform). Morgan gave a typically rousing performance; gracious in defeat, generous towards his opponent, eloquent about his decision to run and passionate about the need for the Party to unite to fight the Assembly election. Davies' response disappointed even some of his own supporters. Sticking rigidly to a prepared script, he plodded through his text, before going off to do the usual frenetic round of interviews and photo-calls.

Morgan had lost – and so, too, in many respects, had the Labour Party in Wales. Morgan had done much better than most had expected. He had enhanced his reputation and certainly added to his moral authority inside and outside of the Party. But if Morgan could take some comfort in defeat, the same could not be said of the Party itself – or rather those who controlled the decision-making.

There were those who saw the conduct of the election as having diminished the Party's standing, both among many of its own supporters and the broader electorate in Wales. It also revealed some potentially damaging fault lines running through Welsh Labour. The engineering of the electoral college had driven a wedge between the Party hierarchy and grassroots members. Ironically, some of those who had happily gone along with an arrangement that had disen-franchised most Party members, had written of the importance of listening to the Party's grassroots. At the beginning of the year Terry Thomas, a leading member of the Executive of the Wales Labour Party and an old-style Party 'fixer' had pontificated in an article in *Tribune*: "there must be an active, participatory democracy at every level of the Labour Party... I support a strong and dynamic grassroots party" (30th January).

Intended or not, the election had created first and second class Labour Party members, where some were 'voting early and voting often' and others – the vast majority – were effectively denied a vote at all. For some, the electoral college had echoes of eighteenth century 'rotten borough' politics, where votes were bundled up by small groups meeting behind closed doors. All this sat uncomfortably with the 'new' kind of politics the Assembly was supposed to usher in. The post-devolution rhetoric was replete with phrases calling for a more transparent, accountable and inclusive politics. But what many saw in the anointing of Ron Davies, were aspects of the worst of the old kind of machine politics at play.

The one 'virtue' of the process that produced victory for Davies was that it had all been done relatively speedily. There will have been those who thought that with the election settled, the bad memories of the campaign would quickly fade. This was to prove wishful thinking. With the dramatic resignation of Ron Davies, the Party was plunged into a second leadership contest. And those who sought to 'fix' the first contest, were confident they could do so again.

The Second Contest: "Labour's Worst Nightmare"

On 27th October 1998 Ron Davies resigned as Secretary of State for Wales. Two days later, and after mounting pressure, he stepped down as Labour's prospective Leader in the Assembly. The stage was now set for a second leadership contest, a contest that was to prove far more bitter and divisive than the first.

Once again, Morgan rapidly made his intentions clear. In what was to become a much quoted response to a question from the BBC's Jeremy Paxman about whether he planned to stand again, Morgan replied: "Does a one-legged duck swim in circles?" This was immediately followed by a wave of speculation about other possible contenders being encouraged to come forward, in order to block Morgan. Heading the list was Alun Michael (who had been given Davies' old job as Welsh Secretary), though there were also rumours of approaches being made to Wayne David and to Paul Murphy, the Northern Ireland Minister and MP for Torfaen. Morgan supporters were quick to claim to see the hand of London at work, and warned of the consequences of trying to 'parachute' in a replacement leader. As one of them put it: "If London tries to impose someone unpopular or unelected, there will be an almighty row" (*Tribune*, 30th October). Those who may have been thinking along these lines needed to be mindful of two other episodes that were troubling the Party in Wales. There was the argument over the selection of the MEP candidates' list, where a sitting MEP (Lyndon Harrison) from outside Wales was widely seen to have been 'imposed' over the heads of two sitting Welsh MEPs. Feeling was so strong over this issue that at Labour's September 1998 Annual Conference, Welsh delegates had voted unanimously not to accept the leadership's official list, with delegates from North Wales threatening to resign as constituency delegates if the list was imposed. At the same time, the Party was also faced with the problem of several Welsh constituency parties refusing to co-operate with the Party's policy on 'twinning'.

In one respect, *Tribune*'s anonymous source had no need to worry. No one was going to be 'imposed' on the Party without an election. In another, the source was wrong. The contest about to unfold was not to be shaped and driven by 'string-pullers' and 'agenda-setters' in London. The turmoil into which the Party in Wales was to be plunged was largely 'made in Wales'. The principal designers of Labour's crisis were those who controlled the Party machine in Wales. For their own reasons they were determined to stop Morgan at any cost. Their problem was how to lever in their preferred candidate – Alun Michael – when it was already clear that the Party's ordinary members were beginning to line up behind Morgan.

The question which puzzled many people was why so many of the key 'power-brokers' inside the WLP were so strongly against Morgan's candidature. One illuminating answer came from a very senior WLP source, who offered this explanation: "People like Terry [Thomas], Ken [Hopkins], Anita [Gale] and George [Wright] were totally opposed to Rhodri. They saw him as being not 'one of us', as a bit of an 'outsider'. They saw him as eccentric, as not dependable – putting him down as a middle class Cardiff guy who had had it too easy". Certainly something close to this view was shared by Labour apparachiks in London. But whatever the reason, one thing was clear. Those at the top of the WLP "egged on by interests in London" were prepared to go to any length to block Morgan's path to the leader-ship. In other words they had their own reasons for opposing Rhodri Morgan, even though the desire to please the Prime Minister was also a key factor.

Monday 2nd November saw the first meeting of the Task Force (chaired by Jim Hancock, member of the WLP Executive and Deputy Regional Secretary of the TGWU) set up to discuss 'options and procedures' for a new election. The meeting removed the first obsta-cle in Michael's way by recommending the panel of Assembly candi-dates be re-opened, a decision heavily criticised by sections of the Party. The Task Force's next step was to settle on a method of elec-tion. Here they were in some difficulty. Although they had cleared a path for Michael to enter the race, he had still not announced his intention to stand. Some in the Party were urging him not to, like the Newport West MP, Paul Flynn. Flynn's own account of the advice he gave Michael, when the latter sought his support for the Leadership, is worth recording, since it anticipated so many of Labour's subse-quent troubles. Flynn wrote: "I begged him not to stand... This time, Rhodri should lead the campaign, I argued... I believed Alun would lose any fair vote. He would be seen as another Lyndon Harrison, being parachuted into Wales... [but].... There was no meeting of minds. The impression I had was that Downing Street had decided that Alun should force an election. Not for the first or last time the neurotic need of Downing Street to control everything was poisoning the harmony of the Labour Party".

Flynn's closing claim is questionable. Before throwing his hat in the ring for a second time, Morgan had asked Blair if he (Blair) would be opposing his bid. Blair assured him he would have no problems with Morgan as Leader of Labour in Wales. (It was strongly rumoured that a week later Blair had a second meeting with Morgan, but this time to tell him that the job should go to Michael and suggesting that Morgan become his deputy). While there was no doubt Michael would be the preferred candidate of Downing Street, if the Party controllers in Wales opted for a method of election giving Morgan a fair chance of winning, there was little London could do about it. This path, though, was not one they were prepared to consider. And this takes us back to the dilemma now facing the Task Force. They needed to know if Michael was actually going to run, before deciding on the election process. The implication was clear. Any system they devised had to give him the prospect of victory, while also trying to avoid the criticisms over the electoral college used in the earlier Davies-Morgan contest.

The portents were not good. As Michael was still canvassing views, a grassroots bandwagon of support for Morgan was starting to roll. A *South Wales Echo* survey (3rd November) of Labour councillors across Wales showed Morgan polling twice as many votes as Michael as their choice of a successor to Davies. More ominously for Michael's backers, the survey revealed that many of those who had gone for Davies in the first election, were not automatically transferring their allegiance to the next machine-sponsored candidate. On the same day, the *Western Mail* reported "deep concern among MPs and Party members that Mr Michael was being 'parachuted' into the gap left by Ron Davies" ('parachute' imagery was to become one of the dominant motifs of the campaign).

Despite these warning shots, Michael declared his intention to stand on 5th November. Over the next three days hurried attempts were made to head off an election. Flynn issued a statement calling for a 'Peace Ticket', his formula to "end the in-fighting in Wales" by calling on Michael "to accept the overwhelming view of the Labour Party in Wales that Rhodri Morgan should be their Leader during the election campaign with the final election of the Leader by the Assembly members after the election". This was countered by a proposal, brokered by George Wright, of a 'Unity Ticket', where the Leadership would be gifted to Michael, with Morgan and Wayne David as his two deputies. The ticket touts found no takers, with the 'Wright Solution' being curtly dismissed by Morgan as "sadly typical of the old-style love of back-stage fixing", pointing out that when this 'ticket' was proposed, Michael was not even on the Panel of Assembly candidates (and wouldn't be until 20th November).

In the meantime there was further gloomy news for Michael. An NOP poll for S4C saw him trailing Morgan by 26% as the Task Force announced it would meet on 13th November to recommend the method of election, so delaying a final decision at its 9th November meeting. After this meeting Don Touhig, Islwyn MP and a member of the Task Force (and the Welsh Executive) issued a statement that was to prove woefully wide of the mark: "we don't want to rush head-long into a bitter and divisive campaign... we don't intend to let that happen". On the same day, Michael began his own campaign by saying, "I believe that we need to take a fresh look at the matter of selections," adding, "I stress for future occasions, not for ones which the Executive is already engaged in". As his message was being delivered, grassroots Labour members held a demonstration outside the Party's HQ in Transport House, Cardiff, calling for the OMOV system to be adopted in any leadership contest. Although the 'demo' was a small-scale affair, it did draw into the limelight someone who was later to described as "Rhodri's secret weapon". This 'weapon' was not one of Morgan's own supporters, but George Wright, Regional Secretary of the powerful TGWU. Wright was to make regular attacks on those calling for union OMOV ballots. His language was so contemptously dismissive it moved one journalist to say, "even Alun Michael must be cringeing".

Even before the Task Force made its formal recommendations, there was growing speculation it would opt for another electoral college arrangement, which would fall well short of full OMOV and keep intact the influence of the four big trade unions (TGWU, UNISON, AEEU, GMB), who between them would control 25% of the total vote. When it was suggested to George Wright that his grass-roots members wanted OMOV he deployed a familiar argument: "We can't afford it.... It would break the [union's] political fund.... It's a terrible idea". As Wright went on to expound his philosophy of "representative democracy", Party officials were forced to cancel a meeting between Michael, Morgan and David after Morgan again made it clear he would not drop out of the race.

As the Party waited for the Task Force's recommendations, the contest was steadily becoming more rancorous. Michael's camp accused Morgan of a having a "separatist, crypto-nationalist agenda". If the campaign was already showing signs of being rough-edged, it was also dividing the Party along some unexpected lines. "Former enemies have become friends, hatchets have been buried and long remembered insults generously reclassified as trivialities no sensible person would dwell on" (*The Independent on Sunday*, 15th November). No-one embodied these shifting allegiances better than Llew Smith, the deeply devo-sceptical Labour MP for Blaenau Gwent. A supporter last time of Morgan (a support fed by a dislike of Davies), he was now declaring for Michael, on the grounds that his new favourite was less enthusiastic about devolution than his opponent!

The Task Force at last declared its hand on 19th November. Its proposed electoral college was cleverly constructed, carefully aimed at trying to appease those lobbying for OMOV while at the same time keeping in place mechanisms designed to give Michael every possible assistance. The package was made up of the following key elements:

1. each section of the college would have 33% of the total vote

2. the Party units section should be polled using OMOV, giving every member of the WLP a vote

3. the section comprising 'affiliated bodies' should 'consult their members as appropriate to their own rules and procedures'

4. the third section would consist of MPs/MEPs and 'those candidates who have been selected to contest a seat or to appear on the additional members list'

5. those voting in the third section would be required to give in their ballot paper to the Party's office in Cardiff

To those unschooled in the ways of Labour 'fixing', the proposals would seem reasonable enough. They gave (under 2) ordinary Party members a vote denied to most of them in the first leadership contest. And measures (3) and (4) appeared to grant all other sections of the Party a chance to have their say. In reality this piece of electoral machinery had been finely tuned to favour Michael. These subtle changes would help Michael in several important ways:

– the wording of proposal (2) would allow the trade unions (who dominated this section, controlling over 90% of its vote) the option of not balloting their members. The calculation here was simple and, for many, cynical – the unions were almost certainly going to deliver their block vote to Michael.

– in the contest between Davies and Morgan *all* 163 candidates on Labour's approved Panel could vote. But now that right was withdrawn, in favour only of those selected to fight a seat or finding a place on the 'top-up' list. The thinking of the Party managers here was clear. First, it was known that a big majority of *all* candidates supported Morgan (an opinion poll for Radio 4's *The World At One* showed candidates backing Morgan by nearly three to one), so if as many as possible could be 'culled', it would boost Michael's prospects. Second, those who controlled the selection of candidates for the additional members list could, in effect, deliver vital votes for Michael.

– the proposed college offered a peculiar form of OMOV. It meant, for example that the section one vote (the 25,000 WLP members) would count for no more than the handful of people making up section three (MPs, MEPs and selected candidates) who, between them, were likely to number under 100. And it was also very likely that section three would lean towards Michael – who would be able to rely on the MP 'payroll' vote, (MPs on, or aspiring to be on, the payroll) and pliant Michael loyalists slipped in through the list system selection process.

– the offer of OMOV to all ordinary WLP members was also carefully calculated, using the assumption that 'armchair' Party members (those – the majority – who tended to participate only minimally in Party activities), would be more likely to favour Michael than the constituencies 'activists'. Had the vote in this section been settled on the basis of 'OMOV by attendance' – at hustings and branch meetings – then it was always probable that the 'activist vote' would have gone to Morgan by a ratio of four or five to one (enough to have propelled him home).

– finally, the apparently trivial matter of where votes were to be cast. Ordinary Party members were to send their ballot papers to London, for counting by Unity Security Balloting Services. But those in the section three mini-electorate were being asked to return their voting papers to the Party's HQ in Cardiff, along with their name and address. Why? Some came to suspect that some nervous MPs and Assembly candidates who were to privately indicate their intention to vote for Morgan, might change their minds if they thought there was even the faintest chance of having their vote identified.

To further improve Michael's chances, the election date was set for Saturday 20th February, giving him three months to raise his profile in Wales.

Morgan's supporters were under no illusions about what the Task Force package meant, though many of them – like most of the media – appeared to focus only on the role of the union 'block vote'. If it was true that in endorsing the electoral college the Party had, as the *Western Mail* put it, "reaffirmed union barons' power over the choice of Labour leader for the National Assembly" (20th November), this was only one part of what was now becoming widely seen as an election 'stitch-up'. For Michael to win there would have been a mosaic of fixes and deals which went well beyond the unions and reached into many corners of Labour's machine in Wales.

Suspicion that the Task Force had been less than even-handed in plotting this latest version of an electoral college was further fuelled when, the day after the package was unveiled, Don Touhig – a Task Force member – came out in support of Michael. His backing was followed by a statement from the TGWU (whose Deputy Leader had been another Task Force member), saying it would make its leadership decision on the basis of "representative democracy" (union-speak for OMOV only for union officers). Equally encouraging for Michael the AEEU announced, on the same day, that it would leave the decision to its regional political committee.

Amid these developments, there was also good news for Morgan's team. A telephone poll run by the *South Wales Echo* showed Morgan running eight to one ahead of Michael. Much more significant were signs that UNISON – the biggest of the 'Big Four' trade unions in Wales, with over 50,000 members – was thinking of balloting its members. Although Jean Brady, the union's Senior Regional Officer in Wales, and another member of the Task Force, had backed the electoral college system, there were reports of other UNISON officials being 'swamped' by demands from members for an OMOV ballot.

The launch of Morgan's campaign came shortly before the first of what would be three Prime Ministerial visits to Wales before the contest was over. Blair used the visit to declare: "I make no apologies for being a strong supporter of Alun Michael. I think he is a great guy". Though careful to distance himself from the election campaign,

Blair was disingenuous when he argued that the electoral college was the one used to elect him as leader. There was one crucial difference: under the electoral college which had returned Blair the trade unions were forced to ballot their members. His warm words for Michael were also widely judged to have been a mistake. Given the growing grassroots support for Morgan, and the strong belief that Michael had been 'parachuted' in from London, there were those who felt "Being a Blair protege could damage your health" (*Western Mail* editorial, 28th November).

At the beginning of December Peter Hain – Michael's campaign manager – picked on what was to become a regular feature of the Michael campaign. "I am astonished that the *Western Mail* has forgotten its usual fairness and news judgement to such an extent that it has become a propaganda sheet for Rhodri Morgan" (1st December). Blaming the messenger for the message was perhaps an indication of how badly Michael's team were doing in the battle to win hearts and minds. Attacks on the press were followed the next day by a recycling of old accusations that Morgan was displaying "nationalist tendencies". Michael then announced he would be going on a 'Meet the People' tour, by visiting each of the 22 local authority areas in Wales, starting in Newport on 6th December.

Before the tour got underway, Morgan received a major boost when, on 2nd December, UNISON's leadership voted to ballot its members. "Democracy," as a *Western Mail* editorialist noted, "appears at last to be breaking out in the Labour leadership contest". Any break-out, though, looked like being quickly brought under control, with none of the other three big unions showing any sign of embracing OMOV.

Over the next few days, the Michael campaign had mixed fortunes. Criticism of Hain for allegedly improperly using his role as Labour's Assembly election campaign co-ordinator to promote Michael's leadership bid, was followed by embarrassment when his own Neath constituency voted to back Morgan. Better news came in the shape of Mo Mowlam, who turned up in Cwmbran on 11th December with Michael in attendance, though she seemed reluctant to offer a direct endorsement.

The New Year started with Morgan's team highlighting the 'astonishing' turnaround in his support in North Wales. Morgan had done badly against Davies in seeking nominations in North Wales, trailing 9 to 2. This time, however, he was ahead 7 to 4, allowing his campaign manager to claim Morgan was now the popular "all-

Wales" choice. Things were going less well in terms of Morgan's relationship with Labour Party officers in Transport House. Early in January they were still awaiting a ruling from Anita Gale on whether telephone canvassing was permitted under the election's 'Code of Conduct'. As they waited, reports filtered back that Michael's team had already been phoning, even though such activity had not been officially sanctioned (at least as far as Morgan's camp were concerned). It isn't clear if approval was ever formally given, but Morgan's team started picking up the phones anyway.

Potential damage to the Morgan campaign came from an unexpected source in the second week of January. An unidentified former member of the Welsh Executive issued a warning – through the *Western Mail* – that if Michael won, "There is every chance that a lot of people will consider their position in the Party.... Let's say a group of people on the nationalist wing of the Party" (13th January). The so-called 'nationalist wing' was a reference to Welsh Labour Action, the ginger group pushing for an Assembly with more powers. Because at least one person in Morgan's team was a prominent member of the group, it gave Michael's camp the opportunity to again raise the spectre of Morgan's supposed 'separatist agenda'.

As the flurry of claims and counter-claims about a "breakaway Party" faded, attention turned to two of the Big Four Welsh unions. On 14th January the GMB's Regional Political Officer, John Franks, wrote to its Branch Secretaries in Wales. His letter contained three key elements. OMOV was not an option (rejected on grounds of cost); "Branches should be consulted and that Branches in Wales should then cast their votes on behalf of their Branch membership for one of the candidates"; and a strongly implied backing for Michael. In providing information about the two candidates, Morgan's qualifications were compressed into one sentence (he "is a backbench MP and a member of the TGWU"), while Michael's credentials – with the stress on his GMB membership – were set out at some length and in warm terms. Exactly how this process of 'Branch consultation' would work was to be a matter of some controversy.

The AEEU then moved to centre stage. Union delegates were due to meet in Swansea on Saturday 16th January, to be addressed by the two candidates and then vote. Both Michael's team and Labour's machine had worked hard to make sure the union delivered. Winning the AEEU was crucial for Michael. As one Party official commented: "If Alun does not win, I am not saying he is finished, but it will be very hard" (*The Guardian*, 15th January). On 14th January Blair held a reception at Downing Street to butter up Welsh MPs, Assembly candidates and union representatives. Next day – on the eve of the vote – Blair, accompanied by Michael, visited North Wales touring engineering works where there was a large AEEU membership. The union's national leadership also signalled its support for Michael. Ken Jackson, the AEEU's General Secretary and one of the union leaders closest to Blair, issued a statement saying the Party should not use the selection process "as some sort of protest". Blair's tour of North Wales was followed by an invasion of Cabinet Ministers – Prescott, Cook and Mowlam. But there were some who thought these tactics were ill-judged, given the well-established image in Wales of Michael as 'Millbank's puppet'. One Welsh Labour MP commented on Michael's campaign: "It has been a diary of disaster. If someone was to write a book on how not to run a campaign, this would be it. Everything they do turns to dung".

Whatever the ordure level, the AEEU delegates came out for Michael. The 72 delegates present in Swansea (out of the 200 eligible to attend) voted 42 to 28 in his favour, with 2 abstentions. While some delegates had balloted their Branch members, others had not, telling the press beforehand they intended to vote for the person they believed would best serve the interests of the union and the Party in Wales. Despite his comfortable margin of victory, Michael was not given an easy time at the hustings. One delegate – Tom Williams, a senior union official and former Deputy Leader of the old Council of Welsh Districts – wanted to know why Michael had not originally bid for an Assembly seat. Another challenged him on why he had apparently done so little during the referendum campaign.

Although the loss was a setback for Morgan, it was not unexpected. He was sanguine about the result, pointing out afterwards that "I always said I could survive today, but Alun could not". The Welsh press were less relaxed about the affair. In a biting editorial, the *Western Mail* observed: "...Labour's failure to insist on internal union democracy in this election has meant that a huge amount of power is in the hands of a relatively small number of union officials" (18th November), followed by a scathing attack on those unions – like the AEEU – "who place their faith in what they call representative democracy". These arguments cut little ice with most trade union leaders in Wales. Asked for his view of criticisms of the AEEU method of balloting, George Wright remained defiant. We are, he said, "not going to be bounced by opportunists" into spending money on OMOV ballots (BBC Radio 4, *World At One*, 16th

November). If the Welsh press were cynical about the conduct of the election, Michael could at least rely upon the support of the Labour loyalist Mirror newspaper group. The day after the AEEU declared, the *Sunday People*, a paper which normally ignored Welsh affairs, gave Michael a full page to expound his views, backing him with a glowing editorial endorsement.

More strikes against Morgan were to shortly follow. On 20th January a letter from Harry Jones – Newport Council Leader and Chair of the WLGA – to Welsh Labour Council Group Leaders was leaked to the *Western Mail*. The letter referred to a plea from Terry Thomas (former chair of the WLP, member of the Welsh Executive and part of Michael's team) for group leaders to help identify councillors who might be prepared to switch their support to Michael. This intervention was attacked by Morgan as 'dirty tricks', arguing that the official Labour Party line was supposed to be one of neutrality. On the same day the Chair of the Wales Council of the Co-operative Party confirmed the Party's support for Michael and urged all Co-op members to vote for him where they could. Like many of the unions, the Co-operative Party had declared for Michael without consultation with its membership.

A further blow for Morgan came with the widely predicted recommendation by the TGWU's Finance and General Purposes Committee to back Michael. The decision came on the same day (22nd January) as the visit of yet another Cabinet Minister to Wales. On a trip to Cardiff, accompanied by Michael, Jack Straw paid tribute to Michael's "leadership skills", though stopping short of making an outright endorsement. While the TGWU's verdict was expected, it was mired in controversy. Before the decision was made, the union had rejected an offer by a charitable trust to pay for a poll of union members' views, for "legal and policy reasons". This had not deterred Channel 4's *Despatches* programme from conducting its own workplace poll of TGWU members. The results, broadcast on 11th February, showed grassroots union members favouring Morgan by a majority of nearly three to one, in line with the size of the majorities he was getting from union OMOV ballots.

Nor did the TGWU leadership do much to further its own cause. It had previously refused to run an OMOV ballot on cost grounds. Now – in an attempt to justify its leadership selection procedures – it sent a lengthy letter along with Michael's campaign literature, recommending that "our members inside the Labour Party" vote for him. The mailing was an inept move on two counts. First, many could not understand why the union could afford to send an expensive mailing to every member, after claiming it had no money to post out ballot papers. Second, by including promotional material from Alun Michael they were clearly in breach of the election's 'Code of Conduct'. A letter of complaint was sent to Anita Gale by Morgan's Campaign Manager on 29th January. There was no reply.

More controversy was soon to follow, this time around the distribution of ballot papers to the Party's 25,000 members in Wales. Morgan's team had been told the papers would be sent out, by USBS, on Monday 1st February. They had, at best, been misled. The papers were posted (second class) on Thursday 28th January, arriving in most cases on Saturday 30th January. The fine detail of the timing was important. Moving the time-table forward happened to 'coincide' with an orchestrated pro-Michael propaganda offensive. Twenty pro-Michael Welsh MPs played their part by writing to their constituency members, urging a vote for Michael. Each MP seemed to be chanting the same mantra from the same centrally supplied script, since they contained near identical phrasing and placed particular stress on the role of 'the media' in the contest ("I urge you not to let the media dictate the outcome.... You and I know those newspapers have never been friends of Labour").

Presumably their jaundiced view of 'the media' did not extend to the *Mirror*. On the day before most Party members would receive their ballot paper, the *Mirror* – the most widely read London paper sold in Wales – carried a front-page plug for Michael. The headline, 'Why the *Mirror* is backing Alun Michael for Wales', was supported by an editorial endorsement, a highly flattering piece by its political correspondent on Michael's campaign and a picture of Michael being warmly embraced by Blair. True, it also found space for Morgan as well – but only to run a nasty little item headed 'SWP for Morgan', an attempt to smear Morgan by trying to link him with the hard left Socialist Workers' Party:

> Left-wing extremists are backing Rhodri Morgan for leader. The Socialist Workers Party is lobbying Labour members to support him. SWP leaflets claim Alun Michael should be rejected because he's New Labour's choice. The SWP backs nationalisation, a 35-hour week and higher tax on the rich.

There was a strong suspicion amongst Morgan supporters that Party officials had tipped-off Michael's campaign that the despatch of ballot papers was being brought forward, but Morgan's team were not told. Morgan's Campaign Manager wrote to Gale on 29 January to complain, forcibly making the point that what had happened "falls well short of the even handedness from the Party's organisation to which Rhodri, as a properly nominated candidate, is entitled and which was promised in writing by the General Secretary of the Labour Party, Margaret McDonagh". Once again, there was no reply. The reason why Morgan's camp was concerned about the change in the time-table was compellingly simply. It is generally believed that in a postal ballot, most people fill in and return their papers within two to three days of receiving them. In other words, Michael's team and Labour's machine in London would have calculated the benefit of having the ballot papers arrive at the same time as the appearance of a flood of pro-Michael publicity.

In the midst of what looked, to many, as collusion between Party officials and Michael's camp, there was some real encouragement for Morgan. On 31st January *Wales on Sunday* published the results of the first Wales-wide canvass of public opinion on the leadership issue. The telephone poll (run in partnership with its sister paper, the *Western Mail*) showed Morgan winning over 90% of votes cast (5,518 to just 519 for Michael). Some of the results, by area, were extraordinary. In Neath (home of Michael's Campaign Manager, Peter Hain) the figure was 389-11 in Morgan's favour; in Swansea, 304-14. Equally spectacular were the polls from Carmarthen (170-3), Ammanford (230-1) and Cardigan (144-3). Though curtly dismissed by Michael as "crude entertainment", the poll was a major boost for Morgan, allowing his team to claim in a press release: "It's now crystal clear that when people get a chance to have their say in this contest, they want Rhodri. Every poll and every ballot from Day One of this campaign has given Rhodri overwhelming backing".

With now less than three weeks before the vote would be announced, Blair made a third visit to Wales on 2 February. His trip to Cardiff, though meant to boost Michael, was widely regarded as counter-productive. While the *Mirror* played its usual cheer-leader role, the Welsh press took a more sceptical line over the visit. A *Western Mail* editorial seemed to capture the prevailing mood: "the suspicion lingers that this latest visit was a mistake... the over-use of the Downing Street card may well do more harm to Mr Michael's campaign than any other single factor... it does his cause little good to be seen to be relying so heavily on the endorsement of Mr Blair" (3rd February). Forced repeatedly during his visit to deny he was there just to help prop up Michael, the Prime Minister appeared to recognise the possibility of Michael losing. Asked about the consequences of a Morgan victory, he replied: "I've made it clear all the way through, I've got nothing against Rhodri and whoever wins I will work with."

On the eve of the UNISON ballot result on 6th February, and with the final overall result looking too close to call, the press began to play on the theme of the 'nightmare scenarios' now facing the WLP. One would follow from a narrow Michael victory won on the backs of union block votes. The other stemmed from Michael becoming leader, then failing to win a seat on the Assembly. There was perhaps also a third 'nightmare' in the offing. This would turn on the relationship between Morgan and Hain. Hain had run two campaigns against Morgan (first for Davies, now for Michael) and had also been put in charge of Labour's Assembly election campaign. So what if Morgan won? As the *Western Mail* put it: "How easily and convincingly could Hain tell Wales to vote for Mr Morgan as First Secretary-elect? How could Labour sell a leader it had painted as crypto-nationalist and a loose cannon?" (5th February).

As expected, members of UNISON voted strongly for Morgan, giving him 7,101 votes to 2,557 for Michael. Hain tried to play down the result by claiming, "With just one in five members voting, this was more a vote for apathy than for Rhodri." He received a sharp response from Morgan's campaign manager: "It's very much in line with the level of turnout in 1994 when Blair was elected Party leader," adding pointedly, "And 19% of 50,000 is better than 19 men in a room."

The next decisive moment in the leadership battle – the selection of Labour candidates for the additional members list – was to be fought out largely in private. It proved to be one of the most notorious episodes in a campaign already scarred by accusations of 'fixes' and 'stitch-ups'. To understand why, we need to return again to examine the detailed workings of Labour's electoral college.

The last of Labour's 40 Assembly constituency candidates had been selected on 7th February. They would take their place in section three of the electoral college, along with MPs, MEPs and an as yet unknown number of people on the list. This section, as we saw earlier, was always going to play a vital role in the election outcome. This miniature electorate (made up of the 40 candidates, 34 MPs, 5 MEPs and an 'X' number of list members) controlled 33% of the total vote. Every single vote would, therefore, be precious, in a tight contest. Both sides were keenly aware of the political arithmetic. Michael's camp had two causes for concern. First, 27 of the 40 Assembly candidates had pledged for Morgan, which helped off-set the lead Michael enjoyed among MPs and MEPs. Second, the UNISON vote, together with the very strong support Morgan had from ordinary Party members and the wider public, had fed rumours that some selected Assembly candidates who had declared for Michael, might now be thinking of switching sides.

It was not hard to see why some might be wavering. An NOP poll commissioned by HTV, released on 12 February, produced some significant findings for candidates who would have to face the voters on 6th May. The poll – based on a sample of 1,500 people – showed, 75% of Labour voters and 78% of all voters expressing a preference for Morgan over Michael for the leadership. But the real interest for Labour's Assembly candidates came in the answers to the questions that followed. When people were asked which Party they would vote for in their constituency if Michael was Labour's leader, the figures were: Labour 55%; Plaid Cymru 19%; Conservatives 16%; Liberal-Democrats 6%; and others 1%. However, with Morgan as leader, the figures showed a dramatic shift to Labour, putting Labour at 64%; Plaid Cymru 16%; Conservatives 14%; Liberal-Democrats 6%; and others 1%.

The message was clear: Labour would get a 9% 'election day bonus' if Morgan was leader, with a drop in support for Plaid Cymru, the party tipped to be Labour's main threat in the forthcoming elections. Faced with these figures it was not difficult to see why Assembly candidates who had committed themselves to Michael, might now be having second thoughts. The message coming from the poll was certainly grasped by Plaid Cymru leaders. As one senior member of the party put it: "Privately we're hoping Alun will win. That would be the best result for Plaid".

In these circumstances, the selection of list members became increasingly important. *Who* was to do the selecting and *who* and *how many* were to be selected now became a major battleground.

There were five regional lists. In every area, the selection process was to be decided by representatives from each of the constituencies in each region, presided over by a Panel made up of three members from the WLP Executive, two NEC members and two Party officials. Candidates for a list place would be given five minutes to address the meeting and then, in theory, the delegates and Panel would decide on who they wanted. The theory ran foul of machine politics. The Panel was packed with known Michael supporters. In January Morgan, correctly anticipating there would be attempts to fix the list if the contest was close, had questioned the participation on the Panel of Terry Thomas. Thomas, despite running Michael's election campaign office, refused to withdraw. His involvement was then discussed at January's meeting of the WLP Executive, where a resolution was passed asking Panel members to be "fair and even-handed". They were to be neither.

The list selection process was bizarre. If constituency delegates present thought they were there to decide on list places, they were sadly mistaken. The decision on placings was going to be made by the Panel alone. After the candidates had made their presentations, the Panel then left the meeting, to return with their recommended list of names and their placing on the list. The delegates were then invited to either approve or reject the list. In three of the five regions delegates moved for rejection. In the Mid and West Wales region, the official list – which placed Michael top – was rejected four times, in what one Morgan supporter described as a "heated meeting lasting more than four hours". Another Morgan supporter present said local members were convinced of a stitch-up before the meeting had begun. He went on: "Their fears were realised when the Panel's recommendations came. Predictably Alun Michael was number one, followed by three known supporters of his – Sioned Mair Richards, Vaughan Gethin and Delyth Evans" (Evans was later appointed by Michael as one of his Special Advisors; Gethin now works for Lorraine Barrett, Assembly Member for Cardiff South and Penarth and formerly Michael's constituency secretary).

That Michael was himself directly caught up in the politics of the list, was another factor that hurt his credibility. He had entered the race late. By the time he arrived many of the safe Labour seats had already been selected. His options were further reduced by Labour's 'twinning policy', which set aside 50% of the constituency seats for women. At one stage there had been speculation that he might find a home in Blaenau Gwent, but this route was blocked when it was realised that most of its constituency members were strongly backing Morgan's leadership bid. Being effectively cut out of the process of seat selection, he was forced to retreat to a place on the list. From here he could move only in the direction of Mid and West Wales, the only region in Wales where Labour was reasonably sure of picking up list seats.

There was similar uproar in deciding Labour's list for the South

Wales Central and the South Wales East regions, where the Panel's
list were also thrown out by delegates. Not that a deadlock between
Panels and delegates counted for much. Panel recommendations
were simply taken for endorsement by the WLP Executive (dominated by Michael supporters) at its meeting on 13th February, a decision that would then be rubber-stamped by the UK's Party's ruling
NEC in London.

If the Panel composition and the selection were fixed, the Party
also had to do some fine calculations about the number of candidates
to be chosen, again with an eye to what best served Michael's interests. Whatever number was chosen, it was only ever going to be likely
that one, or at best two Labour list candidates would actually win a
seat. But then they were not being placed on the list to win seats, but
to deliver votes. Before the list selection got underway it was strongly
rumoured the Party was thinking of selecting up to twelve list candidates for each region – which would have produced a total of 60 list
members. Any thoughts along these lines would have been rapidly
abandoned, as soon as it was realised that 60 people, taken from a list
of those approved Assembly candidates who had not found a seat to
fight, was bound to have contained a high proportion of Morgan
supporters. In the end, the Party settled for four list members per
region, a number finely calibrated to achieve the objective for which
the exercise was designed.

In squaring the lists, the WLP attracted some if its worst local and
national press to date. 'What a Stitch-Up!', 'Failed in Wales', 'Labour
in Disarray', 'Puppets of Blair' were just some of the headlines. From
the point of view of the Party fixers however, this was a price worth
paying for having successfully packed the list with Michael supporters. Around 100 people applied for a list place. It was thought these
were probably split 60:40 in Morgan's favour. But when the list was
published, the balance was heavily in favour of those travelling on
Michael's ticket. And they would be voting in that section of the electoral college where just 94 people represented 33% of the total vote.
Put another way, each vote in this section was worth 0.37% of the
section total. A couple of votes here counted for as much as the
percentage of the vote delivered by one of the smaller unions, or by
roughly 450 ordinary Party members.

There were three other significant episodes between the massag-
ing of the list and declaration of the vote: the decision of the GMB
(the last of the Big Four unions to declare), the counting of Party
members' ballot papers by USBS and an intervention by Lord

Hattersley, former Deputy Leader of the Labour Party. Writing in *The Guardian* (16th February), Hattersley lashed out at the way the contest was being run. Accusing Michael of being the Prime Minister's "poodle", he claimed Blair had a passion for uniformity and a fear of the slightest dissent. He went on: "Nicolas Ceaucescu did not live in vain. Elections begin with the identification of the winning candidate. The voting system is then adjusted to guarantee the desired result."

The GMB came out for Michael on 19th February on the eve-of-poll, giving him their 6.2% of the overall vote. In many respects the electoral process adopted by the GMB had been the most byzantine of all the big unions not balloting their members. Their preferred method had been the device of the 'branch consultation'. It was a method that left many questions unanswered. Exactly what did 'consultation' mean? Were the views of members in all branches that were 'consulted' binding on the person who actually cast the branch vote? How many branches were consulted and by what method? The GMB leadership were not willing to discuss these finer points, simply dressing up the result as 24,520 votes for Michael, against 11,060 for Morgan.

In an attack on political fixing *The Independent* newspaper quoted an eminent political figure who had addressed just this issue in a speech in 1992: "If we can't actually trust Labour Party members with decision-making within the Labour Party, how on earth are we going to go out and try to win support for the Party in the wider community?" The words were telling. They were spoken by Tony Blair.

Morgan's team knew all along that with three of the four big Welsh unions always going to back Michael, together with Michael gathering in the MP payroll vote and benefiting from a list fix, they would have to poll at least 72% of the vote of Party members. This was a tall order, but not impossible. Their telephone canvass returns, plus their other forms of political intelligence gathering, suggested Morgan was well on course to get at least 70% of this section's votes. But there were concerns in Morgan's camp about the precise nature of the relationship between Unity Security Balloting Services (USBS), the firm employed by the Party to count the votes, and the Party machine. USBS Ltd had been set up when Conservative government legislation in the 1980s forced trade unions to ballot their members on more issues than they had done in the past. A party political ballot does not require the organisers to meet statutory standards or controls. According to one source, there had been "consistent complaints from individual members of trade unions [about USBS], which tended to mirror those of Rhodri Morgan" (*Private Eye*, 5th March).

The first concerns surfaced, as we saw, at the end of January when the Morgan team lodged a complaint about the decision to bring forward the release of Party members' ballot papers. They later asked if they could send someone to scrutinise the count (in London), to ensure that ballot papers had been properly received and counted, only to be told this would not be necessary since the counting process was computerised "so there was no point as the computer would count the votes in twenty minutes". Two journalists from *The Times* took up the story, but made little progress, reporting: "A spokesman at USBS declined to reveal details of the count or when and where ballot papers were opened before being counted, because of its contract with Labour" (19th February).

Morgan's team did not press the point (though later they wished they had). Their unease about USBS was reinforced with the declaration of the final, overall result, on 20th February in Cardiff's new five-star St. David's Hotel. They were clearly taken aback by the size of Michael's vote among ordinary Party members. All the work they had done had pointed strongly towards Morgan getting at least 70% of the vote in this section. In the event he polled only 64.35%. This was a considerable achievement by any measure, but the difference between the two figures was enough to cost him the election. Shortly after the election Morgan wrote to USBS, with questions about the way they had administered the ballot. As well as raising the issue of how and why the date was changed for the sending out of ballot papers, he put two further questions. Were the ballot papers counted as they came in? And was any information about ballot returns leaked to the Michael camp? (The inference being that if Michael's team had inside knowledge about, say, voting patterns and response levels, they could redirect their telephone canvass.) Morgan's letter was given short shrift by both USBS and the Party.

Despite this set back, Morgan refused to drop the matter. On March 10th he wrote to Clive Soley, Chairman of the PLP, setting down his worries about links between USBS and the Labour Party. Morgan raised a number of interesting points. He claimed that it was "common knowledge in Cardiff and London" five days before the ballot closed that there was a 65:35% split between himself and Michael in the Party membership ballot. Further, the "circumstantial evidence suggests there must have been an interim count and that interim count was not secure". Morgan went on to suggest that either a progress report was requested and given, or an "unintentional leak" occurred. How, then, might information have been leaked, unintentionally or otherwise? Morgan provided a plausible explanation: "My campaign team had assumed... that since the closing date for postal ballots was 19th February, envelopes would be opened that day and counted. I now understand that this is not the procedure followed by USBS. I am informed that USBS hire electronic counting machines from Zetters, the pools company.... An interim count has to take place because at weekends the pools company uses the machine for their more usual purpose. It is at the point of changeover from pools to political work that a leak is more likely to occur, or the basis for a requested 'progress report' is provided."

If Morgan was right in implying information had leaked out, this might help explain why, a few days before the ballot closed, several pro-Michael Welsh Labour MPs had issued a statement calling upon Morgan to accept the eventual result without challenge. Although the issues raised by Morgan were serious ones, the Labour Party showed no willingness to carry out an inquiry. Instead, it proposed a series of drastic measures to strike off the ballot any candidate who publicly protested about the way in which an election contest is being conducted.

Table 5.2. The Second Labour Leadership Election

	Alun Michael	Rhodri Morgan
Trade Union/Affiliated Bodies	63.96%	36.04%
MPs, MEPs, Assembly Candidates	58.43%	41.57%
Party Members	35.65%	64.35%
TOTAL	**52.68%**	**47.32%**

The final result gave Michael victory by 52.68% to 47.32%. Morgan, as we saw, won well among WLP members (with 64.35% of their votes), but not well enough. He also scored solidly in the MPs/MEPs/Assembly candidates section, picking up 41.57% of the vote, which was probably about as well as he could have expected to have done, since he was up against the MP payroll vote and a fixed additional list. Where he lost decisively was among the trade unions and other affiliated bodies, where he gained only 36% of votes cast, against 63.96% for Michael. The size of Michael's majority in this section was, of course, underpinned by the union block vote, which accounted for nearly 50% of this section's total vote.

These headline figures hid the fact that whenever an OMOV ballot had been conducted, Morgan had won comfortably, and in many cases overwhelmingly. He was typically generous in conceding to his opponent, but said: "I recognise that I have not won this contest. But I have to tell you I do not feel like a loser." A member of the public waiting outside the hotel on being told the result was less gracious: "This is devolution on a dog lead".

On the Monday before the result, the BBC *Panorama* programme had claimed the controversial electoral college system had been cooked up at the Party's Millbank headquarters in London. Their claim was immediately dismissed by Peter Hain as a lie because "it was decided by Wales". Sadly, for the Labour Party in Wales, Hain was right. It was, in the end, those who controlled the different parts of the Party's machine in Wales who had set the rules for a disastrous and damaging leadership contest. Trying to explain Labour's troubles in Wales by conjuring up demons from Millbank was to miss the point. While 'London' obviously wanted Michael – and Millbank moved heaven and earth to help him – it was not within Blair's considerable powers to lever him in without the active help and connivance of Labour's power brokers in Wales. They were the real architects of the Party's misfortunes.

6. The New Ambassadors: Selecting the Candidates

Well before the WLP formally launched its formal process of candidate selection in March 1998, some figures in the Party indicated they wanted the Assembly to be a 'show-case' for the best talent Labour could muster. Indeed the issue had been raised in a discussion between Tony Blair and Ron Davies, the day after the referendum result had been declared. It was certainly an issue about which Davies felt deeply. In his speech to the Party's 1997 Annual Conference he restated his view that Labour's Assembly candidates should be the brightest and most able that Wales had to offer: "We must open up to the many, both men and women, who have given service to Wales – to business, universities, sport or culture, the media, public and private sector alike" (4th October). He went on: selection should reflect "Service to our country, not just to our Party". The message was clear. The doors should be held wide open and the test of selection should be quality and merit – not length of service. Implicit in Davies' speech was an appeal to the Party to avoid selecting candidates drawn just from the ranks of time-served Labour activists.

His call was never likely to be answered. Even before speaking to conference, Davies had been admonished by "a source close to Tony Blair" for suggesting a relaxation of the rule that Labour candidates should be Party members for at least two years to be eligible for selection.

There were sound reasons why Davies wanted to re-write the script for candidate selection. The low public standing of politicians in Wales was one reason why the prospect of an Assembly had failed to impress many voters during the referendum campaign. There were fears that low calibre local councillors would seek – and get – Assembly places, turning it into what some critics referred to as "Glamorgan County Council on stilts". This spectre was not likely to enthral the electorate. As we saw earlier, local government in much of Wales was close to being a one-party state, and councillors in Wales were more likely to be over 70 than under 45, men outnumbered women by 8:2 and fewer than one in a hundred were from ethnic backgrounds. As Wales' dominant Party, it was incumbent on Labour to prove it was genuinely committed to a more representative style of politics, where women were promoted as readily as men and quality and diversity were valued above length of service to the Party.

Preparing the Ground

The first steps taken by the Party were encouraging. As part of its preparations for the Assembly elections (and the Scottish Parliament) it introduced three novel procedures to try to ensure Labour candidates met the twin criteria of high calibre and gender balance. First, *self-nomination* meant any Party member could apply to become a candidate, thereby opening the process beyond the usual local networks of referral, patronage and sponsorship. Second, the Party designed a rigorous *selection panel process*, where applicants would have to pass a gruelling interview before qualifying for the list of approved Assembly candidates. The third institutional innovation was *twinning*, aimed at ensuring gender balance within the Labour group of Assembly members. This was to prove the most controversial of all the new procedures. Twinning was to be achieved by obliging each CLP to 'twin' with another, so as to select a male and female candidate, thus producing a 20:20 gender balance in the 40 constituency seats in Wales (the same principle was to apply to the placing of candidates on the additional members' list).

Enter the Gladiators

The deadline for applications was set for the end of March 1998, by which time the Party had received over 600 expressions of interest. Each inquirer was sent a package detailing the selection procedure, the qualifications the Party would be looking for, a four-page application form, an outline of the functions and responsibilities of the Assembly and an invitation to attend briefing meetings to advise and prepare applicants for the panel selection process. In the briefing meetings – conducted by Andrew Davies, then a Labour Party Officer – it was stressed that the Party would be looking for candidates of real calibre and was keen to encourage applications from those who could claim neither lengthy Party membership nor a long history of local political involvement. The number of initial inquiries was welcomed by both the Party and the press. Ron Davies and Anita

Gale declared themselves "happy" with the response, while the *Western Mail* was moved to comment: "Ron Davies was emphatic that the National Assembly would usher in a new era of Welsh politics. Integral to that has been his stated aim of attracting a new generation of politicians to become the new Assembly [persons]... With such a lengthy list [of applicants] Mr Davies' dream of an inclusive Assembly of men and women drawn from all areas of Welsh life... does not seem so far-fetched" (20th January 1998)

In the event, around 450 formal applications were returned and these were vetted by a selection board. The initial 'culling' was done on the basis of a 'blind trawl', where selection was based entirely on the content of the forms (while only candidates' membership numbers – not names or gender – appeared on the form, some applicants were later to complain that in the small world of Welsh Labour politics, it would not have been difficult to identify many people through the information they provided). Those approved passed to the second stage (the interview). Unsuccessful applicants were given reasons for their rejection and the right of appeal. It is thought that about 120 candidates fell at the first hurdle, including some well known names in Welsh Labour politics, like Tyrone O'Sullivan, Keith Griffiths, Jeff Jones, Tom Middlehurst and Janice Gregory. All were reinstated on appeal, but not before one of them – Griffiths – had threatened to mount a legal challenge.

The Party's attempt to produce a selection process that was open, fair and meritocratic, was not universally applauded. As applications were still coming in, Ogmore MP, Sir Ray Powell, was attacking the new procedures. Claiming to speak for many ordinary Party members, Powell said the new selection methods represented some kind of "devolution loyalty oath", where only those 'New Labour' candidates supporting the Government's line on the Asembly would get chosen. The same line was taken by other Party members. One rejected applicant – Hedley McCarthy, an Islwyn councillor, and opponent of both devolution and twinning – claimed: "They don't want individuals. It's a cloning situation".

Much more worrying for those committed to a more 'inclusive' form of selection were the rumours, circulating in March, that certain safe Labour seats had been earmarked for favoured local candidates. One hopeful candidate related how she was advised to avoid certain seats which had already been set-aside for local Party members (like Cardiff South and Penarth, for example, which was allegedly earmarked for Lorraine Barrett, who was Alun Michael's assistant).

Panel Beating

Candidates who had cleared the first hurdle did not move rapidly to stage two. The Party managers were facing two major distractions. The start of the leadership battle between Davies and Morgan and an ongoing and increasingly fractious internal Party struggle over the twinning policy. The first signal that the selection process was about to move on did not come until 3rd June 1998 (nearly three months since the briefing meetings), with an invitation to attend a half-day session at Cardiff County Council HQ for a discussion of 'interviewing procedures'. The day (6th June) was one most candidates were not likely to forget. It gave them the first sight of their 'opposition', which was a little unnerving for some, especially those new to the candidate selection game. After some routine information had been given out, candidates were then 'invited' to do exercises designed to help them relax before going into an interview room. Most found these sub-aerobic maneouvres – based on a series of breathing exercises and a bit of what christian evangelicals would no doubt call 'touchy-feely work' – deeply embarrassing, but politely went along with it. The manic enthusiasm of the instructor was not, it is fair to say, widely shared by most candidates (a group of grizzled old Labour stalwarts from the Valleys was especially sceptical). Of much more interest to them was the announcement that the Party hoped to complete all interviews in the period, 8-28th June.

In the event, the time-table was not met. Interviews were not finally completed until the end of July. In addition to its other problems, the Party found difficulty sometimes in assembling its selection panels. Candidates were supposed to be interviewed by a four person panel, comprising the following: a member of the WLP Executive; a nominee from the NEC; an 'independent' member of the WLP; and a professional adviser to the panel. Understandably, it would never be easy to put together full panels to interview around 300 candidates in the time set by the WLP, given panel members' other commitments and the time and travel involved.

From the viewpoint of most candidates the actual interviews, once underway, were not too daunting. Candidates had, after all, been carefully briefed about the procedure, had time to prepare an initial five-minute presentation to set out their stall, been told well in advance of the policy areas they would be questioned on and were made well aware of the criteria they would be judged upon. There was no obvious reason why a well-prepared and reasonably well-informed applicant should not get through. The panel chairs were generally judged to have been scrupulously fair in dealing with candidates. In instances where it either had not been possible to assemble a full panel on the day, or when candidates knew one or more of the panel (which was often the case), chairs would give candidates the option of leaving and being interviewed by another panel.

Of course none of this stopped the rumours, gossip and information-swapping among candidates waiting for interview. Inevitably those who had been interviewed early in the process were frequently swamped with calls from those waiting their turn, probing for information. Sue Essex – a Cardiff councillor and among the first to be interviewed – has described how: "Suddenly my phone never stopped ringing. Candidates from everywhere wanted to know who interviewed me, what they were like, the questions I was asked – all the usual things. I tried to be reassuring. I didn't find it a massive ordeal". Nevertheless, the rumour mill ground on. Some panel members rapidly became 'demonised' by anxious candidates, others were labelled as a 'soft touch' as candidates traded stories about how the panels were working. The paranoia of some of them was fed by a spate of stories in the press over allegations that, in Scotland, the selection panels were in the business of 'dumping leftists' and anyone else who had upset the Party's managers in some way. The well publicised failure of two well known left-wing Scottish MPs – Denis Canavan and Ian Davidson – to get on Labour's list of approved candidates for the Scottish Parliament, was hailed as "proof" that the new selection process was just an excuse for a "vendetta" against "Old Labour" by "New Labour modernisers" (14th June, *The Observer*). This mindset found full expression in an editorial in the left-leaning *Tribune*, which spoke of our "worst fears" being realised if the selection panels in Scotland and Wales "have engaged in a purge" (12th June). The paper then raised the temperature further by linking together the selection processes in Scotland and Wales with growing protests from sections of the Labour Party over the battle for places on the NEC (the annual election round to Labour's ruling body was by now underway) and places on the all-important lists for the 1999 MEPs selection. The implication was clear. The Party was using these various selection processes to reward loyalists and weed out suspected 'dissidents'.

Those taking the *Tribune* line would have found it difficult to make the 'purge' charge stick when the WLP at last produced the list of those who had passed the panel interviews in Wales. Published on 6th August – the 151 names on the list (or, more accurately, an interim list, since appeals were still being heard) were greeted as "good value" by Paul Flynn in his weekly *South Wales Echo* column. Anticipating criticism from some of "Labour's Welsh awkward squad of MPs", he pointed out with evident feeling: "Most of them were selected by processes riddled with patronage and favours stitched up with secret plots. The rotten past is being replaced by systems that are open, rational and fair" (7th August). The list was also warmly endorsed by the *Western Mail*. In an editorial titled, 'Slow-moving Labour has chosen well', the paper highlighted the presence on the list of 52 women and 9 black or ethnic minority candidates and added: "By choosing such a large shortlist [Labour] has given plenty of leeway to its constituencies who have a broad field to pick from" (7th August). But just how the constituencies were to play their part was to be a matter of some controversy. More immediately, though, the Party was plunged into a row over the handling of its appeals procedure.

'I've Got a Little List'

Among the 150 or so who had failed to make the shortlist were a number of prominent names and some less well known, but who had powerful patrons. The first category included Tyrone O'Sullivan (something of a Welsh folk-hero for having led the fight to save Tower colliery), John Adams (who became Ron Davies' chief policy adviser in 1996) Tom Middlehurst (a Labour council leader from North Wales) and Gareth Hughes (former member of the Welsh Executive), the last two lodging appeals. The second category included Lorraine Barrett (assistant to Alun Michael MP), Janice Gregory (Sir Ray Powell's daughter) and Christine Gwyther (an ally of Nick Ainger MP), all of whom put in appeals. In total, 58 people appealed, but only 12 were upheld.

The trouble was to centre on the appeals procedure, which was handled by a three-person panel headed by Terry Thomas. It was never clear how the Thomas panel arrived at the conclusions it did. Candidates who had been rejected at stage one, were sent a letter outlining the reasons why they had failed. Then, if they wished, they could submit a written appeal (to the written part of the selection process), responding to the points that had been raised. No such formal procedure was operated for stage two appeals. Some rejected candidates gave odd reasons for their failure. For example one claimed she had been distracted by the noise of a builder's drill; another appealed because there were only two people sitting on her panel (grounds which should have been discounted since, as we saw, applicants were given the option to withdraw if there were aspects of the panel they were dissatisfied with). The fair and logical way to treat appeals would have been for candidates to be reassessed by a different panel.

Thomas presented his 'add-ons' to the final meeting of the WLP panel, which had laboured long and conscientiously to select the original list of 151 candidates. The original choice had been executed in a transparent and impartial way and in many cases the panels had been painstaking in discussing and 'grading' marginal interviewees. Now they were being asked to accept the appeals list, without Thomas offering any explanation as to why some had been accepted and most refused. It made a nonsense of the selection procedure and, not surprisingly, the panel unanimously refused to accept Thomas' recommendations. Thomas responded in typical style: "If we cannot go ahead with you, we will go ahead without you".

At this point Paul Flynn enters the story. Flynn was, at the time, a member of the Welsh Executive. Thomas had taken his list to a Newport meeting of the Executive for their approval and again declined to give reasons for his selection. Flynn, in recounting the episode later, wrote: "I said that unless some pretext was provided for these decisions, the belief would spread that those who were being added to the Panel had friends in high places, or were 'the favourite sons and daughters' of influential people in the Party" (Flynn, 1999). This was denied, but Flynn claimed other MPs have since told him they did intervene to help their local favourites. The Executive, as might have been predicted, endorsed Thomas' little list. Among the appeals allowed were Barrett, Gregory, Gwyther and Middlehurst. All are now Assembly Members and the latter hold two Cabinet posts.

One who certainly made no secret of his intention to do some lobbying was Martyn Jones, Clwyd South MP. After Labour's list of approved candidates for Assembly selection had been published, he made it clear he was unhappy that no applicants from his constituency had got through. He announced at a constituency meeting that he would be "working very hard" to get three rejected Clwyd South applicants put back on the list. The three all won their appeals. One – Karen Sinclair – is now the Assembly Member for Clwyd South.

Flynn, however, refused to let the matter drop. In December 1998 Alun Michael had written to Flynn saying he was determined to "correct the abuses of democracy and fair play in the Labour Party in Wales". In replying Flynn seized the opportunity to raise again the issue of the use and abuse of patronage in the appeals process.

He wrote: "Briefly I discussed this with you the other day involving one individual close to you whose appeal was successful and another fine candidate whose appeal failed. Other MPs have told me that they did intervene to help their favourite sons and daughters. One person whose appeal succeeded is, I understand, a close relative of an MP and an aspirant candidate in the MP's seat. I did not intervene on behalf of three aspirant candidates from Newport West, because I thought it was wrong. Did you?" There was no reply to Flynn's letter. For many in the Party the micro-politics of the appeals process had adulterated the orginal process of candidate selection.

Campaign Charlies: The Slaughter of the Innocents

There were now 163 approved Labour candidates set to compete for 40 Assembly constituency seats. Twinning arrangements meant that there were 105 men and 58 women running for 20 places apiece. The struggle for a place was given an extra intensity by other factors. First, at best Labour could really only hope to win 34 of the 40 constituency seats in Wales (i.e. by being returned in those areas it had won in the 1997 General Election). Second, there were several constituencies where it was allegedly common knowledge that the seat had been 'reserved' for a local favourite (among them: Lorraine Barrett (Cardiff South and Penarth), Janice Gregory (Ogmore), Wayne David (Rhondda), John Marek (Wrexham) and Tom Middlehurst (Alyn and Deeside)). Nor was anyone likely to relish the prospect of taking on the immensely popular Rhodri Morgan, in Cardiff West. Third, even where there was no single local favourite there were, in many other seats, a clutch of local candidates who enjoyed strong local support. There were perhaps just three or four seats where there was no obvious local claimant and all except one of these (Monmouth) were reckoned to be unwinnable by Labour (e.g. Brecon and Radnor, Ceredigion, Montgomeryshire, Meirionnydd Nant Conwy). Finally, the 163 candidates who started the race, were joined by a further eight after the Executive's decision to re-open the Panel on 2nd November, for the purpose of finding a perch for Alun

Michael (a move which let in Jane Davidson – who was to be selected for the safe Pontypridd seat). Candidates experienced in the ways of Labour constituency politics knew what to expect. For the rest, though, it was to be what one seasoned party member described as "the slaughter of the innocents". It was all a far cry from the days when Ron Davies had called for the Assembly to be a 'showcase' for the best talent Labour in Wales could muster.

The first decision facing most candidates was how wide to cast their net in the search for a seat. Some opted for a complete trawl, applying to all 40 constituencies. Others, probably the majority, settled for more limited fishing expeditions, trying to target seats rumoured to have no local person in line – or maybe seats where they thought competing 'insiders' might provide a chance for an unfancied 'outsider' to slip in. A handful made no applications anywhere, being content, just to have won a place on the approved list, perhaps using it as a marker for later bids for Parliamentary seats. Some decided to go for just one seat, invariably their home constituency. Candidates casting just a single line, were of two types. Those who had neither the time, nor the inclination to look beyond their home territory. And those earmarked as the clearly favoured local son or daughter; these were candidates who had, in effect, their nomination 'in the bag', well before the constituency selection had formally started (indeed, in some cases, well before the list of approved candidates had been released).

Having settled on a strategy, the candidates' next step was to produce a CV. Usually no more than a double-sided 'flyer', their production values ranged from the slickly professional (glossily printed, smartly designed, multi-coloured creations) to the engagingly amateurish looking (home-produced and clumsily laid-out). The next step was to get this material circulated – the first point at which those having to travel to find a seat, began to realise the cost of their candidacy. Bidding for a seat involved having to send multiple CVs to constituency officers, branch secretaries, union branch secretaries and to all those affiliates who had a finger in the selection process. This was an expensive business, with no certainty the material sent would ever get to its intended destination (no-one knew how many secretaries or affiliates would make an attempt to circulate this material to their members). Among the candidates looking for possible seats across Wales, some spent several hundred pounds in the course of their search.

Added to financial costs were what might be called the 'social costs' of candidacy – the *time* many candidates had to invest in the process. Travelling long distances, often at night, on roads of indifferent quality, meant that candidates with other obligations (family, work, as a carer) were effectively ruled out from competing for distant seats. For example, a candidate from South Wales, or South-West Wales, interested in finding a seat in North Wales, faced serious logistical problems (the same, of course, would also apply for those looking south). Twinned constituencies might contain up to twenty separate local Party branches. Because branch selection meetings were (quite understandably) organised to suit the convenience of the local members, not the candidates, branches made their own arrangements. There was rarely any attempt to co-ordinate candidate selection.

Branches generally opted for one of three methods of candidate nomination. The first was to invite no candidates at all, but simply decide on the basis of the CVs sent through by hopeful supplicants. This was a common practice and one most often followed in constituencies where there was a favourite son or daughter already waiting in the wings. Hence the thinking was 'why bother to go to the trouble of setting up a hustings, when we know who we want'. These decisions were usually made either by branch officers, or by those actually attending branch meetings (normally only a fraction of the total branch membership). In the event for most candidates the only indication they had that the branch had met, was a 'dear John' letter some days later (if they got one at all).

Rejection letters were a minor art form in their own right. Some were encouraging while expressing regrets and fulsome in their hope that the candidate would do better elsewhere. Others were curt (or at least this is how it appeared to those on the receiving end) one-liners, recording the failure and oblivious to the sensitivities of some applicants. One candidate – who had collected more than her fair share of rejection slips – later recalled: "After a while I used to dread the sound of the morning mail being delivered. It put me in my mind of those stories I'd read about of World War wives living in fear of the postman turning up with a black-edged telegram". Some replies could barely contain their surprise that outsiders could think of applying, like the reply from Broughton and Bretton, which said "I must inform you that two of our county councillors were selected at a Branch Meeting.... I think the general pattern will emerge throughout the various constituencies".

The second method of nomination was the one preferred by most candidates: an invitation to a formal hustings giving the opportunity to make a short speech and sometimes answer questions. Even these sessions, came in a variety of guises. At best (from the candidate's viewpoint) they allowed for a ten minute speech and a few minutes for questions. If the speech was a disaster, at least it was one of their own making. The questions, though, were a different matter. While most branches played it fair, pitching in with general policy questions, there were, inevitably, some who played the game by their own set of rules, posing questions answerable only by someone with an encyclopaedic knowledge of the local area. One candidate who ran into this type of inquisition remembers how: "As the questions started I could see this person straining to get in to ask a question. When it came, it floored me. It was about some obscure local issue – obscure to me anyway – and I had no idea how to answer it. In fact I had no idea what he was talking about. I lost confidence after that and things went down-hill from then on. My inquisitor seemed very pleased with himself, but I thought 'what a bastard'. I'd spent two hours travelling there and came away feeling like a complete idiot".

This tragi-comic experience highlights a more important general point. 'Outsider' candidates on the selection trail were always very conscious of their lack of local knowledge. In most cases this was not a problem, since most branch hustings tried hard to provide a level playing field, by asking all candidates the same, general questions. But a good answer to even a general question really required candidates to provide a local illustration or example. As a result, candidates on the road in the search for seats had to put in a huge amount of basic research work, trying to find as much as they could about the constituencies they were bidding for.

Not all branch hustings allowed for questions. Some wanted only speeches from the candidates. This often meant a severe test of the stamina of those branches where a large number of applicants were seeking a nomination, as a procession of supplicants came and went. For example, the Fishguard branch (in the Preseli-Pembrokeshire constituency) was addressed by no less than 23 candidates, speaking to an audience of less than a dozen. This was not untypical. Quite often branch selection meetings saw the members present well out numbered by the applicants. The Preseli-Pembrokeshire constituency was unusual in setting up a selection procedure that gave some thought to the problems facing candidates from outside the area. Instead of holding separate branch meetings, all branch members were invited to Narberth to hear the candidates at a single 'sitting'. Around

150 turned up, to listen to 22 candidates. Going in, in alphabetical order, each had just two minutes to impress. At the end of their two minutes of fame, a bell was rung and they were ordered off, whether in mid-sentence or not. Once the entire 22 had been processed, candidates were then invited to 'mingle' with the delegates to press their claims further. As one candidate present that night recalls: "I was near the end of the list of speakers. By the time I walked in, the audience looked a bit shell-shocked. Like everyone else I rattled through my speech at a pace that must have been barely comprehensible. I managed to squeeze it all in just before the bell tolled. Afterwards, mixing with branch members an elderly lady took me to one side and said, 'You were very good dear'. My spirits rose, but soon sank again when she whispered, 'but we don't want anyone from Cardiff'. I still remember the stress she placed on the word Cardiff. I felt a bit depressed by this, but took some perverse pleasure from thinking that every other outside candidate was probably in the same boat".

Whether they were or not, it was very apparent that 'localism' was a major barrier in the way of most 'outsider' candidates and one that proved almost impossible to surmount. Candidates, whatever their intrinsic merits, had little chance of making progress unless they could find a constituency where they had a personal connection, or influential local patrons willing to lobby on their behalf. Most candidates quickly resigned themselves to these realities. The geography of Wales, the tight time-table for selection followed by many constituencies and limits on some 'outsider' candidates' time and resources, combined to help reinforce 'localism'. Those who had started out in the innocent belief that the Party had embraced the idea of the 'new politics', would incubate a 'new breed' of political representative, rapidly became disillusioned. One – with a distinguished background in the health sector – wrote: "I was attracted to standing for the Assembly because of my understanding that the Labour Party in Wales wanted candidates with relevant experience.... I thought the initial process was fair and conducted along modern personnel lines. However after that all the selected candidates were left very much on their own.... It became very clear to me that those people who were within the Constituency Organisations and Labour Party hierarchy had huge advantages and indeed this proved to be the case.... The constituency meeting system..emphasised the advantage to internal candidates". He added: "I also feel for Labour to succeed in the Assembly there must be fundamental democratic reforms within the Party in Wales".

A third method used by some branches to assess candidates was the 'informal' branch meeting. Under this arrangement candidates were invited along not to give speeches and take questions, but to meet and talk informally with branch members. For most candidates, this was the most painful selection ordeal of them all. To begin with, candidates nearly always outnumbered branch members, sometimes by a ratio of three to one. Candidates never quite knew how to handle these encounters. On occasions there were embarrassing mistakes, as one female candidate recalls: "It was a dark winter's night and my very first invitation to attend a local branch. They were meeting in the local rugby club and I felt very nervous. I walked into one of the club rooms, pulled a chair up and greeted everyone effusively. They were lovely. Lots of jokey exchanges. After about 10 minutes they asked who I was. It turned out I'd wandered into a meeting of the rugby club's social committee".

Another account captures very well the awkwardness of many informal branch meetings. "All of us had our applications displayed on two notice boards. They looked liked the 'wanted' posters you see in police stations. The meeting was in the bar of a social club. About a dozen, rather elderly local members sat at tables around the room, clinging to each other for comfort and throwing occasional glances in our direction. There were 24 of us, hanging around awkwardly like teenagers going to their first dance – waiting to see who was going to make the first move. A few members came over – more to take advantage of the buffet on offer than from any great desire to talk to us. Some used this captive audience to talk about themselves. In the rare gaps your pedigree was explored to establish which part of the constituency you, your father, grandfather, etc. came from. Groups of three or more candidates would be competing furiously for the attention of one branch member. I don't think politics was ever mentioned".

Accounts like this could be almost endless, from every corner of Wales. One woman was to memorably describe the attempts by candidates to make an impression as they tried to 'work' a room at these informal sessions, as "a political version of lap-dancing". Most candidates enjoyed these encounters if only in what one described as "a morbid sort of way", and as they met up on the seat selection trail, would often swop stories about the latest indignation or humiliation, all stoically borne. If nothing else, when it was all over, new friendships had been forged under fire, and those unschooled in the ways of the Labour Party emerged wiser, if chastened by their experiences.

What we have been relating here is the prosaic detail of the Assembly selection process, which was crucial in determining who was brought on and who was turned back. In so many cases, the branch selections were mere formalities; where those petitioning were listened to politely, but where a local had usually already been promised the prize of the nomination. The procedure adopted varied, but the outcome was often pre-determined. Branches which operated by 'informal' selection rarely set about their business in a rigorous or systematic way. They had, after all, no need to. Most knew who they wanted long before selection had even formally started.

The odds were stacked against 'outside' candidates in other ways as well. In some instances, the timetable for the selection process was so tightly drawn, they had no time to circulate material, or to lobby. To take one example, candidates from outside one constituency were told of its selection timetable on a Friday. Those who phoned the constituency's Procedural Secretary (the person responsible for running the selection process) the next day asking for the names and addresses of branch secretaries (for mailing purposes), received the information the following Monday. Candidates phoning the secretaries on Monday evening for more information were told they were too late. Nominations had been made and gone, of course, to local applicants.

Even when the selection schedule was more leisurely, outsiders were in no real position to contact all constituency members; either because they had no full membership list, or – if they did – no time or resources to do a full mailing (remembering that constituencies could have anything between 300 and 1,000 members). This inability of candidates to reach the wider membership, meant in effect that nomination decisions were controlled by branch officers and the fraction of the branch membership attending selection meetings.

The politics of selection moved up a level once branch nominations were in and the twinned constituencies began to decide on the short-listing for the final hustings. As some candidates soon discovered, holding a clutch of nominations was no guarantee of getting short-listed. This stage of the selection process – a vital one – was often as much about local horse-trading, as it was the 'objective' merits of the candidates. Twinning gave it all an extra edge. In some cases the process was reduced to a trade-off along the lines of 'you support our woman and we'll support your man'. Often, of course, it was more complicated than this, especially in those constituencies where more than one man or woman enjoyed substantial local backing.

Once the short-listing was settled, each candidate could then ask for a full membership list from the paired constituencies. This at least gave all candidates the chance to write to, or telephone canvass all individual Party members in the two areas. This was helpful – particularly for 'outside' candidates – but only up to a point. They found major problems in the control of *postal votes*. To understand why, we need to understand the procedural arrangements leading up to the final hustings.

Husting meetings were arranged where those shortlisted would speak and answer set questions. Members present would then vote, ranking candidates in order of preference. Husting meetings varied in number. Some twinned constituencies had just one (e.g. Cardiff North and West); others five (like Monmouth and Brecon and Radnor). The number chosen usually reflected the geography of the area. If the territory covered by the twinning arrangements was large, then more hustings tended to be held. Hustings at least gave those present the opportunity to see and hear candidates perform, though only rarely would an 'outsider' be able to overcome the weight of votes already 'pledged' to one favoured local candidate or another. However, a particularly strong performance by a non-local candidate on the day might result in the person picking up a lot of second preference votes and so give them a slim chance of winning the backing of those attending the hustings.

But winning the battle of the hustings was one thing. Winning the postal vote was quite another. And since postal votes and the votes taken at the hustings were totted-up together, a candidate outperformed at the hustings could still come out on top through taking the bulk of the postal vote. In theory, postal vote numbers should have been small. The WLP's procedural guidelines for the award of postal votes made it clear they would "only be granted to those unable to attend a hustings meeting – not to those who choose not to attend". The criteria set down were precise: "Postal votes will only be granted for those who have a physical incapacity, cannot make reasonable travel arrangements, have work commitments or caring responsibilities". They were not, according to the rules, to be made available to Party members choosing to do something else on the day.

The rules were honoured more in the breach than in the observance. To give some examples; in one instance the 'twins' held one joint hustings where just under 200 members turned out. Before the meeting got underway, it was announced that 126 postal votes had been sent in coming mainly, as was discovered later, from just three branches. One was the home branch of one of the shortlisted candidates, the other from branches where the candidate was being backed by local Party officials. In another instance, a branch with around 100 members sent in nearly 80 postal votes; this branch, the biggest in its constituency, owed its size to a sudden surge in membership recruitment at the end of 1997, when 40 new members were signed up in two months.

Allegations about the 'manipulation' of the postal vote broke out into the open on one occasion, after the selection for the twinned constituencies of Ogmore-Rhondda. Jeff Jones, second in the contest for the Rhondda nomination, behind Wayne David, argued he had won a "moral victory" after winning most of the votes at the two hustings meetings, claiming David had won only because he had more postal votes. David, of course, strongly rejected Jones' claims. The cause of Jones' concerns would have been the relatively high postal vote recorded (108) against the number attending the hustings (187) in constituencies which between them claimed a total of nearly 1,500 members. Another dispute about postal votes surfaced at the end of January 1999, leading to the postponement of the selection process at Islwyn-Torfaen. Last minute objections were made to the way Islwyn had carried out is postal vote. Torfaen CLP members were concerned about the large number of postal votes submitted when Islwyn had been allowed to extend the deadline by three days.

The role of the postal vote raises a number of issues. First, Party officers appear to have made no rigorous attempt to vet postal vote applications. Second, organising the postal vote (and their concentration in some branches in some constituencies, suggest postal votes were being harvested), put outside candidates at a major disadvantage. Collecting postal votes is an intensely local affair, requiring local knowledge and support and input from those local Party activists backing one local candidate or another. Unless an outsider could find an 'insider' to do this work, they would be in difficulty. Next, trawling for postal votes had the effect of helping undermine the hustings as a forum for open debate and discussion, by reducing attendance. This, in turn, raised another issue of concern. In many twinned constituencies member participation in the final selection process was low. Numbers voting (in whatever way) was often only a small proportion of the total membership – for some yet another indication that many Party members remained unenthused about the Assembly.

Labour's selection of seat candidates was painfully slow. It was not until 14th November 1998 that the first two were chosen (for the 'twins' of Cardiff North and West), by which time the other parties had all their candidates in place. Complicating the selection process was the re-opening of the panel on 2nd November (to provide the window of opportunity for Alun Michael, a move deeply resented by many candidates on the original list) and the continued skirmishing over twinning (see below).

When Labour at last published its list of 40 constituency candidates, its composition came in for some criticism (Table 6.1 gives the candidates' profiles). The commitment to gender balance was welcomed (where Labour did much better than other Parties: the Liberal-Democrats selected only 12 women, the Conservatives 11 and Plaid Cymru only 8); so too was the relative 'youthfulness' of Labour's candidates. The average age of 46 was younger than that of Welsh Labour MPs (averaging 54) and much younger than the average for local councillors. Concern, though, was expressed about what was called the "overwhelming public sector bias" of the list. Of Labour's constituency candidates, nearly 50% were councillors or former councillors and if lawyers and public relations consultants are excluded, none came from the private sector. The conclusion was inescapable: "If Labour scores well on gender and age, the bias towards local government and the public sector means it has failed to select from a wide range of professional backgrounds" (Morgan, 1999). This raises the fundamental, but perhaps intractable, issue of selection. Intractable, that is, unless the Party, at the most local level, is ready to radically rethink its traditional methods of candidate selection. As one of the authors commented: "The first stage did secure the kind of applicant that Ron Davies said he wanted. But... how do you widen the area of talent when they have to go through the narrow confines of a local party selection process?" (Horton, 1999).

The 'calibre' issue was always going to be a point of tension in the candidate selection process. When Ron Davies spoke of his hope that Labour might attract candidates of high merit, who were "above the fray" of day-to-day politics, he brought an angry response from Terry Thomas. For many long serving, hardworking Party activists, the 'c' word was a code for a process aimed at cutting them out, while ushering in newcomers who had served no proper political apprenticeship. Any thoughts that Assembly place selection would – or should – produce some kind of 'samurai' class of political warriors, was hopelessly idealistic. It was an aspiration that was always bound to come to grief when coming against the realities of an entrenched political culture, determined to protect its own local interests and

Table 6.1 Labour's Constituency Candidates for the National Assembly

Constituency	Name	Occupation	Political Experience	Age
Aberavon	Mr Gibbons	GP		49
Alyn and Deeside	Mr Middlehurst	Retired	Councillor	63
Blaenau Gwent	Mr Law	Consultant	Councillor	51
Brecon & Radnor	Mr Jones	Lecturer	Councillor	29
Bridgend	Mr Jomes	Barrister	Councillor	32
Caernarfon	Ms Jones	Union Official		54
Caerphilly	Mr Davies	MP	MP	52
Cardiff Central	Mr Drakeford	Lecturer	Councillor	45
Cardiff North	Ms Essex	Lecturer	Councillor	54
Cardiff S & Pen	Ms Barrett	MP's Assistant	CLP Secretary	49
Cardiff West	Mr Morgan	MP	MP	60
Carm E & Dinefwr	Mr Llewellyn	Voluntary Sector	Councillor	37
Carm W & S Pemb	Ms Gwyther	Local Govt Officer	MP's Agent	40
Ceredigion	Ms Battle	Lawyer		42
Clwyd South	Ms Sinclair		Councillor	47
Clwyd West	Mr Pugh	College Manager		44
Conwy	Ms Sherrington	Teacher	Branch Chair	37
Cynon Valley	Ms Chapman	Local Govt Officer	Councillor	43
Delyn	Ms Halford	Ex-Police Force	Councillor	59
Gower	Ms Hart	Officer	Wales TUC	42
Islwyn	Mr Williams	MP's Assistant		31
Llanelli	Ms Garrard	Lawyer		49
Merionydd NC	Ms Jones	Teacher	Councillor	49
MT & Rhymney	Mr Lewis	Officer	Labour Party	35
Monmouth	Ms Short	Social Worker	Councillor	47
Montgomeryshire	Mr Hewitt	Civil Servant		47
Neath	Ms Thomas	Social Services	Councillor	57
Newport East	Mr Griffiths	Solicitor	Councillor	43
Newport West	Ms Butler		Councillor	56
Ogmore	Ms Gregory	MP's Assistant	CLP Secretary	44
Pontypridd	Ms Davidson	Local Govt Assn		42
Preseli Pemb	Mr Edwards	Pol Researcher	CLP Secretary	43
Rhondda	Mr David	MEP	MEP	42
Swansea East	Ms Feld	Voluntary Sector		52
Swansea West	Mr Davies	Consultant	Councillor	47
Torfaen	Ms Neagle	Voluntary Sector	MEP Assistant	31
Vale of Clwyd	Ms Jones		Councillor	46
Vale of Glamorgan	Ms Hutt	Voluntary Sector	Councillor	49
Wrexham	Mr Marek	MP	MP	59
Ynys Mon	Mr Owen	Voluntary Sector	Councillor	40

fierce in its defence of traditional custom and practice. All the rhetoric about a 'new politics' meant little, unless the Party was ready to radically reform its own internal structures.

Candidates with no seat to fight had one more opportunity to find an Assembly place – by trying to get on Labour's additional members list (the proportional representation top-up). These selections took place between 8-10th February 1999. In an earlier chapter we described how the conduct of these list selections were caught up in, and disfigured by, the leadership battle between Michael and Morgan. There are other points to be made about this corner of the selection process. These were eloquently summarised in a letter of complaint sent to Anita Gale by Mark Drakeford, one of Labour's Assembly candidates. Drakeford wrote: "The preparation of candidates for interview lacked equity and transparency. The selection process was intended to operate according to criteria against which individual candidates were to be assessed. Yet these criteria were not available to candidates.... The tragedy for the Labour Party is that the incompetencies and inadequacies which have come to the fore during the week have so badly undone the good which earlier rounds in the selection process had produced.... In the public mind, the Labour Party machine has been wheeled in to conduct the old-fashioned machine politics" (11th February).

Drakeford was wrong on one point. Some candidates did seem to know what the criteria for selection were. Though the fact of partial disclosure helps underline his claim about the lack of "equity and transparency".

It had taken Labour nearly a year (from March 1998) to produce its full slate of Assembly candidates. The selection process had been dogged by controversy and cross-cut by two bruising and demoralising leadership contests. From here, the Party was shortly to plunge into the Assembly election campaign. Any thoughts it might have entertained that its troubles had finally been laid to rest, were to be badly disappointed.

Twin to Win

Producing an approved list of Assembly candidates had taken a month longer than expected. Hopes that the selection process would henceforward move rapidly fell victim to two factors: Labour's leadership contests and the bitter internal battle over the Party's twinning policy. At the Special Conference on 19th September 1998 which marked the end of the first leadership race, one delegate tartly remarked: "A full year has passed since the referendum and we possess neither candidates nor a policy".

Labour's internal battle over twinning first broke out at the end of 1997. A month after the referendum vote, Cardiff North MP Julie Morgan led a delegation to the Welsh Office of women interested in becoming Assembly candidates. The purpose of the delegation was to ask Ron Davies for assurances that women would have equal representation on the new body. According to Morgan, the Assembly offered the opportunity for "the first time in the world to start a political institution with equal representation" (21st October).

By the middle of January the WLP Executive had adopted the principle of twinned constituencies, though Anita Gale pointed out that the precise mechanism for delivering gender balance had still to be resolved. Opposition to the principle began to escalate. Representatives of 17 CLPs, the Wales Co-operative Party and some trade unions planned to meet in Ebbw Vale, on 7th February, to set up a working party to co-ordinate resistance to what was labelled as a 'Party diktat'. Two CLP Chairmen (Tom Williams, Islwyn and Malcolm Thomas, Blaenau Gwent) were reporting widespread unease about the proposal, arguing that ordinary members had not been consulted. Similar noises were coming from the Cynon Valley, Llanelli, Merthyr Tydfil and Rhymney CLPs. According to Williams: "They [the Executive] should be listening to us, not dictating to us. They are riding roughshod over the views of the constituencies" (21st January). One sign of the strength of local feeling on the issue was the decision by the Risca and Cross Keys wards (in the Islwyn CLP) to withdraw a speaking invitation to Glenys Kinnock, because of her support for the twinning arrangement.

The following month the twinning policy looked vulnerable when a meeting of the Welsh PLP voted to call on the Welsh Executive to 'shelve' the scheme as too divisive. Don Touhig, the Islwyn MP, mindful of his local party's hostility to twinning, wrote to Gale asking the Executive to "reconsider their position" and to put the issue out for wider consultation to avoid the "perception of foisting" the policy on the Party (21st February). Soon afterwards, the ever-litigious Keith Griffiths, Deputy Leader of Caerphilly County Borough Council, revealed his intention to launch a court challenge to twinning, a move inspired by a leaked document suggesting that the Lord Chancellor, Lord Irvine, had doubts about the policy's legality under European law.

Under mounting pressure the Executive gave ground at its meeting on 16th March. Its new line was to reaffirm the policy of gender balance, but to have a period of consultation – until 23rd April – to allow alternatives to be put forward. The Executive was clearly deeply divided over the issue. One of them, Annabelle Harle (Cardiff West), attacked what she called: "a camp of angry men shouting loudly and using bully-boy tactics" (17th Match). This brought the retort from Llew Smith that "she is talking nonsense", claiming strong opposition to twinning among women Party members in his own constituency. He added: "This is not about gender balance, but about centralising power within the Party. If it's not, why are we talking about having a panel of selected candidates?" Smith's comments are interesting. They show that many of those opposed to twinning, were also hostile to the Party's proposals to bring in a new method of Assembly candidate selection. For them, the process of change was driven not by the desire to reform the Party, but to control it more effectively. Politics, though, is a multi-layered game. Smith, who was so strong in his defence of the rights of grassroots members on these matters, remained silent about the use of the union 'block vote' in the leadership contests.

With the WLP's Annual Conference in Swansea looming closer, the battle intensified. Lord Irvine's opinion that twinning was unlawful, was condemned by Labour's four Welsh women MPs. A letter from Ron Davies to the Executive warned that the issue would cause the Party "major difficulties" if pursued and said – pointedly – that if there was a legal challenge, the Party centrally would not fight it. His sentiments came in for strong criticism from Labour Welsh MEPs, led by Wayne David. "This is not about legality or illegality;" David argued, "it's a political issue. If we want to see a genuine new politics in Wales, we have to have gender balance among our candidates" (25th April).

The WLP was split between 'The Twin to Win' campaign and 'The Campaign Against Twinning'. Both were out in force when the Executive met in Cardiff on 27th April to discuss twinning and its possible alternatives. By now the anti-twinners were claiming the support of 20 of the 40 CLPs in Wales, two of the four big unions (TGWU and the AEEU) and the majority of Welsh MPs. The meeting ended with the Executive still undecided as to the best way to proceed. A statement from its Chair, Terry Thomas, said it had been "agreed to make a final decision... at its pre-conference meeting on 7th May". After the 7th May session, Thomas isssued another statement: "This is so important an issue that Conference should make the final decision". A sure sign of the turmoil inside the Party was the declaration by Liz Pleece, Secretary of Blaenau Gwent CLP and – more significantly – Chairperson designate of the WLP – that her constituency viewed twinning as "undemocratic and unlawful" and would not implement the policy. The scene was set for a major confrontation at the Party's Annual Conference.

Arguments raged over two motions. One, that Conference accept one of two gender balance options, was carried overwhelmingly by 80.57 to 19.43%. The real heat was then generated when delegates had to choose between the Party managers' favoured twinning formula and the so-called 'Ponty Option', dreamed up by Party officers in the Pontypridd CLP. After an intense – and sometimes ill-tempered 100 minute debate – the 'Ponty Option' was narrowly rejected by 51.95% to 48.41%. In this way the Party had, on 16th May, made an historic decision to select an equal number of men and women candidates to contest the 1999 Assembly elections.

While the decision may have been historic, the row rumbled on. In July Griffiths restated his intention to mount a legal challenge to twinning. The following month Hain – after reports that the five CLPs of Blaenau Gwent, Cynon Valley, Caerphilly, Llanelli and Newport East were preparing to fund a court challenge – urged them to back off. By October it was clear that this residual opposition to twinning was holding up the selection of Labour's Assembly candidates in South Wales. At the end of October a quarter of the Party's CLPs had still to agree on the seat with which they would be 'twinned'. At the beginning of November four of the most stubborn 'refuseniks' – Blaenau Gwent, Cynon Valley, Islwyn and Llanelli CLPs – were given an ultimatum by Gale: either co-operate or have the twinning process imposed by the WLP. It was no idle threat. On 11th November she wrote to all those on Labour's list of approved Assembly candidates, saying: "For all of you interested in the constituencies of Islwyn, Blaenau Gwent, Llanelli and Cynon Valley, would you contact me as I shall be running the selection process in these seats".

Undeterred, hard-core anti-twinners – now organised into 'Members Against Twinning' – renewed their threat to make a High Court challenge. Claiming they would need £2,000 to begin an action and £20,000 to see it through, they opened a 'fighting fund' and claimed to have already raised £1,200. In the event, the money was not forthcoming and there was no legal challenge.

But if formal opposition to twinning had collapsed, it was to leave a poisonous legacy. In a bitter rejoinder to Gale's 'take-over' letter, Diane Darby, a leading anti-twinner and a member of Llanelli CLP said: "If [Gale] goes ahead with the selection process in the anti-twinning constituencies the feeling amongst most members is that when the Assembly election campaign starts she can do it all on her own, canvassing, the lot" (8th January 1999, *Tribune*).

When the time came, Labour was to do badly in those areas which had stood out longest against the twinning policy. While there were also other reasons why Labour was to do poorly, there could be no doubt that the lingering resentment over twinning played its part. Stretching over almost 18 months, Labour's twinning battle had helped sap the Party's energies, seriously delayed candidate selection and left many Party activists disaffected and demotivated.

7. The National Assembly Election

Several months before the election campaign opened, Peter Hain had warned that Labour might not win control of the Assembly. In a conference speech in Aberystwyth, in June 1998, he suggested that a possible low voter turnout and the vagaries of the new voting system might combine to deny the Party overall control. Similar sentiments were also expressed by Wayne David, MEP. Both held that Labour's fortunes in May would depend on the quality and strength of the Party's election campaign. Their views were attacked by one Labour peer – the recently ennobled Roy Hughes, formerly the MP for Newport East – on the rather curious grounds that if "we are not going to control the Assembly, then it's better we do not have it" (30th June).

On the face of it, there was no need for Labour to have been unduly concerned. A BBC poll published the following month (27th July), gave Labour 34 seats, a predicted overall majority of 8 seats. In October a poll for the *Western Mail* suggested Labour would win 36 seats. A pre-Christmas poll, again for the *Western Mail*, seemed to bring further encouraging news. Under the headline, 'Labour is still No 1 despite scandal' (a reference to Ron Davies' resignation after his 'moment of madness'), the story said the poll findings pointed to Labour emerging with 36 Assembly seats (22nd December). At the end of January, a 'poll of polls' review (examining the polls carried out in the second half of 1998), indicated that Labour was poised to take 35 seats and to win a comfortable overall majority.

But a glance behind these headline figures showed a more complex picture and one not quite so flattering for Labour. As the national polls were rolled out, little attention was given to a string of post-general election defeats for Labour in council seat by-elections, with Plaid Cymru as the main beneficiary, quietly picking up seats in Labour's traditional core areas like Caerphilly. The national polls in the pre-Assembly election campaign period also suggested support for Plaid was rising, with every result putting them second to Labour. Further, while the media were largely fixated on the headline figure (how many declared a preference for what party and how this translated into seats), sight was often lost of the numbers of those polled saying they were either 'undecided' or refused to declare how they would be voting. The former figure was running at around 25%; among the latter would almost certainly have been Conservative Party supporters reluctant – or perhaps just embarrassed – to declare openly.

Nor could the polls hope to accurately predict the actual turn-out on the day. This last issue was of particular concern to Labour, which had often found it difficult to mobilise its vote. Given the well known lack of enthusiasm for the Assembly among many of Labour's activists and traditional supporters, voter turn-out in May would be a bigger problem than usual. Finally, in the run-up to the launch of the Assembly election campaign, no one could be sure of the impact of the battles over twinning and the second leadership contest on Labour's ability to mount a vigorous, hard-hitting and persuasive campaign.

Working Hard for Wales

Labour's campaign was launched on 15th March, amid press reports that Blair had given his "personal authority" for the Party in Wales to "take off the gloves" and take on the Nationalists (15th March, *The Guardian*). Taking his cue, Alun Michael used Labour's first campaign press conference (in Cardiff's City Hall) to attack Plaid Cymru and its "loony policies" through a pamphlet entitled *The A to Z of Nationalist Madness*. The line did not play well in the Welsh press. The *Western Mail* dismissed it as a "juvenile assault" and even some in Labour's own ranks, like Ron Davies and Paul Flynn, thought it "infantile".

At the same time Labour was putting in its campaign 'war-room' at Transport House, equipped with all the usual paraphernalia of modern electioneering. Labour was prepared to spend to win, with up to £1m said to be available for campaigning (a sum which, if true, was more than the money on hand for the other three main parties put together). Labour was also ready to employ some of the techniques which had served it so well in the 1997 General Election. Pledge cards would be issued, a rapid rebuttal team set up, election campaign material was to be centrally co-ordinated and an intensive telephone canvass planned for key target seats. Hain was the campaign co-ordinator. Key members of his team included John

Braggins (more usually found working on Labour's by-election victories), Huw Evans (London's Press Officer on loan from Millbank), and Julie Crowley, a former Millbank Press Officer who resigned as one of Michael's special advisors to work full-time on the campaign. Another echo of 1997 was the campaign 'battle bus' complete, according to one reporter, "with computers, internet access, faxes and three types of mobile phones to cope with reception in the rugged countryside", to allow Michael to criss-cross Wales on his campaign trail.

Little of this appeared to impress the voters, or indeed many Party workers. Criticism of Labour's fabled election machine raises issues we take up at the end of this chapter. For the moment, though, our focus is on the extraordinary extent to which Labour's election campaign was shaped – some would say burdened – in one way or another by the legacy of the Party's second leadership contest. It did so in several significant ways.

First, the contest, together with those other events that had made the previous 18 months difficult ones for Labour, meant the Party was poorly prepared for an election campaign. It had started its campaign without a manifesto. This was not to appear until 14th April, nearly a month after the campaign launch and only three weeks before polling day. There had been little discussion within the Party about the manifesto. True, Hain had produced a draft manifesto on the day of Davies' election as leader, for 'debate', but the Party's attention was soon drawn away elsewhere, as the second leadership battle got underway. The document, when it finally appeared, was pretty anodyne, looking, as one Labour Assembly candidate described it, "like a watered down version of our 1997 General Election manifesto". The manifesto's title, which became Labour's campaign theme – *Working Hard for Wales* – was also thought to be worthy, but unexciting. An earlier suggestion for a campaign logo – Standing Up for Wales – might well have been a more inspired choice, given the effective play the nationalists were to make by presenting themselves as the 'Party of Wales' and Labour as the 'Party of London'.

Nor was there much evidence that Labour's Assembly candidates had had the opportunity to spend much time in thinking about election policy and strategy (and they were, after all, going to be the principal standard bearers). Delays and arguments about candidate selection (another partial by-product of the Morgan-Michael contest) meant that the final slate of candidates was not agreed, as we saw, until barely a month before Labour launched its campaign. Between the finalising of the list and the start of the campaign, only one meeting was arranged for Labour's candidates. Even this, a day and half in a hotel in Merthyr, was missed by some candidates after the date was changed at short notice to allow Michael to attend a family wedding.

Second, a planned 'Key Seat Strategy' (modelled on the one Labour had developed so successfully for the 1997 elections) failed to materialise. Early in 1998 Welsh Labour MPs had met with Party officials to sketch out a strategy. Three seats in particular – Cardiff Central, Cardiff North and the Vale of Glamorgan – were identified as needing particular support and extra resources. These were all marginal seats in the South Wales Central region. The new electoral arithmetic – based on the formula for the distribution of seats on the additional members' list – meant that if Labour were to lose one, or even two of these seats, it would be unlikely to pick up list places. In other words, a loss here could not be 'compensated'. But if Labour began the campaign with the idea of a key seats strategy, this rapidly unravelled, to be replaced by a key seat strategy. As the campaign unfolded and it looked as if Michael's own prospects for a seat (as the top of Labour's list in Mid and West Wales) might be in jeopardy, the focus of attention turned to Labour's fight against Plaid Cymru in Mid and West Wales. Even without this 'distraction' the 'marginals' had problems. The centrally-produced election material was sometimes slow in being delivered, promises of help were not always forthcoming and a full telephone canvass was never carried out. Arguably, of course, if there had been a key target seats strategy, it would have had little impact. Labour's key seats approach in 1997 had worked so well because the ground had been intensively tilled long before the General Election was called. This was not the case in 1999, and gives weight to the old adage that elections are not won or lost during the formal election campaign period itself.

Third, one obvious leadership hang-over was the resentment and hostility many Labour canvassers met on the doorsteps (or on the telephone) over the way the Party was seen to have treated Morgan. As one Party worker put it, after an evening's door-knocking in what had traditionally been a safe Labour seat: "I was taken aback by the strength of people's feelings. There was no point in trying to talk about the issues. People just wanted to have a go at us about the leadership thing. It was very discouraging. It cost us badly". Anti-Michael feeling led some candidates to try to rethink their tactics, wanting to put as much distance as they safely could between themselves and the Party leadership. This was particularly true for those who had supported Morgan for the leadership and who now felt at risk from the backlash from his defeat. Trying to convince the Party's campaign managers of the problems being caused by the leadership 'hang-over' was not always easy, as one candidate recalled: "At one of my public meetings I got the predictable question about the leadership issue. I made it clear I'd backed Rhodri. This got reported in the local rag. That night I had a phone call from Peter Hain saying I shouldn't have said it. I asked him – what should I have said? Hain said the line must be 'that's all behind us now'. I tried to tell him that's not how the voters see it. What are you supposed to do when you have people walking out of public meeting shouting they had always voted Labour in the past – but not this time".

Where they could these candidates put out literature picturing themselves with Morgan and not Michael. They were keen to have Morgan out canvassing with them and equally reluctant to be seen with Michael. One candidate recalled: "One day I was told Alun and his 'battle-bus' were going to be in my constituency and was told to be there when he turned up. Frankly, this was the last thing I wanted. I like Alun, but he was doing me no favours by coming. There was so much feeling about Rhodri on my 'patch', that I felt having Alun here would lose me votes – not increase my chances of winning". Candidates like these were in an impossible situation. They recognised that Michael, a Party leader, had to have a prominent place in the campaign, would have to feature on Labour's election material, and be expected to make frequent media appearances. Yet, they also knew that the more intrusive Michael was, the more it simply served to remind people of what they saw as the leadership 'fix'.

Fourth, we have already alluded to how much of the campaign became fixated on Mid and West Wales. There was endless media speculation about the electoral dynamics of this corner of Wales, as Michael's prospects were talked down and talked up. Much of the interest (and there was much interest, to the despair of those who wanted an issues driven campaign) was concentrated on the fate of Labour's candidate standing in Carmarthen East and Dinefwr, in a heavily Welsh-speaking area, with a Welsh Labour MP. To explain this fascination, we need first to briefly summarise the new electoral system Assembly members were to be elected under.

It was a hybrid system, in which people had two votes. Each Euro-constituency in Wales had eight members chosen on a first-past-the-post basis. These winners would then be 'topped up' with four other candidates from the party lists, in proportion to how voters used their second vote. If Labour took (as was expected) four of the eight seats and between 30-33% of the popular vote in Mid and West Wales, it was unlikely that Michael would be elected. The only way it was thought this could be prevented, was if Labour lost what was described as its 'shakiest seat' – Carmarthen East and Dinefwr.

Given these fine electoral calculations and what was at stake – the real possibility of Labour's leader not actually getting a seat after a bitter leadership contest – the media, naturally, found the story irresistible. Among the many commentators drawn to this drama was Simon Hoggart, who wrote the following, highly mischievous account: "Plaid Cymru... want to lose the seat to Labour. But official Labour wants to lose it too. Supporters of Rhodri Morgan, however, will be wholeheartedly backing Labour in order to squeeze Mr. Michael out. It's a confused situation with the two main parties both ostensibly wanting to win and privately wanting to lose, except for rebel elements in Labour, who are so rebellious that they want to win" (27th March, *The Guardian*).

Although a slightly tongue-in-cheek account, delivered in typical Hoggart style, it was one reflection of the growing speculation about what might be afoot in Mid and West Wales. It's also worth noting that Hoggart's piece came early in the campaign; an indication of how quickly the electoral politics of this part of Wales was beginning to exercise journalists and psephologists alike.

On 30th March a poll for the *Western Mail* reported a surge in support for Plaid Cymru – with Labour facing one of its biggest slides in support in Mid and West Wales – leading the paper to comment: "The irony is that this could actually help Mr Michael, who will only get elected... via the 'top-up' system if Labour candidates do badly in this area on May 6". A spate of articles throughout April and in the first few days of May kept the issue of the Mid and West Wales vote near the top of the campaign reporting agenda. *Wales on Sunday* carried predictions that the prospects for Michael were looking bleak (4th April) and returned to the subject in every edition up until polling day. The *Western Mail* reported the dilemma facing Labour in Carmarthen East and Dinefwr, where a successful Party campaign might be at Michael's expense (5th April). The issue also surfaced in editorials in *The Independent* and *The Guardian* (9th April) which discussed the possibility of Labour being plunged into a third leadership struggle if Michael failed to get in.

On 14th April the story was given a new twist when a group of disgruntled Labour activists launched a 'Think Twice' campaign in Llanelli (in the Mid and West Wales region). In calling upon Labour supporters to 'split' their vote, a spokesman for the group claimed this would be "a positive way of expressing dissent against Alun Michael being imposed by the party in London by using the second vote for someone else". Although little more was heard of the campaign, its brief flowering drew attention, again, to the scars left by the leadership battle.

The press never relented in its pursuit of the story. Typical headlines as the campaign rolled included: 'Michael's hopes hinge on Labour defeat' (17th April), a reference to Carmarthen East and Dinefwr; 'Nationalists' advance stirs fear for Labour list' (19th April, *The Independent*), a report on how Labour was suffering from Michael's "relative unpopularity"; and 'Labour strains loyalties in valleys', a lengthy profile of the Rhondda constituency campaign by *The Guardian*'s Matthew Engel, where he raised the previously unthinkable idea that Labour actually might lose a seat that was at the heart of its heartland. Searching for reasons why, Engel wrote: "The disgust [with Labour] is general.... There are three elements to it... [including)]... a profound bitterness – and here disgust is truly the word – at the grubby fix which secured the leadership of Welsh Labour for Alun Michael" (28th April). And just two days before the election, the *Western Mail*'s front-page lead, 'Tactic to sink Michael denied', reported claims that both Plaid and Labour supporters were being privately encouraged to back Labour's candidate in the crucial seat of Carmarthen East and Dinefwr.

Running alongside this stream of stories, were a clutch of opinion polls, which offered Michael varying degrees of comfort as polling day approached. What is important in all this was not the accuracy of the speculation around the likely result in the Mid and West Wales region (in fact, in the end, while Michael got his seat, it was by an unexpected route when Labour lost not only Carmarthen East and Dinefwr, but the supposedly safe Llanelli seat as well), but the sheer *volume* of media coverage on one corner of a national election campaign.

Fifth, this fixation on Michael's prospects, allowed Ron Davies back onto the campaign agenda. Doubts about Michael winning a seat, fuelled media interest in Davies' political future. Months before Davies had pledged support for Michael in his leadership bid. Cynics, at the time, took the view that Davies' endorsement was more to do with how he calculated his own leadership chances, rather than with any deep commitment to Michael's cause. These chances, it was suggested, would look more promising with Michael as a leader who might not win a seat.

Early into Labour's campaign there were signs that Davies was quietly positioning himself to make a move if Michael came to grief. He had been making public appearances about his vision for devolution, including a keynote speech to the Institute of Welsh Affairs and an address to the prestigious Institute of European Affairs in Dublin. He had also been contacting Labour candidates with offers of campaign help (by voting day his well publicised itinerary had taken him to half of the 40 Welsh constituencies), and was to make frequent radio and TV appearances before 6th May. "This exhausting schedule," as a *Financial Times* reporter later noted, "is beyond the call of duty to enable him to win his Caerphilly seat" (4th May).

Amid denials from Davies, several Labour sources had told the *Western Mail* (25th March) that he was preparing the ground for an eventual strike if the opportunity arose. The next day the paper reported a friend of Davies as saying: "The rehabilitation phase is over; we are now into post-rehabilitation", in an article headed, 'Davies sets out his stall as contender for First Secretary'. In anticipation, perhaps, of the leadership issue being forced open again in the event of Michael's failure to get a seat, the WLP – at its 1999 Annual Conference in Llandudno – adopted a new set of Standing Orders for the election of the leader of Labour's Assembly Group. Under the new dispensation, Labour AMs would vote with the Party's 30-strong Executive to decide the outcome. If this was seen by some as a potential 'blocking mechanism' to stop Davies, others saw it as a device for blocking Morgan as well.

Whatever his actual intentions, there was little doubt, as *The Sunday Times* put it, as the campaign drew to a close, that: "Amid the back-stabbing and confusion, Davies haunts Michael's campaign like Banquo's ghost. Despite pledging his full support, Davies has distributed weekly newsletters about Michael's policies and his friends have been associated with a whispering campaign against him [Michael]" (2nd May). In the event, any hopes Davies might have had were dashed. Not only did Michael win a seat, he also – as the new First Secretary – declined to give Davies a cabinet post. Among the privately stated reasons for this decision was resentment about what was seen as Davies' attempts during the campaign to quietly undermine Michael, while publicly endorsing him. While this brought to a close the (then) latest chapter in the Davies saga, the episode served to underline the extent to which the main contours of the campaign had followed the fall-out from the second leadership contest.

Sixth, the success Plaid Cymru enjoyed in the campaign was to a large extent built upon the legacy of Labour's leadership battle. Although every poll suggested Plaid would be able to turn-out its core vote, it was always clear Labour would be struggling to enthuse its traditional supporters. Many were indifferent to the Assembly 'project'. To stir their interest and to persuade the sceptics, would require the full commitment of Party grassroots workers and activists. But many of these had been disaffected by the conduct of the leadership contest (for some, of course, the twinning issue added to their discontents) and in some areas found difficulty in getting Party workers out in strength.

Again, Plaid's clever rebranding of itself as 'The Party of Wales' worked so successfully because it could brand Labour as 'The Party of London'. Labelling Labour in this way would simply not have worked had Morgan been Labour's leader, as Plaid were well aware. Ironically Morgan, tagged as a 'crypto-nationalist' by Michael's team during the election contest, was the one person who could have checked the surge to Plaid. The HTV/NOP poll (12 February) was clear evidence that a Morgan-led Labour Party would have produced an election day 'bonus' for Labour of close to 10%, and largely gained at Plaid's expense. But 'The Party of London' charge resonated with voters for the reason that Michael was seen as London's creature. The accusation was wrong but it is a truism in politics that perceptions are everything. And if, as Robert Worcester claims, voters increasingly identify with parties through their leaders, then Labour had a further problem. Dafydd Wigley, the Plaid leader, consistently polled more strongly than Alun Michael when voters were asked who would make the best leader for Wales.

Finally, the salience of the leadership legacy, which found expression in the ways we have described, made for an election campaign where policy issues were largely pushed to one side. Apart from a brief confrontation between Plaid and other parties over Plaid's stance on 'independence', and a longer-run debate over Objective One matched-funding (an issue which the wider public found it difficult to engage with), too often media attention was diverted onto matters concerning Labour's leadership. This was particularly true of the London press, which dominate the newspaper market in Wales. Their reports focused almost exclusively on Michael's prospects, the Ron Davies factor and what they liked to call "the rising tide of nationalism" in Wales.

Less than a week before polling day, the *Western Mail* ran a front-page lead highly critical of the parties' election campaigns. Under pictures of the four main party leaders it carried the headline: 'Gentlemen: What is dull, boring and grey? Your campaigns. What are you going to do about it?'. The accompanying commentary described their campaigns, so far, as "drab" and as a virtual "non-event"; the parties, it claimed, "have failed to transmit their ideas to the voters" (30th April). To some extent, the criticism was unfair. Labour – like the other parties – certainly had policies but, again like the other parties, depended on the media to carry these to the electorate. If the media thought there was little worth transmitting, then perhaps this was a judgement on the Assembly itself. A body with no primary law-making or tax-varying powers, was one hard to enthuse many people about. Further, since the Assembly had small room for manoeuvre in policy terms (it would have to operate within a fixed budget) there was, in reality, not a great deal of scope for the parties to promise major policy initiatives. However, what could have been provided was persuasive leadership, of a kind able to excite and inspire; a leadership capable of offering the electorate a vision of Wales to which the voters could respond. Michael, for all his qualities, was never able to do this. There were two in Labour's ranks who might have done so. One – Ron Davies – had lost the leadership because of his own foolishness. The other – Rhodri Morgan – had had a glimpse of the leadership but was, in the end, cheated out of it.

The Results: "A Quiet Electoral Earthquake"

Like the earlier referendum result the Assembly election result was examined over and over again to discover what portents it held for the future of Welsh politics, as though a single election could ever do such a thing. As we can see from Table 7.1 Labour's expected haul of 34-36 seats was reduced to just 28 in what was arguably its worst ever electoral result in Wales. With just 37.6% of the constituency votes and 35.5% of the regional votes the Labour Party found itself

Table 7.1   Assembly Election Results

Party	Seats	Constituency Votes	%	Regional	%
Votes					
Labour	28	384,671	37.6	361,657	35.5
Plaid Cymru	17	290,572	28.4	312,048	30.6
Conservatives	9	162,133	15.9	168,206	16.5
Liberal Dems	6	137,657	13.5	128,008	12.6
Others	0	47,992	4.9	50,068	4.7

in the ignominious position of not having a working majority, an outcome which confounded the pollsters and chastened the party. Straining to find the appropriate metaphor to describe the Assembly results, along with some equally unprecedented local results on the same day, like the loss of Rhondda Cynon Taff in the heart of the valleys, polling experts could not have done better than "a quiet electoral earthquake" (Trystan and Jones, 1999).

The other side of Labour's woe was Plaid Cymru's joy: the nationalists had trebled their percentage share of the vote since the 1997 General Election, overwhelmingly at the expense of the Labour Party. Swings of some 35% enabled Plaid to capture such heartland Labour seats as Rhondda, Islwyn and Llanelli and the swings were almost as impressive in seats like Cynon Valley (31.9%), Neath (27.6%), Merthyr (26.9%) and Pontypridd (26.5%), seats which Labour narrowly retained. These disastrous results can be attributed to a combination of general factors (like disunity over the leadership question, disquiet with New Labour and low turnout) and local factors (like the profound unpopularity of RCT council for example).

The Assembly election results cannot be dismissed as an aberration because, as Table 7.2 shows, Plaid Cymru's vote held up well in the European elections a month later. On the other hand the low turnout in both elections means that we cannot read too much into the results of 1999, and we certainly cannot compare a Westminster election with an Assembly election because voters, it seems, are able and willing to distinguish between the two and engage in tactical voting. Optimists in the Labour Party interpreted the results as nothing more than a protest vote against the governing party combined with a low turnout. In contrast, pessimists saw deeper problems in the results, like an ill-organised party which was disconnected from, and

Table 7.2   European Election Results in Wales

Party	Votes	%	Seats
Labour	199,690	31.9	2
Plaid Cymru	185,235	29.6	2
Conservatives	142,631	22.8	1
Liberal Dems	51,283	8.2	0
UKIP	19,702	3.1	0
Green	16,146	2.6	0
Others	11,738	1.9	0

contemptuous of, members and voters alike. While the former are waiting for normal service to be resumed so to speak, the latter are intent on reforming the party to make it more internally democratic and more externally relevant.

Understandably perhaps, Plaid Cymru lost no time in claiming that the results presaged a historic realignment of Welsh politics: just as Labour had displaced the Liberals as the dominant party in the 1920s, they argued, so Plaid is now beginning to supplant Labour. These claims will be tested at the ballot box in the future, when Plaid will have a much tougher fight on its hands. As the official opposition in the Assembly the nationalists will now attract much greater scrutiny than before, especially on the issue of independence. During the Assembly election campaign Plaid got off lightly when its leader, Dafydd Wigley, made the astonishing claim that "Plaid Cymru has never advanced independence, never ever on any occasion" (Jowit, 1999). Adopting the English suffix 'The Party of Wales', Plaid prefers to use such terms as 'self-government' and 'full national status in Europe', terms which are less threatening than 'independence' or 'separatism' but which amount to the same thing according to critics. As we argue in chapter eight, this ambiguity will be exposed to the full in future elections.

Equally important, Plaid will have records to defend in the future, with none more significant than Rhondda Cynon Taff, where the nationalists inherited a poisoned chalice from Labour. RCT is the most important showcase for Plaid Cymru as a governing party because of its symbolic location in the heart of Labourland: the key question here is whether RCT is a springboard for further advances or, to mix a metaphor, a grave for Plaid's ambitions in the valleys.

The full implications of 1999 will not register for years to come, in the meantime the battle has been joined to control the 'narrative'

– that is, the way we think and feel about the events, and this depends on whose 'story' comes out on top. Ceri Evans and Ed George have produced the most convincing story to date: among other things they argue that it was not the leadership contests themselves that hurt Labour, but rather the conduct of them, because free debate and elections are not the signs of a weak party but a vibrant one. As they argue:

> Neither should we take the view that the enormous swing from Labour to Plaid in the south Wales coalfield represents a rejection of 'Labourism' itself in any fundamental sense.... Labour's 'nationalist madness' campaign failed so abjectly because its authors failed to understand that the appeal of Plaid to Labour voters lay not in its 'nationalism' but rather in the perception that Plaid were better defenders of their interests – were, in fact, better 'Labourites' – than New Labour itself (Evans and George, 1999).

This interpretation fully accords with that of Paul Flynn, who argued that Plaid wanted pensions to be increased by earnings levels and student loans to be replaced by grants and "the Labour voters of Islwyn, Rhondda and Llanelli found that 'insanity' irresistible" (Flynn, 1999a). It also helps to explain why voters were not frightened when the Labour Party in Islwyn resorted to the most desperate measure of all – the language card. In a last minute election leaflet called *Fact not Fiction* the Labour Party warned voters that "you must speak Welsh" if you live in Gwynedd, at that time the only Plaid-controlled authority in Wales. Plumbing the depths it said "How long before this happens here if the Nationalists take control?" A desperate measure from a desperate party.

The Inquest: Time for a Change?

The immediate aftermath of Labour's poor performances in the Assembly and Euro elections induced a spate of instant judgements about what had gone wrong. On 8th May Peter Hain conceded that the leadership row had cost Labour seats. The following day the *Wales on Sunday* took the same line, with the front page header: 'Wales Strikes Back: The People Punish Blair for Treating Democracy with Contempt'. John Prescott, commenting on the low turn-out of Labour supporters, saw no real cause for concern: "It's the politics of contentment, it's people thinking we don't need to turn out, we're satisfied with the Government we've got" (8th May, *The Mirror*). Writing in the *Western Mail*, Hain tried to broaden the hunt for scapegoats. While again – briefly – mentioning the "deep scars" left by the leadership contest, he also pointed the finger at badly performing local Labour councils (to explain away the loss of Islwyn and the Rhondda); the "lack of enthusiam for the Assembly amongst many of our traditional supporters" (to explain the low turn-out); the "impression" created that Labour lacked a "distinctive Welsh policy agenda"; and a failure to motivate "our 'Old Labour' vote" (those unimpressed by what Hain described as the "brilliantly maintained 'New Labour' coalition Tony Blair assembled for our [general] election landslide"). There was no suggestion in this and subsequent articles Hain wrote on the subject that he bore any particular responsibility for Labour's plight. Hain's attempts to explain away Labour's defeats brought a ferocious response from Paul Flynn. Claiming Hain was one of those busy trying to "falsify" the very recent past in the Wales Labour Party, Flynn condemned those leading it as "unprincipled and undemocratic" (14th May, *Tribune*).

A month later Labour was forced into another post-mortem, this time over its even worse showing in the Euro elections, where the Party had lost more than half of its voters since the last Euro poll. These successive setbacks brought the first formal response from the WLP. In June its Executive agreed to set up a small working party to inquire into what had gone wrong and to "devise a practical action plan to help prepare us for the next General and Assembly elections". On 6th July Jessica Morden, who had recently replaced Anita Gale as General Secretary, wrote to all CLP Secretaries, Assembly election agents and Assembly candidates inviting them to attend one of three election 'debriefing' meetings at Cardiff and Carmarthen.

But even as the working party was being set up, Morden received a letter, written on behalf of the Rhondda Cynon Taff County Borough Council Labour Group, saying why they thought Labour had its "biggest rebuff" from the people of Wales in a 100 years. Many of their views were to be echoed by others in the coming months. Although acknowledging that local council issues had played some part in the reaction against Labour, the Group honed in on what it regarded as the three really decisive factors. First, the impact of the 'twinning' issue on a section of the voters in their area (an area where several CLPs had been strongly anti-twinning). But as they went on to point out: "By itself, the controversy surrounding twinning could not have sustained this resentment through to May 6. It was the leadership contest... that caused incalculable harm to the party". Adding: "Those of us with long-standing commitments to the GMB, the AEEU and the TGWU should also have the courage to admit that the way that they cast their block vote seriously undermined the credibility of the WLP and the whole Labour movement in Wales". The third factor was the claim that 'New Labour' policies and ideology did not sit well with the people they represented. This was coupled with a warning that if the Party failed to reassure its traditional supporters, then the future looked bleak for the survival of "AMs such as Christine Chapman, Ron Davies, Jane Davidson and Jane Hutt" in the next round of Assembly elections. The letter closed with a call for the WLP to "evolve Wales-specific policies that will win back this lost support" (Willis, 1999).

While the Party waited on Morden's 'debriefing' sessions to begin, the Welsh PLP produced its own report on the Assembly election results. The report, circulated on 14th July, was terse and damning. It also tried to put a 'spin' on the reasons for failure, not surprisingly perhaps, since most Welsh MPs had backed Michael in the leadership battle. For example, the report's account of the damage done by the leadership issue sought to reduce this to perception, rather than substance. Thus:

> The process by which Alun Michael was elected leader (which) created an indelible perception in the minds of the Welsh public that there had been a 'fix', a 'stitch-up' arranged by London, Millbank and Tony Blair. This perception, actively promoted by the media, left a lasting impression on the party and the electorate and contributed to our poor performance. The decision not to adopt OMOV in the trade union section... conjured the image of New Labour adopting old-fashioned fixing techniques to get in 'its man' as Leader. The mishandling of the issue by the Welsh Executive compounded our problems. (Wales PLP, 1999)

Much of this diagnosis misses the point. There *was* a 'fix'. The story *was* the 'stitch-up'. To blame the messenger or to depict the electorate as gullible, is to refuse to face reality. This piece of 'spin' serves to deceive only the 'spinners', though their point about the ineptitude of the WLP Executive was certainly a good one.

Many of the report's other findings covered ground addressed in the submission from the RCT Labour Group, but also introduced two other factors. The report was fiercely critical of the organisation and content of Labour's Assembly election campaign. It wrote:

The campaign... was inefficient and misdirected. This was best illustrated by the centrally-produced election literature emphasising Tony Blair and Alun Michael and only served to remind people of a perceived leadership election 'fix'. The literature did not allow for the effective promotion of the local candidates and local issues. The WLP manifesto was unimaginative and dull and seemed to offer nothing new. We have heard of numerous complaints of delays and mistakes in the centralised literature, and of a disorganised Regional Office.

The second factor concerned the nationalist 'spectre':

We did not appear to have an effective response to the nationalist challenge, and when we did, it was ill-directed and facile as for example our 'A-Z of Nationalism'. A belated attack on the nationalists fitted ill with the impression given during the previous two years when we extolled the virtue of collaboration and 'inclusiveness'... cosying-up to the nationalists before, during and after the referendum did considerable damage to the Labour Party.

The last line was a clearly aimed 'dig' at Ron Davies, the architect of inclusiveness, and while it was true that the WLP had no coherent anti-nationalist strategy, the authors of the report failed to pick up on three key points. First, the one Labour politican – Morgan – capable of checking the nationalist surge, had been the victim of a leadership fix in which most Welsh MPs had been culpable. Second, the nationalists' own campaign was all the more effective for having Michael as Labour's leader. And third, the Assembly's hybrid electoral system will mean that from here on, Plaid is likely to have a significant presence in the Assembly and to deal with them, Labour has to develop an approach based on something more subtle than the old politics of condemnation and confrontation.

Four months before the WLP had put its 'inquest team' in place, a group of Labour delegates had met at the Party's Annual Conference in Llandudno, to discuss the fall-out from the second leadership contest. At a Conference fringe meeting, on 'Democracy and the WLP', the decision was made to start a campaign for internal Party reform, once the May and June elections had passed. The group, going under the name of 'Cyfle' ('Campaigning for Your Franchise on the Labour Executive'), was formally launched at a meeting on 17th July in Transport House, Cardiff (to be followed a week later with a North Wales launch).

Cyfle had assembled an impressive roll-call of supporters signing up for its call for a reform of the Executive. They included 15 AMs (among them the Assembly's Business Manager – Andrew Davies – and 5 Cabinet members, Rosemary Butler, Edwina Hart, Christine Gwyther, Jane Hutt and Rhodri Morgan); 5 Welsh MPs, an MEP and several leading councillors from all parts of Wales. Over 100 Labour activists turned out for the Cardiff launch, to take part in an intense two hour discussion, ranging over the causes of Labour's recent troubles. Opening the meeting Catherine Thomas (from the Pontypridd CLP and an aide to Julie Morgan MP), spelled out what was at stake: "this must be our opportunity to make a fundamental difference to the WLP... the time is now right... and our focus must be on the reform of the WLP Executive".

As speaker followed speaker, three clear themes emerged. The first was forcefully expressed by Richard Edwards (the Preseli-Pembrokeshire AM), when he said: "There is no use blaming Blair or Millbank – the problem is with the Executive. They organised the calamity of the leadership stitch-up". Labelling the Executive as "both dysfunctional and disconnected", Edwards continued: "what sort of Party is it that allowed the selection of list candidates to be so shamelessly rigged?... I feel deeply ashamed by some of the things that have been done in our name in the last 12 months.... We gave Wales a new democratic settlement, but have not delivered one for ourselves". Edwards' point about the politics of the list was delivered with special feeling. He was from the region – Mid and West Wales – where the fight over list selection had been especially bitter.

The second theme concerned criticism of the 'ecology' of the Executive itself: its composition, methods of membership selection and mode of operation. At the time of Labour's leadership 'troubles' there was a 47 person Executive (since slimmed down to 30), whose composition was meant to reflect the diverse sectional interests that make-up the Labour Party in Wales. This justified representation from: the trade unions (18 members); the CLPs (12); Women's Organisations (3) the County CLPs, the WLGA Labour Group, the WPLP and Young Labour Wales (2 each); and 1 each from the ECLPs, the Co-op Party, the Socialist Societies, and the EPLP Welsh Group, plus the Secretary of State for Wales (as an ex-officio member).

On the face of it, the Executive seemed to be a rich mosaic, drawing together the multiple interest groups working under the banner of Welsh Labour. In reality, the composition was weighted in favour of the trade union interest. Not only were they clearly the biggest bloc within the Executive (with nearly 40% of the total membership), but their nominees were all full-time trade union officials. This simple fact had a major bearing on the operation of and attendance at Executive meetings. Those on the Executive with regular work commitments often found meetings were held at times and places which made it difficult for them to attend, though this posed no problem for the unions 'full-timers'. And there was never any doubt that if WLP Party organisers at Transport House wanted something steered through the Executive, they would invariably get their way, as long as they had union backing as we saw in Chapter 3. By these means, as one CLP Executive member put it "most of the decisions the Executive takes are usually about rubber-stamping reports coming from Party officers".

The method of electing members of the Executive was also contentious, especially among the various 'Party Units' and among the smaller affiliated bodies (e.g. the 'Socialist Societies'). None adopted the OMOV principle, so denying the wider Party membership any say in who sat on the WLPs 'governing body'. Instead, the process of selection came down to favours exchanged and deals done at the WLP Annual Conference. As one Cyfle supporter put it, describing how she was levered onto the Executive: "It all really comes down to making deals and lobbying in the Conference bars. There's nothing open or democratic about it. It's just horse-trading. There's no circulation of biographical details, so the system favours those already known – those who go to Conference most often".

This last point is important in trying to understand both the structure of the Executive and who comes to exert the greatest influence within it. As we have seen, the CLPs had 12 Executive places. Often the most active and lively CLPs would change the delegates they sent to Conference each year. While the reason was laudable – to give as many ordinary Party members as possible a chance to go to Conference – the practice worked against them. Novice delegates were at a major disadvantage when the 'horse-trading' started for seats on the Executive. Other CLPs, in contrast, would send the same delegates year after year (e.g. Rhondda, which made Ken Hopkins a permanent fixture at Conference), making them much better placed to put the necessary deals together and so get their people in place. These customs and practices also worked against the North Wales CLP delegates. There was, as one speaker pointed out, a clear regional bias in the make-up of the CLP 'bloc' on the Executive, favouring delegates from south-east Wales. Almost inevitably, those CLP and other non-union representatives who sat longest on the Executive, came to exercise the greatest influence, often finding common cause with the trade union interest.

The issue was then raised as to the relationship between the Executive and the wider Party membership it was supposed to represent. The picture that emerges was not an encouraging one. "In effect, we meet in secret every couple of months or so", said one Executive member, "no reports are circulated. Indeed, most Party members have no idea who is on the Executive and even less idea about how they got there". A Cyfle member, formerly on the Executive, gave an account of the problems he ran into when trying, as he put it, to "throw a ray of light" on its proceedings. "I wanted," he recalled, "to send reports to members of my CLP about what the Executive was doing. I told Anita Gale about this. She wanted to vet my reports before they went out. So I sent them to her. But they were so long in coming back that by the time they did, they were of little use."

What is being described here is a political culture with a bias against disclosure and the sharing of information, a political culture which *disempowers* and de-mobilises its members and its *supporters*. In lobbying for a reform of the Executive, Cyfle (which wants a directly elected body, a membership from each of the regions of Wales and a requirement to be accountable to their constituencies) are pushing for significant changes to a body which is, in essence, the political 'powerhouse' of the WLP. We have seen how it used that power in successive leadership struggles and in candidate selection. For many inside the WLP, the case for reform is now compelling.

The third of the themes which ran through Cyfle's launch meeting, was the equally urgent need for the Party – through the Assembly – to produce a distinctive Welsh political agenda. Several of the AMs present at the meeting warned of the consequences of not going down this path. According to one: "Unlike the other parties, we went into the Assembly unprepared. In the lead-up to the elections, the Executive did nothing. It provided no leadership, no sense of direction. As a result we are being wrong-footed all the time by the Nationalists and the Liberal Democrats".

For another, it still seemed as if "the Whitehall tail is still wagging the Welsh dog", an inelegant proposition, but one which touched upon the widespread feeling that the Assembly still lives too much in the shadow of London.

The WLP's own post-mortem meetings were to go over much of

the same ground covered in the RCT letter, the Welsh PLP report and the Cyfle meetings. The Cardiff session and the meeting in Carmarthen raised criticisms concerning: poor communications with the Regional Office during the election; the legacy of the twinning and leadership issues; problems with the print consortium – producing material that was often delivered late, lacked specific Welsh policy content and where the Welsh language versions were marred by spelling and grammatical errors; delays in candidate selection, with the result other parties were a long way ahead on the campaign trail; and the failure to respond to the Nationalist challenge. Some areas were singled out for special mention. In Llanelli, Labour – unlike Plaid – had no local office and where strong local feeling against twinning meant that because Labour's candidate (Ann Garrard) was not from the area, she found local party activists and councillors refusing to work for her. In Islwyn – with only 6 Labour councillors left out of 28 after the May election cull – Labour faced a party (Plaid) which had invested in a full-time local organiser and extensive telephone canvassing. In some constituencies the Labour MP offered minimal help. The example was given of Rhondda, where Allan Rogers did not even make his office available during the campaign.

The factors which bedevilled Labour's Assembly election campaign were, in many respects, the culmination of the Party's troubles over the previous eighteen months. Without doubt, the second leadership contest inflicted the biggest wounds, with all those many-layered consequences we have explored in previous chapters. At the very centre of these disastrous machinations was the WLP Executive. Calls for its reform have now spread beyond disaffected Labour workers to the highest reaches of the Party in Wales. The recommendation from the WPLP that "There has to be a restructuring of the Welsh Executive so that it can more accurately reflect the feelings and wishes of the Party membership" is surely a strong sign that pressure for change is beginning to build up. How far and how fast reform proceeds is a matter for speculation. In our next and final chapter we examine the prospects for a 'new politics' in Wales and the challenge of democratic devolution in and beyond the Labour Party.

THREE: THE CHALLENGE

8. The National Assembly and its Futures

The creation of the National Assembly for Wales was little short of a miracle. However close the result, however low the turnout, the referendum vote in favour of a National Assembly in 1997 was an extraordinary event by any standards, a triumph of hope over fear, the hope being that the future could be something better than the past. It seems little short of a miracle for two reasons. First, for a majority of voters to support a new tier of government when politicians are held in such low public esteem seems somewhat miraculous. Secondly, for the very poorest communities in Wales, in the west and the valleys, to vote 'yes' when the resources for an Assembly could have been used to improve public services in some of the most deprived parts of the UK is perhaps even more startling. In their different ways these voters clearly hoped that the National Assembly would be an investment and not just a cost, a new departure rather than business as usual. For some of them it was a means to improve public services, for others it afforded a more powerful voice for Wales in the corridors of power and, for each and every one of them, hope sprang eternal that the Assembly would signal the beginning of a new, more inclusive and more relevant kind of politics. Whatever their reasons, those who voted for an Assembly clearly did so because they hoped or believed that, in the fullness of time, it would make a difference to the quality of life in Wales.

In this final chapter we set these hopes and aspirations against the early experience of the Assembly, which has been a learning exercise for all concerned. First we look at the prospects for a new politics in Wales, focusing on the two largest parties, Labour and Plaid Cymru. Secondly, we examine the Assembly in action, looking at its powers and constraints in the context of the two issues which have dominated the agenda in the early days, agriculture and EU regional aid. Finally, we outline two futures for the Assembly: a pessimistic, *business as usual* scenario versus a more optimistic scenario in which the Assembly is perceived to be *making a difference*. Scenarios may seem fanciful, but they remind us that the future is not out there waiting to unfold like some pre-ordained Hegelian script; on the contrary, the future, lest we forget, is partly in our own hands.

Towards a New Politics?

The days have gone when the national politics of Wales were largely an extension of the internal politics of the Labour Party: one-party-ism, in other words, is an idea whose time has gone. A new politics tentatively began to show its face in Wales in the 1990s, as Ron Davies recalled in his personal memoir:

> From 1994 a new vocabulary had crept into Labour's lexicon. Party members were now supposed to be... either New Labour or Old Labour, although truth to tell many of us were neither. Old Labour had little time for devolution. They wanted statist solutions to our problems and they thought devolution pandered to Nationalism. New Labour had scarcely more enthusiasm – it certainly wasn't part of the original 'project', but Tony Blair to his credit honoured the commitment inherited from John Smith. There was, I always thought, a third strand. Not New Labour or Old Labour but Welsh Labour.... We wanted greater co-operation and a new pluralist approach to Welsh politics which was libertarian, decentralist and patriotic (Davies, 1999).

Davies' call for a new politics resonated with all parties, especially with the nationalist wing of the WLP and with Plaid Cymru, where Davies seemed to have more supporters than in his own party. During the 1997 referendum campaign, as we have seen, a new pluralist politics did indeed emerge, as Ron Davies and Peter Hain sought to forge new alliances with pro-devolution parties and civic movements like the Yes For Wales Campaign. Whatever political capital the WLP had earned by introducing a new democratic era to Wales was quickly squandered by the undemocratic behaviour it displayed during the leadership debacle. The new era of democratic devolution had been demeaned by the Labour Party failing to live up to the standards required by the new era. If there was a silver lining to the Labour leadership cloud it was that the WLP Executive was seen for what it was, a superannuated rotten borough in urgent need of reform.

The Welsh electorate seems to support the cause of co-operative politics, having tired of the tribal politics to which it had been treated for so long. In July 1998 a National Assembly poll conducted by BBC Wales asked: would you like to see a coalition of two or more parties running the Assembly or one party in control? The answer was revealing: while 21% of respondents favoured one-party control, 51% preferred a coalition. More by default than design the Labour group in the National Assembly has been obliged to engage in co-operative politics because it was denied an absolute majority. Having decided to go it alone as a minority administration, rather than form a coalition like its Scottish counterpart, the Labour group needs to make common cause with others since its very life depends upon it. Although the First Secretary, Alun Michael, would ideally like to have as little as possible to do with Plaid Cymru, a minority government can't be too fussy about how it stays in office. Hence the most remarkable feature of the Assembly's early career, the *de facto* coalition between Labour and Plaid Cymru, may not have been made in heaven, but here on earth it is no less important for that.

There are Assembly Members (AMs) across the political spectrum who understand that, to be effective, the Assembly will have to pioneer a new kind of politics, a politics in which their own party is no longer considered to have a monopoly on wisdom, truth and good ideas, a politics in which collaboration with other parties is not considered treasonable or, perhaps worse, a sackable offence. As the two largest parties it is incumbent on Labour and Plaid to demonstrate that party rivalry does not preclude co-operation for the sake of something that is larger and more important than either of them, namely Wales.

To be fair, Labour and Plaid have both evinced a laudable determination to get the Assembly up and running, not least because the very credibility of the new institution is on the line. A combination of factors – pragmatism, statesmanship and enlightened self-interest – helps to explain why Labour and Plaid have forged a *de facto* coalition to launch the Assembly, a stance which has its critics in both parties. The Plaid leader, Dafydd Wigley, has been criticised by sectarian elements inside his party for being too accommodating towards and too supportive of the minority Labour administration. But Wigley has astutely recognised that the very vulnerability of the minority Labour government places an extra burden of responsibility on Plaid as the official opposition. At Plaid's 1999 annual conference Wigley warned his party of the consequences of bringing down a government in an irresponsible fashion, which might create "a new First Minister every three months, as used to happen in Italy".

Conscious of the value of statesmanship Wigley refused to engage in what he called "the meaningless politics of perpetual confrontation" (Wigley, 1999).

Wigley did well to maintain this tone because, in an attempt to spike the Plaid conference, the Labour Party released a 'dirty tricks' briefing document which included a number of controversial charges, including the claim that Plaid (through its links with the Greens in the European Parliament, a party which favours legalising cannabis) was giving "the green light to drug-abusers in many of Wales' poorest communities". This document, considered to be tasteless even within the WLP, was hardly calculated to enhance co-operative politics in Wales. Though clearly aimed at the party conference season, when tribalism and posture politics are at a premium, the briefing document may have unintended longer term consequences. For example, the weekly meeting between Alun Michael and Dafydd Wigley, a formal mechanism designed to regulate their informal compact, has been cancelled by the Plaid leader until the Labour leader disowns the 'dirty tricks' document.

Although Plaid entered the National Assembly with more confidence than Labour, a legacy of the election results, it has some way to go before it can credibly claim to have re-invented itself. If it is to pose a *sustained* challenge in Labour's heartlands, particularly in the valleys, Plaid will have to do more to dissociate itself from the charge that it is, essentially, a separatist party hell bent on taking Wales out of the UK. The party will have to ask itself whether the benefits of this 'southern strategy' are outweighed by the costs of losing support among traditionalists in the west and the north, many of whom still favour full independence for Wales. Plaid's policy director, Cynog Dafis, insists that the party's immediate aim is "parity with Scotland" and, after that, Wales in some federalised union inside the UK and the EU (Starling, 1999). In other words Plaid's longer term aims are still unclear, not least because there is no common agreement about these inside the party, an ambiguity which could cost the party dear in future elections.

For its part Labour entered the Assembly shell-shocked. Despite being the largest group, Labour was still coming to terms with demoralising results in the local government, Assembly and European elections; the group was also trying to forge a common identity after the bloodiest internal conflicts in living memory. In short, it could hardly have been a less auspicious start for the Labour Party. Partly because of this post-election atmosphere, and partly because of the proprietorial leadership style of the First Secretary, which makes him unable or unwilling to delegate, many Labour AMs feel that the group lacks strategic direction and common purpose, a problem compounded by the fact that there are limited opportunities for free and frank debate within the Labour group. This is one reason, perhaps, why Labour is so unsure as to how it should relate to Plaid: should it build links with progressive elements in Plaid and recognise that the nationalists are *de facto* coalition partners, or should it attack them all without fear or favour on the grounds that Plaid are the only serious electoral threat? The truth of the matter is that each of these views has its adherents inside the Labour group; as with Plaid Cymru, there is no commonly agreed code as to how to behave towards 'the other'.

One of the few things we can say with certainty is that the relationship between Labour and Plaid at Westminster, remote and asymmetrical as it is, will furnish few answers as to how Labour AMs should proceed in Wales. The Assembly signals a wholly new political arena, with its own rules, its own codes and its own networks of trust and reciprocity: it is not, in other words, Westminster writ small and to treat it as such would almost certainly spell disaster for the Labour Party. There are a number of reasons why the Assembly will be different from the 'Wales at Westminster' model. First, a measure of proportional representation in the Assembly electoral system means that Labour will have to shed the mindset of one-partyism, a mindset in which co-operation with others was rendered superfluous by the Eiger-like majorities that were (and still are) possible under the first past the post system. Second, the intensity of the workload in the Assembly, particularly in the over-burdened subject committees, means that stronger inter-party links need to be developed if the Assembly is to deliver the goods. Third, the Welsh media will be monitoring the work of AMs much more thoroughly than has been possible at Westminster, not least because the Assembly is closer and more visible, and this will make it more difficult to engage in gesture politics. Fourthly, the gender composition of the Assembly is much more balanced than in Westminster (especially in the Labour group, where women account for 14 of the 28 AMs) and it has been suggested that this could yield a more co-operative style of politics (Osmond, 1998).

The prospects for a new politics in Wales will depend in no small way on how the AMs choose to conduct themselves, internally within the Assembly and externally with respect to civil society. What the

Assembly does is important, but of far greater importance is what the Assembly enables others to do for themselves. To this end the Assembly would be well-advised to use the spotlight of publicity creatively, not just to enhance its own status but, more importantly, to highlight models of best practice in Wales: in business, healthcare, education, training and the voluntary sector for example. Politicians have more power than they realise. They do not have the power to dispense material largesse, the power they would like to have, but they do have the power to influence perceptions, priorities and practices, in other words our "cognitive maps" (Morgan, 1999). Indeed, they exercise this immaterial power in a whole series of ways: in the people whom they choose to address, the projects they extol, the firms they visit and the events they commemorate. In all these ways, consciously or not, politicians exert influence by accentuating certain aspects of our lives, both past and present, and the Assembly's politicians would do well to utilise this power in a more conscious and purposive fashion. To make this immaterial power count in a material world, however, the Assembly will need sufficient wisdom and humility to recognise that it is wholly dependent on its partners in the outside world if it is going to make a difference.

The Assembly in Action: The Powers and the Practice

When the National Assembly formally assumed its powers, on 1 July 1999, the *Western Mail* proudly announced that Wales had finally acquired control over its own destiny. The fact that the Assembly has neither tax-raising powers nor primary legislative powers makes it highly dependent on Westminster, underlining the point that *executive* devolution (as opposed to *legislative* devolution) leaves Wales a long way short of controlling its own destiny – whatever that means in today's inter-dependent world. This does not mean that the Assembly is not worth having, as some critics have alleged. Whatever the limits of executive devolution the Assembly has acquired some important functions, including:

> Powers which give the Assembly full discretion to allocate its annual budget between its responsibilities
>
> Powers to make rules and regulations (secondary legislation) which expand Acts of Parliament (primary legislation) and flesh out the detail

Powers to make appointments to public bodies in Wales, an important function given the turbulent history of the quango state in Wales

Powers to acquire land and property and to undertake works such as the building of new roads

Powers to decide disputes and appeals, such as those relating to planning inspections (Welsh Office, 1999).

As regards finance the Assembly will control a budget of some £8 billion per annum, larger than many regional budgets in the European Union, and for the first time this will be rendered directly accountable to the Welsh electorate. This is a major advance on the Welsh Office era, when there was no accountability to Wales. On the other hand the main criticism to be made of these financial arrangements is that they are "hardly compatible with the dispersal of power that devolution is intended to achieve" (Bogdanor, 1999). According to this view the financial formula for the Welsh Assembly runs counter to the first principle of sound government, namely that the power to spend money must not be divorced from the power to raise it, otherwise all the problems can be attributed to the parsimony of the revenue-raising body (the Treasury) and all the credit can be taken by the spending body (the Assembly), which has a weaker incentive to economise than if it were spending money which it had to raise itself.

As for the Assembly's legislative powers these are not unimportant either because secondary legislation – statutory instruments and the like – has evolved into a significant capability, hence it would be wrong to dismiss secondary legislation as 'second class' legislation. However, the key point to remember about the Assembly's legislative powers is that they depend not merely on the provisions of the Government of Wales Act, but also upon the way in which legislation for Wales is drafted by Westminster and the degree of discretion which central government decides to confer on the Assembly. The looser it is drafted the greater the discretion available to the Assembly, and vice versa of course. Executive devolution, in other words, is not so much a milder variant of legislative devolution. It is, in fact, a completely different model: while legislative devolution involves a *transfer* of powers, executive devolution involves a *division* of powers as well as a transfer of powers (Bogdanor, 1999). In short, executive devolution requires a closer and more co-operative relationship between devolved and central governments than legislative devolution, which means the Assembly needs to pay far more attention to the legislative drafting process at Westminster than the Scottish Parliament.

The scope and limits of the Assembly's powers will become clearer the more they are tested, and the one thing the new institution has not been short of is testing situations. From the moment it began its life the Assembly has lived in a seemingly permanent state of crisis and controversy. Leaving aside the fact that the Cabinet was described as "the weakest in Western Europe" (Betts, 1999a), the Assembly has had a baptism of fire, born as into the worst agricultural crisis in living memory. On top of that was the mixed blessing of gaining Objective One regional aid for the west and the valleys, a status which the European Commission awards only to the very poorest regions in the EU. This is a mixed blessing because the Assembly needs to persuade the Treasury to release more money for Wales so that the EU rules on additionality and match-funding are respected, otherwise the Assembly will be faced with two equally unpalatable choices: either find the match-funds from its existing budget, which would displace current expenditure, or leave the money unclaimed in Brussels. These two issues – agriculture and regional aid – have cast such an awesome shadow over the Assembly that we examine each in turn to discover what they tell us about executive devolution in Wales today.

The Crisis in Agriculture: In Search of Subsidiarity

It was a cruel coincidence that the Assembly should have to take responsibility for an agricultural crisis which was none of its making. Welsh agriculture (which basically consists of beef, lamb and dairy) has been hit right across the product range by a combination of factors, including falling (farm gate) prices, food scares like BSE, belated reforms to the Common Agricultural Policy which are gradually reducing subsidies and growing exposure to world market competition. Taken together these trends have had a devastating effect on farm incomes. The origins of the crisis may be largely European in nature, but the effects in Wales are to be seen in rising suicide rates among farmers and in livestock being dumped or killed because its price is lower than the cost of taking it to market. Although the crisis is UK-wide it seems to be more acute in Wales, where hill farmers have long been the poor cousins of the wealthy 'barley barons' of East Anglia.

Everyone agrees that the long term future of Welsh agriculture lies in the creation of premium, branded products with an environmentally positive image with more of the value-added processing in Wales. Everyone can also agree that farming needs to move away from industrial agriculture towards a more sustainable agriculture, like organic production for example (Morgan and Murdoch, 2000). In the long term, as Keynes famously said, we are all dead, hence the problem is what to do in the short term. Although the Assembly assumed responsibility for agriculture, the real decisions in this field are actually made at the EU level, and the Ministry of Agriculture, Fisheries and Food (MAFF) is the lead department in negotiations between the UK and the EU. We need to remember these institutional niceties because they help us to understand why the agricultural crisis exploded into a political crisis of the Assembly itself.

Of all the portfolios in the Cabinet none was condemned to live in such 'interesting times' as the Secretary for Agriculture and Rural Development, a post given to Christine Gwyther, a former local government officer from Pembrokeshire. Even her selection was contentious because, being a vegetarian, the farming community felt that she could never be a credible ambassador for Welsh lamb and beef products. To sack her on these grounds, as some farmers demanded, would have set a dangerous precedent; even so, it was an unfortunate choice because it distanced her from the very people with whom she needed to build a close relationship.

From the outset AMs were anxious to prove that the Assembly could do something, however modest, to ease the agricultural crisis and to signal to the farming community that they were not just receptive but *relevant*. The early efforts revolved around lifting the beef-on-the-bone ban, which was controversially imposed in the wake of the 1997 general election. Following appeals from the chief medical officer for Wales, who opposed unilaterally lifting the ban, a view shared by the Labour Cabinet, the ban stayed in force. The real irony of the beef-on-the-bone story was that the Assembly, which had hoped to be the first to lift the ban in the UK, was eventually cast as one of the laggards when, on 20 September 1999, MAFF suddenly turned the tables by announcing it was prepared to lift the ban but was prevented from doing so because of opposition from Cardiff and Edinburgh. If the pressure to maintain a single UK message on food safety was understandable, it nevertheless raised questions as to whether the Assembly would ever take independent action ahead of Whitehall.

The answer was not long in coming and took the unlikely form of a calf-processing scheme to slaughter and render unwanted animals. A similar scheme for disposing of unwanted ewes was thought to be viable only as a UK-wide scheme because, unlike cattle, sheep did not have identification tags, therefore the scope for cross-border fraud was deemed to be unacceptably large since English farmers would have an incentive to claim the cull-ewe subsidy. As an agitated Welsh farmer told a bemused BBC TV crew: "the nationality of sheep would change overnight if we just had a Welsh scheme".

Despite the misgivings of some MAFF officials the Assembly was prepared to go it alone with a calf-processing scheme if need be. At a specially convened meeting between Alun Michael and Christine Gwyther for Labour and Dafydd Wigley, Ieuan Wyn Jones and Rhodri Glyn Thomas for Plaid, it was agreed that the Assembly should first try to secure two UK-wide schemes (one for surplus ewes and one for surplus calves) because this would reduce the scope for fraud and also allow the Assembly to draw funds from central government. As a second best solution they also agreed to press ahead with their own Welsh calf-processing scheme in the absence of UK action, and this private agreement formed the basis of a Plaid Cymru motion unanimously passed by the Assembly on 15 September. Having failed to persuade Nick Brown, the UK Agriculture Minister, of the need for UK action, Gwyther announced that £750,000 had been set aside for Wales to operate its own calf-processing scheme from 1 October 1999 to the end of the year, when such schemes were due to expire under EU rules. Asked whether the deadline could be met Gwyther was reported to have said "I am confident that we can do it" (Betts, 1999b).

Friday 1 October passed without a calf-processing scheme and it was not until the following Wednesday that Gwyther informed the Assembly that the scheme faced "serious legal obstacles". She later went on to say that the scheme "is a measure for member states, and discussions so far have not found a way in which it would be legally possible to operate it in part of a member state". But before Franz Fischler, the EU Commissioner for Agriculture, could make a formal pronouncement on the calf-processing scheme, it was technically killed off on 12 October when the opposition parties pressed for an unequivocal announcement on the future of the scheme, a move which forced Labour to formally abandon it once and for all.

The reaction was swift and furious because the calf-processing scheme had acquired a totemic significance way beyond its actual value to the farming community: like a rite of passage it was the first time that the Assembly had tried to act independently of Whitehall. Equally important, it was the Assembly's way of *doing something* to help the beleagured farmers, not so much economically – the scheme was too modest for that – but psychologically, to show it cared about their plight. Furthermore, opposition AMs felt that Labour had raised the Assembly's expectations about the feasiblity of a Wales-only scheme, when the problems had not been fully ironed out. For all these reasons the three opposition parties combined for the first time to table a motion calling for Gwyther to be censured for failing to secure the calf-processing scheme demanded by the Assembly, a move which threatened to create the Assembly's first constitutional crisis when Gwyther said she had no intention of resigning in response to a censure motion which was passed by 30 votes to 27.

In her defence Gwyther could claim that the obstacles to the scheme had been under-estimated by all concerned. Some three weeks earlier, for example, the Labour MEPs Glenys Kinnock and Eluned Morgan publicly announced they had won positive assurances directly from the EU Agriculture Commissioner after meeting him in Brussels to clarify matters. Given subsequent events however the only credible explanation for Fischler's U-turn is that he had not been fully briefed by his officials when he had met the MEPs, hence he was not aware of the obstacles himself at that stage. In a later statement, issued on 6 October, Fischler declared that EU rules prevented Wales from going it alone:

> We have to avoid market distortions within a country. If we don't follow the regulations then the consequences will be that the other farmers have the right to go to the Court of Justice. I hope that the Welsh farmers will understand that I've no alternative than to follow the regulations (*Western Mail*, 7 October, 1999).

Fischler was nevertheless keen for Nick Brown to make more of the running on behalf of the Welsh scheme since it is the UK, not Wales, which is the member state. Because Brown did not do more to help the Welsh scheme, questions will naturally be asked as to whether the UK Agriculture Minister really wanted the Assembly to appear to be doing more for Welsh farmers than MAFF was doing for English farmers. Looking back it is still not clear whether the

Wales-only scheme was actually illegal under EU regulations or whether it was doomed by its *novelty,* in other words that it was something which had not been tried before. Either way, the fate of the Welsh calf-processing scheme highlights the fact that subsidiarity – the principle of devolving power to the lowest level where it can be effectively executed – is easier to preach than to practice, even though the European Commission likes to parade its attachment to the principle. If there is no scope for policy divergence within a member state, because of 'market distortions' for example, then real subsidiarity is a chimera and devolution will remain more apparent than real.

What the scheme also revealed was that, to be effective, policy-makers need to secure agreement from a complex multi-level governance system which straddles local, regional, national and supra-national institutions. Success, as we know, has many parents but failure is an orphan, an adage especially true of a multi-level governance system where it is virtually impossible to know who to blame when things go wrong. Not surprisingly politicians and officials in Cardiff, London and Brussels all blamed each other for the fate of the hapless calf-processing scheme.

Given the novelty of the scheme and the complexity of the system it is unlikely that anyone could have bettered Gwyther's efforts, a point gracefully acknowledged by the National Farmers' Union, who thought the censure motion against her was a pointless gesture. But politics would not be politics without gestures and the censure motion, though failing to trigger her resignation, was a forlorn expression of collective anger from the opposition parties. Even so, the recriminations over the scheme should not obscure the fact that the Agriculture and Rural Development Committee has been something of a model of co-operative cross-party policy-making, especially with respect to long term initiatives to support young farmers and measures to promote more value-added processing in Wales. The real things that need to be done if Welsh agriculture is to have a viable future.

It was no coincidence that the censure motion against Gwyther was heard on the very day that the Assembly was scheduled to debate the Objective One strategy. Dafydd Elis Thomas, the Assembly's Presiding Officer, postponed the censure motion by almost a week in the hope the opposition parties might "seriously consider" the implications of their motion. He warned that the use of censure motions for party political ends was an abuse of power as well as being "deeply destructive" to the Assembly as a fledgling institution. By scheduling the censure motion for the same day as the Objective One debate, the Presiding Officer hoped the contrast would not be lost on the Assembly: the contrast between an empty gesture about the past and a strategic debate about the future.

The Mixed Blessing of Objective One Status

As domestic regional policy has been progressively cut back the significance of EU regional aid has grown steadily since the late 1980s. When Objective One status was secured for west Wales and the Valleys, a status which triggers the maximum level of grant-aid from Brussels, the news was greeted as a mixed blessing. On the one hand it meant that over £1 billion would be available for the poorest parts of Wales during the 2000-2006 planning period; and with other parts of Wales qualifying for Objective 2 aid and the whole of Wales eligible for Objective 3 aid, the total aid package would actually exceed £1 billion. On the other, there was nothing to celebrate about being badged one of the very poorest regions in the EU. Nor was there unalloyed joy in the Welsh Office when Objective One status was secured because civil servants knew that this could wreak havoc on existing budget lines if additional funds from the Treasury were not forthcoming.

The track record of Objective One programmes in the EU is decidedly mixed: for every Irish Republic, where regional aid has been used intelligently to promote genuine structural change, there is a Campania, where aid is less effective, not least because so much of it goes unspent. In previous programming periods EU aid could not be fully spent in Wales, especially in the Valleys, either because local applicants did not have the matching funds or because the quality of the projects was so poor. In other words the Objective One programme will pose a challenge for every participant to raise their game, irrespective of whether they are a public, private or third sector organisation.

As the Assembly prepared to sign-off its Objective One programme, in a plenary debate held on 19 October 1999, there was a danger that the means had become the end. Most of the debate concerned the issue of whether the Treasury would release additional resources to allow Wales to claim its full entitlement from Brussels, an issue which should have been a formality under EU regulations. What the debate in Wales ought to be focusing on are the projects and the partnerships around which the Objective One programme will stand or fall.

'Partnership' is perhaps the most over-used term in the regional policy lexicon, a term now in danger of moving from obscurity to banality without any intervening reality. Many of the partners in the European Task Force, the main partnership body for EU regional aid in Wales, questioned the Assembly's commitment to partnership when, at its meeting on 28 September 1999, the Director of Economic Development, Derek Jones, unilaterally announced that no further meetings of the Task Force would be held, the implication being that the Assembly would thereafter assume control of the process. The local authority partners were used to this kind of behaviour from the Tory-led Welsh Office, when they acidly called it the "Raj style of management", but were horrified to see it resurrected in the name of the Assembly. But perhaps the old habits of the Welsh Office die hard, as one official conceded off the record:

> We thought that when the Assembly got going we would have 60 Secretaries of State instead of just one. Instead we haven't got any at all and everything is being run by the officials. It's just like the Welsh Office (quoted in Shipton, 1999).

A Raj style of management, with its hierarchical and imperious attitude to others, would be the kiss of death to the Objective One programme, which requires an open and inclusive approach to partnership. Where this is not the case the Assembly will be unable to get its partners to commit their local intelligence to the cause of social and economic renewal, and without active and committed interlocutors the Assembly is nothing.

If the *substance* of Objective One revolves around the quality of the projects and the calibre of the partnerships, the *politics* of the programme seems set to revolve around the issue of additionality, that is whether the Treasury will release additional funds to allow Wales to make full use of EU regional aid. With the enlargement of the EU on the horizon, a process which will admit countries substantially poorer than west Wales and the Valleys, this is the one and only occasion that Wales will qualify for Objective One status. Given this unique historical opportunity Plaid Cymru have clearly decided that Objective One is the only issue on which it is prepared to use the 'nuclear option' of tabling a confidence vote in the Labour administration if there is no *new* money from the Treasury.

In other words, Objective One poses a far greater challenge to the Assembly than the agricultural crisis because the latter never looked like provoking a serious confidence vote in the whole administration. Like the calf-processing scheme, Objective One brutally brings to light what can sometimes be forgotten in the era of democratic devolution, namely that Cardiff is as dependent on London as ever it was in the past. Under executive devolution, the Treasury will ultimately determine whether Objective One is a blessing or a curse for Wales.

For Wales, See Wales?

Given the external constraints on the Assembly, in the form of the powers wielded by London and Brussels, does it make any sense to say that executive devolution gives Wales any control over its own affairs? Power and sovereignty used to be thought of as absolutes which were indivisible, an archaic notion which would scupper the EU if it were true because the Union is based on a sharing of power and sovereignty. The same principle applies to the relationship between Wales and Westminster, even though the powers of the former are strictly limited. Despite its modest powers the Assembly is worth having for two fundamental reasons: it provides accountability in Wales where there was none before and also allows Wales to design policies which are better attuned to its own circumstances, subject to EU regulations of course. Arguably there is a third reason, no less important for being more abstract, namely that the Assembly is the single most important investment in the *national identity* of Wales and has the potential to generate a whole series of tangible and intangible benefits, the kind of benefits associated with the growing self-confidence of a nation for example. Whatever else may be said of it, the Assembly will finally lay to rest that age-old ignominy, 'For Wales, See England', that chillingly simple reference which signals like nothing else how close Wales came to being totally assimilated by its larger neighbour.

But new identities count for little if they are not part of a *purposive* politics which is able and willing to make a difference to the things that resonate most deeply in everyday life – health, education, jobs, transport, the environment and so forth. For all its limitations the Assembly does have the *potential* to make a difference in these spheres of everyday life, not a huge difference admittedly, but enough to justify its existence. But will it *actually* make a difference? When all is said and done this is the only question worth asking about the Assembly. It may take two full terms before we can begin to discern the answer to this question, but the answer is not just a matter of time. More important will be the politics of the Assembly: how it conducts itself and how it interacts with others. Drawing on the experience of the first six months of the Assembly the answer could go either way. We have seen signs of inclusive and co-operative politics, alongside evidence of infantile and destructive politics. In this final section we present two polarised scenarios to highlight the very different futures that could lie ahead of the Assembly, each of which carries radically different implications for Wales in the twenty-first century.

Business as Usual: A Pessimistic Narrative

In the course of writing this book we sought the opinion of a great many people from all walks of life, including friends, foes and officials who obviously wanted to remain anonymous. Commenting on an early draft a senior local government official offered a number of criticisms, one of which was the far from trivial point that we had failed to convey what was most distinctive about political culture in Wales. The point is worth repeating:

> Wales possesses a political culture which is a function of its subservient relationship with England. It is an immature political culture which defines itself solely in its relationship with the more powerful neighbour. It is a culture which has not developed a capacity to tolerate and take advantage of differences within itself. It is a monist rather than pluralist political culture. Within parties, chapels, councils and unions the dominant expectation is one of solidarity; opposition is regarded as illegitimate; dissent is not tolerated; discussion is regarded with deep suspicion. When Rhodri Morgan challenged for the leadership claiming a virtue for democratic choice, he was not just offending the traditions of the Wales Labour Party but the traditions of Welsh political and civic life!

To the extent that this is true the challenge for the Assembly is much greater than we have realised: if we have a monist political culture which, deep down, frowns upon robust debate then this suggests not just a weak political establishment but also a weak civil society because politics reflects civics and vice versa (Putnam, 1993). The argument of our anonymous official seems most compelling when applied to the Wales Labour Party, where the mindset of one-partyism runs deep even when it is a minority government. In earlier chapters we have seen that the struggle for democracy inside the WLP has only just begun and the campaign of Cyfle, for example, is by no means assured of victory. The post-election reorganisation of the WLP is so far notable for the fact that former Millbank officers now occupy the senior positions in the party: will they be the eyes and ears of Millbank in Wales or the voice of Wales in Millbank? Perhaps a bit of both; but where the balance is struck may be all important for the future prospects of the party in Wales.

The Labour administration in the Assembly inevitably reflects the imprimatur of Alun Michael, the first First Secretary. To say he has had a difficult time since being asked to step into Ron Davies' shoes is an understatement, but the personal abuse heaped on him has been unfair and unfortunate for a man whose motto, 'working hard for Wales', is an accurate reflection of reality. Unrivalled in his workrate Alun Michael is generally perceived as a 'safe pair of hands', a politician "who we can trust to make the right decisions" as Tony Blair put it during the Assembly election campaign. These are important assets for a First Secretary in a new and untried institution like the Assembly.

On the other hand members of the Labour group, including some of his own Cabinet, privately concede that he has an anally-retentive management style which makes him unable or unwilling to delegate authority to others. What compounds this obsession with control is that he tends to prevaricate, with the result that decision-making is more protracted than it should be. The obsession with control also showed itself in the composition of the first Cabinet, where it is fair to say that some of the most competent Labour AMs found themselves excluded because control was extolled over competence in the selection process. This style of politics is not conducive to free and frank debate and, allied with the fact that AMs are over-worked and under-resourced, leaves the Labour group with little time to reflect on past actions and future strategies.

Nor is this style of politics conducive to building the cross-party alliances essential if the Assembly is to be a success. What most infuriates the opposition parties is the way in which the *minority* Labour administration acts as if it possessed a substantial majority, a sure sign that the mindset of one-partyism lingers on. Although there were no constitutional obligations on Alun Michael to sack his Agriculture Secretary after she was censured by the Assembly, he could easily have assuaged the anger of the opposition parties by showing a modicum of contrition for the indisputable fact that Labour had raised expectations about the feasibility of the Welsh calf-processing scheme among politicians and farmers alike. In the absence of a contrite gesture the ratchet of destructive politics took on a life of its own, with Tory AMs pursuing a confidence vote in the First Secretary for showing contempt for majority opinion. Dispassionate observers might be forgiven for saying that these actions – Labour's lack of contrition and the Tories' infantile addiction to censure motions – deserve each other. It was a depressing reminder of how far the Assembly has distanced itself from the unpretentious aspirations for a new and inclusive politics in Wales.

As the largest party Labour must take the lion's share of the responsibility for this sad state of affairs, but the opposition parties are also culpable. In Plaid Cymru, for example, there is a good deal of unease about Dafydd Wigley's constant talk about censure and confidence motions, a stance which undermines his more statesmanly tone at the party's 1999 annual conference, when he rejected "the meaningless politics of perpetual confrontation". As the official opposition in the Assembly Plaid must take its share of responsibility for the Assembly being in danger of losing what little credibility it had. Plaid seems to have been hoist on its own petard in agreeing to be part of the joint censure motion against Gwyther; but, unlike the Tories, they wanted to draw a line in the sand when nothing came of their censure victory. The Plaid Group want to reserve a no confidence motion for the issue which dominates all others in their eyes, namely matching funds for Objective One.

The Tories are in danger of becoming the most destructive force in the Assembly by routinely resorting to censure motions, the value of which lies, paradoxically, in them *not* being used. Being the one party which opposed the National Assembly the Tories urgently need to prove their commitment to democratic devolution, especially after their Welsh spokesman at Westminster suggested that the Assembly could be abolished in the future. There are signs they are capable of doing this, especially since the party leadership passed from Rod Richards to Nick Bourne, who is more amenable to the principle of inclusive politics than his atavistic predecessor.

How the Assembly conducts itself is important, but how it relates to others is far more so. One of the great dangers of executive devolution is that the Assembly can abdicate responsibility when things go wrong, by passing the buck to central and local government for example, and taking the credit when things go well. As we have seen, the issue which seems set to dominate the Assembly's first term is Objective One and this is tailor-made for blaming London for all the ills, particularly with respect to matching funds. If London – that is Westminster and Whitehall – ever becomes a dirty word in Wales then the era of democratic devolution will have failed.

But local government could become as much of an issue for the Assembly as central government, both directly and indirectly. First, any partnership between the Assembly and local government will need to be predicated on performance and some local authorities are clearly performing well below what is acceptable. This issue was lurking below the surface of a Partnership Council meeting on 22 October, when a proposal was tabled to raise an extra £28 million from the council tax in Wales, of which some £24 million would be used to clear the debts of four troubled councils, namely RCT, Merthyr, Blaenau Gwent and Neath Port Talbot. One can imagine the hostility from well-managed councils to the idea of a higher council tax to bail out RCT for example, a council which has been mis-managed since its inception.

But there is a less direct sense in which local government can be a problem for the Assembly and this is best expressed through an example. In a little noticed incident on 29 September 1999 the parents and pupils of Trelai Primary School in Ely, a poor district of Cardiff, protested outside the National Assembly about the state of their school building. What triggered the protest was a recent report from the school inspector, which described it as "the worst school seen". Thinking that the buck stops with the Assembly the parents were surprised and frustrated to be told by Rosemary Butler, the Education Secretary, that they "should lobby Cardiff County Council rather than the Assembly" (Hornung, 1999). In contrast to the quango state, where no one was sure who was responsible for what, the Assembly was meant to make it clearer where responsibility lay for public services. A division of labour in which the Assembly holds the purse-strings and local authorities deliver the services can be just as frustrating as the Welsh Office system. Recall the time when Alun Michael announced an additional £70 million for education when he was Secretary of State for Wales, only to find that nothing like this sum found its way into the schools because local education authorities used the money to fund other things. The division of labour between the Assembly and local government, which is right and proper in principle, needs to show that it can work better in practice, otherwise it can easily become a recipe for passing the buck, an outcome which will devalue both institutions.

If the trends outlined here are not checked, in other words if it is business as usual, the Assembly will have completely failed to meet the aspirations of its supporters and, by the same token, this will confirm the worst suspicions of the majority of the electorate who did not vote for it. Above all, this scenario would vindicate the critics who always maintained that Wales was not fit to assume more control over its own affairs because, as Tim Williams put it, a Welsh Assembly would turn the country into "a banana republic without the bananas". If the Assembly fails to realise its potential this will clearly reflect badly on the 60 AMs; but the deeper causes of the failure will have to be sought in Welsh civil society. If civil society in Wales is weak, parochial and short of self-confidence then we must not be surprised if these attributes are reflected in the Assembly itself (Morgan, 1999).

Finally, the Assembly will hopefully come to appreciate the value of constructive criticism because, in its early days at least, it thoroughly resented any form of criticism. This was particularly apparent in the way the First Secretary berated the media for its failure to develop what he called "the new journalism", which would offer more supportive coverage of the Assembly, and for its refusal to join 'Team Wales'. To suggest that the media should suspend its critical faculties to allow the Assembly to find its feet is misplaced because the early days of a new institution are the most important: this is when the tone and the standards are set, when custom and practice are established. In fact it is a myth to suppose that the Assembly is the victim of a hostile media. On the contrary, the evidence suggests that the media remain broadly supportive of the Assembly, and that most of the adverse publicity has been generated by the politicians themselves (Mungham and Bromley, 1999).

The habit of ascribing one's problems to the media could easily induce a 'bunker mentality' in which professional politicians become 'insiders' who are effectively disconnected from 'outsiders' in civil society. If the Assembly, and the Labour group in particular, seeks to elevate itself above criticism, then the fruits of democratic devolution will continue to elude us.

Making a Difference: An Optimistic Narrative

Throughout the twentieth century the UK was a highly centralised political system and Westminster, the 'mother of parliaments', had successfully honed adversary politics to a fine art. Given the fact that old habits die hard, it is perhaps understandable if AMs still use West-minster as the template for political behaviour, even though they may profess otherwise. Like any new institution the Assembly is bound to face a steep learning curve as it struggles to develop its own style of politics and, during this early period especially, we must expect some teething problems. In its first six months the Assembly has certainly not covered itself in glory, with more to criticise than to celebrate; indeed, some supporters have begun to think the unthinkable and wonder if it was all worth it.

A measure of disappointment is understandable after the heady atmosphere of the referendum campaign; but this is nothing compared to how supporters would feel today had Wales voted against the Assembly. Let's picture it. With Scotland, London and the English regions moving ahead with their own devolution plans, to say nothing of the more dynamic regions of the EU, a vote in favour of the status quo would have conveyed the impression that Wales was somehow set in aspic. A nation that showed no confidence in itself could hardly expect others to do so. Most damaging of all though, a No vote would have reinforced the message which has been trans-mitted to young people in Wales for over sixty years: that is, "if you want to get on, you have to get out". To compound this depressing picture a No vote would have allowed that motley band of anti-devo-lution politicians – Rod Richards, Ray Powell and other antediluvian figures – to parade themselves as the true ambassadors of public opinion in Wales. The teething problems of the Assembly pale into insignificance compared to the dystopia which would have followed a No vote in 1997. What this means is we need some perspective when assessing the difficult birth of democratic devolution in Wales.

During the first six months, admittedly, the Welsh public could be forgiven for thinking the Assembly has been a platform for petulant egos and infantile politics. But this perception, fuelled by the gesture politics of the plenary sessions, is not the whole story. At the risk of over-simplifying matters it could be said that the plenary sessions have witnessed the least impressive side of the Assembly, while the subject committees have sown the seeds of a more inclusive, more purposive politics. This contrast is perhaps most compelling in the case of agriculture, where the subject committee is one of the pioneers of a robust cross-party consensus on future rural develop-ment policy, though one might not know it from the plenary sessions.

In other words a more innovative politics has begun to emerge in the prosaic policy-making process, but this is not yet fully appreciated because it has occurred 'below deck', so to speak. Petty party point-scoring is more evident in the plenary sessions because these tend to attract more publicity than the subject committees, where competence, commitment and co-operation are the attributes which command most respect.

In time AMs will have to recognise that competence, commitment and co-operation are the only attributes that can take the Assembly forward, the only things that can genuinely help it to make a difference. Indeed, these attributes constitute the stuff of inclusive politics, a notion often identified with an insipid politics, when in fact it is nothing of the sort. *Inclusive politics*, unlike tribal politics, means engaging with the issues and the policies rather than the ideologies and the personalities, and it is therefore wholly consistent with robust political debate. All too often inclusive politics is seen as a convenient mantra, the political equivalent of a fashion accessory, in short a luxury. But far from being a luxury we can ill-afford, inclusive politics will be what determines whether the Assembly succeeds or fails. Why? For the simple reason that Wales is not over-endowed with political skills, or indeed with any skills, hence national success – in and beyond politics – will depend our ability to harness every ounce of expertise, whatever its political affiliation.

Clearly, we cannot expect inclusive politics to flourish if the Assembly is dominated by an anally-retentive political culture which extols control over competence, if free and frank debate is frowned upon and if all roads lead to the First Secretary, in other words a culture which parodies the very ethos of devolution. All parties have a responsibility to create a more inclusive politics, but Labour, as the largest party, has a special responsibility to do so. The Labour group in the Assembly needs to become a more collegiate body and Alun Michael would be well advised to remember the sagacious words in the *Mabinogion*, "A fo ben bid bont" (Who would be leader let him be a bridge), an old Welsh metaphor for a new Welsh politics. This conception of the leader as a bridge is particularly apposite for the Assembly, where a minority Labour group needs to heal divisions within itself as well as forge alliances with progressives in other parties if it wants the Assembly to make a difference.

But in concrete terms what does *making a difference* actually mean? In our view there are three key tests: first, does the Assembly represent a *new mode of governance*; second, will it have a tangible effect on *economic renewal*; and third, can it enhance civic capacity in Wales. Let us look at each of these tests in turn.

As regards the first test the Assembly will need to demonstrate, in deeds not words, that it constitutes a *new mode of governance* which is open, meritocratic and interactive, both internally with respect to its own operations and externally with respect to its partners. Much will depend on whether the new politics of inclusivity will be valued and nurtured or whether it will be buried under the weight of tribalistic party politics. Many people have argued that a better gender balance will make the Assembly more inclined to pursue a co-operative style of politics, but this thesis needs to be tested in practice. On the external front a more open and interactive political style is of benefit in itself, which is just as well because, given its modest budget, the Assembly cannot afford to engage in cheque-book politics. Indeed, when the dust has settled from the opening skirmishes it will become clear that the Assembly has signalled a new and more open mode of interacting with the main interest groups in Wales.

In the plenary debate on Partnership with Business for example, Alun Michael rightly referred to this as "one of the three golden threads that run through the work of the Assembly", the other two being the partnerships with local government and the voluntary sector (Official Report, 1999). Under the Government of Wales Act 1998 the Assembly has a duty to forge co-operation with these three interest groups and to promote equal opportunities and sustainable development as well, perhaps the first time in history that a government has had a statutory duty to pursue such ends. An obligation to co-operate does not necessarily mean that the Assembly will do so in the intended spirit of course, but there is sufficient commitment to do so across all parties that this duty looks like being met in both the spirit and the letter of the law.

Turning to *economic renewal* we can safely say that of all the challenges facing the Assembly none will be as important, nor as difficult, as the task of raising the level of economic well-being in Wales, particularly in the west and the valleys. Although the Assembly will be subject to EU and UK macro-economic policies, there is still much that it can do to facilitate a more innovative and balanced economic development strategy in Wales. Raising the level of economic well-being is a long-term endeavour, and politicians should not pretend otherwise. Some of the main tasks here are:

To raise the status of business as a respected career and to encourage a new business birth rate strategy which is sufficiently catholic to embrace both conventional enterprise as well as community enterprise, a sector which is too often treated as the Cinderella of the economy

To insist on parity of esteem between inward investment and indigenous development so that local firms are encouraged as much as inward investors

To ensure the institutional framework is sufficiently robust to deliver high-quality business support services, with a clearly understood division of labour between the WDA, TECs, Local Authorities and the four new Regional Economic Forums

To do more to ensure that the university sector, the main source of advanced technology in Wales, is more receptive to and more supportive of indigenous firms

To set a higher premium on education and training and encourage new skill formation within firms because one without the other is a recipe for disaster, either skills without the jobs or jobs without the skills

To promote Wales as a premier location for high quality and sustainable foodstuffs from plough to plate, especially for organic foodstuffs

To raise the status of balanced development as between the regions of Wales (Morgan and Morgan, 1998).

These tasks may seem prosaic but they are no less important for that, and they have the great merit of being feasible, and to be fair the Assembly is addressing some of them already. Since AMs have little business acumen themselves, all the more reason to engage the business community in the design of enterprise support programmes along the lines of the Regional Technology Plan, which sponsors the idea that firms learn best from other firms. In the economic sphere, as in so many others, the Assembly knows full well that it needs to harness external expertise if it is to deliver the goods. Everyone should appreciate, however, that the fruits of a new economic development strategy take time to materialise, though the Objective One windfall (assuming it is a blessing and not a curse) ought to enable those fruits to appear sooner than might otherwise be possible. But make no mistake about it: in the fullness of time the Assembly will be judged on this economic development test before all others.

Building civic capacity is only a marginally less demanding challenge than raising the level of economic well-being. While civic capacity – the norms and networks of trust, reciprocity and civic engagement – is clearly not a responsibility of the Assembly, or *indeed of any government*, it has enormous implications for the ways in which governments conduct themselves. A civil society in which citizens and organisations are well-informed, where they expect high standards of behaviour of themselves and of government and where they are disposed to collaborate for mutually beneficial ends is perhaps the most important ingredient in the recipe for good governance. While it might be unnerving for some politicians, a strong civic capacity provides governments with more demanding and more intelligent interlocutors – be they business networks, community organisations, citizen groups – and these help to ensure that public policy is more creative and more accountable than it would be in their absence.

This means the Assembly would be acting in its own (enlightened) self-interest if it promoted civic capacity in Wales because civics feeds through into politics and vice versa. Without strong and independent civic groups to keep it on its toes, the Assembly could degenerate into an insular and self-referential body surrounded by a bunker mentality. To keep atrophy at bay we need more initiatives like the *Finding Our Voices* forum, organised by Margaret Minhinnick and Martin Fitton, which seeks to promote popular participation in the Assembly as well as providing opportunities for civic groups to articulate their views and exchange experiences about the new institution. The fact that there is a genuine commitment among AMs to engage with civic groups, in sharp contrast to the Welsh Office era, means that there are grounds for being cautiously optimistic about the Assembly on this score.

For Wales, See Wales... London and Brussels

The future of the Assembly will depend partly on what happens in Wales and partly on what happens in the corridors of power in London and Brussels since executive devolution makes Wales beholden to Westminster while the latter is increasingly subject to EU law. To be effective the Assembly will need to familiarise itself with these wider networks of power outside Wales for one very simple reason: if it is not *in* the networks it will be *out* of the reckoning. Rapid constitutional change is underway in both the UK and the EU, which means the Assembly will need to engage with a moving target.

As ever, a rapidly changing environment presents both threats and opportunities and to make the most of the latter the Assembly will need to raise its sights above the prosaic day-to-day business agenda and develop a strategic capacity to think ahead and, crucially, to decide where it wants to be. The worry is that the Assembly may not have the time, the staff nor the resources to develop a sufficiently robust intelligence network to carry out these strategic tasks.

With the advent of democratic devolution the UK has embarked on a radically new constitutional journey with no clear destination in sight. Looking ahead, though, there are three main constitutional options: first, the asymmetrical model of devolution we have at present, which seems unsatisfactory to the English regions; second, there is separatism, which currently commands little support; and third, the intermediate option of federal devolution, which presupposes that the parties desire union but not unity (Bogdanor, 1999). Assuming that the nations and regions of the UK wish to remain in union, but not uniformity, it is difficult to see anything other than federal devolution offering a stable long term solution to the constitutional conundrum. But that's for the future to decide. In the medium term the evolving UK scene presents the Assembly with a whole series of new challenges, two of which merit special attention: legislative discretion and finance, the two issues which most affect the powers and resources of the Assembly.

On the legislative front, as we have seen, the Welsh model of devolution involves not just a transfer but a division of powers between Wales and Westminster, with the result that the discretion available to the Assembly will be determined by the way in which central government drafts legislation – the looser, the greater the discretion and vice versa. In the early days of the Assembly, when energies are inwardly focused on the task of getting the new body up and running, it is natural that civil servants, AMs and the Cabinet Secretaries will be out of the London loop, but if this situation persists it can only spell disaster. To maintain as much discretion as possible the Assembly will need to forge a constructive partnership with Welsh MPs at Westminster, a relationship which deserves to be nurtured more seriously than it is at present.

As well as forging stronger bonds with Westminster the Assembly needs better links with Whitehall because, as the agricultural crisis revealed, MAFF often seemed to be at loggerheads with the Assembly. Relations with Whitehall will be more formal and more structured than in the Welsh Office era and will be managed through a series of non-statutory concordats. To be truly effective, however, the relationship between London and Cardiff will require nothing less than a new form of territorial statecraft, involving trust, reciprocity and mutual adjustment *on both sides* because the 'Whitehall knows best' days are over. It has been alleged that London civil servants are dealing with Assembly officials in Cardiff "as if they were functionaries in some colonial outpost" (Shipton, 1999). If this is true it could trigger a downward spiral of turf fights between Cardiff and London which could fuel separatist sentiments.

On the financial front the present formula for allocating public expenditure between the nations of the UK is not sustainable in the more transparent era of democratic devolution. With the creation of Regional Development Agencies (RDAs) the English regions acquired a political voice for the first time and are collectively lobbying for a reform of the existing Barnett formula, which they claim privileges the Celtic nations over the English regions in the distribution of public expenditure (Morgan, 1999). Designed in 1978 as a population-based formula to allocate changes in public expenditure the Barnett formula has not been adjusted to take account of changing prosperity levels in the UK. Since it was designed, Scotland's per capita income has caught up with England, but Scottish per capita expenditure remains some 20% above the English. Wales, in contrast, has moved in the opposite direction: on every major economic index Welsh prosperity, relative to England, has deteriorated (Institute of Welsh Affairs, 1998). In other words the Assembly has nothing to fear and everything to gain from a new needs assessment since its case for a larger share of UK public expenditure is quite simply unanswerable. In making its case the Assembly will quickly realise that the territorial distribution of public expenditure can excite the passions like no other, especially among the more self-conscious and aggrieved of the English regions.

On the wider EU canvas the challenges are even more momentous, in particular the *deepening* of the Union through Economic and Monetary Union and the *widening* of the Union through enlargement. As the EU embraces the poorer countries of central and eastern Europe areas like Wales will lose their claims on regional aid, which means that Objective One status is a one-off opportunity. But enlargement will force some hard choices on the EU and its member states: either they radically reform the current decision-making machinery to make it leaner, fitter and more accountable or they muddle through until gridlock overwhelms them. We can only hope that they opt for radical reform, in which case they may have to apply the principle of subsidiarity more widely than hitherto. Ever since the Maastricht Treaty subsidiarity has been a governing principle of the EU but, legally speaking, it applies only to the relationship between the Union and its member states and not *within* the latter. In political terms however this potentially empowering principle needs to be practiced within member states as well, as indeed it is in federal states like Germany. Until a deeper concept of subsidiarity is recognised in the EU, devolved bodies like the Assembly will find that they have portfolios without power.

Subsidiarity is actually the biggest political issue in the UK today, even though it is never invoked by name. When one considers that this principle deals with the location of power in a multi-level governance system it is clear that the question of subsidiarity applies to such vexed issues as Economic and Monetary Union, devolution to the regions and nations of the UK and the balance between central and local government to name but three. What is notable here is that anti-Europeanism often goes hand in hand with devo-scepticism, a combination which is becoming ever more pronounced in the Tory party, though it is also apparent among antediluvian Labourists. What animates this twin dislike of Europe and devolution is a narrow sense of nationalism and a hopelessly romantic attachment to the centralised state. Although these Tory icons may command more popular support than we dare to admit, the alternative case needs to be put more forcefully: namely as much external *integration* with Europe as necessary, as much internal *devolution* as possible. The Blair administration would do well to have the courage of its convictions and champion this bold political agenda, a more pluralist Britain in a more diverse Europe.

The Assembly will need to engage with these wider issues because its fate is inextricably tied up with them. In this protean environment, in which change is the only constant, it would be foolish to think that the current devolution settlement is the last word on the subject. There are those, like Paul Murphy, the Welsh Secretary, who claim that devolution is now "a settled question", but this is more an expression of hope than a judicious assessment of the medium term needs of Wales. With so many imponderables and contingencies ahead to talk of the Assembly as "a settled question" is the constitutional equivalent of declaring unilateral disarmament. But quite apart from the practical problems of freezing the existing settlement when things are evolving elsewhere, there is a political problem. The Young

People poll which BBC Wales commissioned in May 1999 showed that the existing settlement commanded less support than parity with Scotland, while an independent Wales proved to be the most popular choice of all (Beaufort Research, 1999). Though we should not make too much of this small poll, it suggests that the status quo may not be as stable nor as attractive as some politicians like to assume.

To suggest the Assembly needs new powers and additional resources will seem comical unless it is perceived to be making a difference. In other words if we see more evidence of the inclusive politics the Assembly was supposed to inaugurate then, in the fullness of time, a credible case can and should be made for a more robust institution. The initial experience of the Assembly in action may have disappointed some seasoned devolutionists but, however unpalatable, Wales will get the Assembly it deserves not the Assembly it desires.

POSTSCRIPT
Anatomy of a Crisis

Alun Michael's sudden fall from office on 9th February 2000 was rooted in the very processes that had brought him into office in the first place. As we have seen, the method of his election had helped deny Labour a majority in the new Assembly. The divisions which had marked the leadership election campaign were carried over into the new administration. Michael faced not only the problem of presiding over a minority Labour administration, he also had to work with a Labour Group in the Assembly in which a clear majority had backed Morgan for the leadership. From this perspective, Michael's exit could be seen as another piece of 'unfinished business', a belated resolution of a leadership contest which had officially closed almost a year to the day of his dramatic resignation.

His resignation had been a desperate gamble to save his job and it failed. As a result, his short-lived career at the helm of Welsh politics had ended as it had begun – in controversy. In the aftermath of his departure, two questions call for an answer: why did it happen so early in the life of the Assembly? And what are the likely political consequences for Wales and Westminster?

The Decline and Fall of Alun Michael

There is no mystery as to what triggered the motion of no confidence in the first First Secretary. All three opposition parties were publicly committed to a vote of no confidence if Michael failed to secure additional funds from the Treasury for the express purpose of matching the £1.2 billion which Wales had secured under the EU's Objective One programme, a sum which had to be matched by UK resources to be utilised to the full. The minority Labour administration claimed that enough matching funds were available for the first year of the programme. The opposition parties, unimpressed with this argument, decided to press on with their no confidence vote. The fact that this problem could not be resolved until later in the year, when the results of the Treasury's Comprehensive Spending Review were released, might have forestalled the no confidence vote had Objective One been the only issue at stake. But something else was animating the opposition parties (together with a growing number of Labour politicians as well) and that was Alun Michael's style of politics, a proprietorial, command and control style of politics which seemed to mock the whole ethos of devolution.

As the largest opposition party Plaid Cymru faced a dilemma with respect to the no confidence vote. Many party activists were keen for Michael to remain in office on the grounds that his unpopularity would encourage traditional Labour voters to switch to Plaid, as many had done in the first Assembly election. As time wore on, however, some of Plaid's leaders were becoming increasingly concerned that Michael's style was damaging the Assembly in the estimation of the Welsh public. In other words narrow party advantage decreed one course of action, namely sticking with Michael, while a broader calculus implied that he should be removed for the sake of devolution – even if this meant facing a more popular Labour leader like Rhodri Morgan. In the run up to the no confidence vote Plaid publicly insisted that the issue was simply one of Objective One match funds, but in reality the latter was inextricably linked with the wider issue of Michael's political style.

For their part the Tories were never in doubt as to what they would do. From the outset they had been the most combative of the opposition parties and the quickest to resort to no confidence motions. The Tories openly conceded that the First Secretary's political style was part of the reason why they would be voting against him, hence Objective One was simply part of a wider problem in the Assembly.

The Liberal Democrats were the most intriguing of the opposition parties, not least because it was widely rumoured that they would provide the 'dinghy' to rescue Michael at the last moment. But they had always maintained they were happy to talk to Labour so long as match-funding was on the table, otherwise there was no prospect of a deal and without a deal there was no 'dinghy'.

As the crisis loomed it was not clear how the 28 members of the Labour Group would react under pressure. As no one wanted to be seen to be disloyal to Michael the Labour Group remained silent, at least in public, a silence which party officers fatally misconstrued as support. Labour AMs had to ask themselves two questions: was Michael the leader to raise the credibility of the Assembly and was he the leader to revive the fortunes of the Labour Party in Wales? The answer to both questions was a resounding 'no' for a growing body of opinion within the party. The Ceredigion by-election (February 3rd, 2000) had confirmed Labour's worst fears: the ignominy of coming fourth, with just 14% of the vote, seemed to reinforce the downward trend that was established in the 1999 elections. However, the Labour members opposed to Michael had a problem: there was no obvious mechanism, short of breaking party unity, for expressing their opposition. Indeed, the mantra of the party officers was that Michael was the only Labour Party nomination for First Secretary, before and after a no confidence vote.

The first serious cracks in this superficial façade of unity came in January with the publication of a letter in support of Michael from Anne Jones (chair of the Labour Group in the Assembly) and Jim Hancock (chair of the Wales Labour Party), the two bodies responsible for electing the leader in Wales under the party's new rules. In reality, however, the letter had been written by Michael's personal advisers and had never been discussed by the Labour Group in the Assembly, consequently many AMs were furious at the crude and undemocratic means employed to misrepresent their views. This letter infuriated Andrew Davies, the Chief Whip, who had not been properly consulted on the matter; so much so that he openly expressed his disquiet at the next Group meeting, a move which led to a furious row with Julie Crowley, Michael's political adviser, who accused Davies of 'disloyalty' to the First Secretary. Such was the command and control culture in Michael's private office that disagreement was tantamount to disloyalty.

This was the context in which the political crisis unfolded in the second week of February and, in retrospect, it seems that four factors killed Michael's hopes for retaining power. In the first place the Labour Group in the Assembly began to assert itself. Having been cowed by a climate of fear, in which speaking one's mind could lead to none-too-gentle reminders about the need for loyalty and so forth, Labour AMs used the occasion of a critically important Group meeting on Monday 7th February to insist that they should play a full and active part in the discussions following the no confidence vote on 9th February. Michael and his advisers had originally wanted to confine the discussion to officers of the Group and officers from the Wales Labour Party, party apparatchiks on whom he could count. But this move was foiled by the Group insisting on a meeting immediately after the no confidence vote to reflect on the situation.

The second factor which worked against him was the response of the Liberal Democrats. Michael's team had privately conceded defeat ahead of the first no confidence vote, but believed there was everything to play for if he could get re-nominated and then secure a deal with the Lib-Dems. What very few people in Wales knew at the time was that Tony Blair was engaged in a frenetic last-ditch attempt to save his First Secretary: among other things Blair urged Charles Kennedy, the Liberal Democrat leader, to persuade the Welsh Lib-Dems to strike a deal with Michael. To his credit Kennedy is reported to have told the Prime Minister that "devolution implied that decisions such as the choice of a First Secretary had to be made locally" (McSmith, 2000).

The Welsh Liberal Democrats took the issue of Objective One funds far more seriously than outsiders ever realised. Mike German, the Group leader, took a personal interest in the issue of EU funds. He had discovered that the problem of Objective One was just the tip of the iceberg. Among other things the Lib-Dems had discovered that up to £250 million still had to be paid to approved projects under the 1994-99 EU programme, a point which Assembly officials had reluctantly conceded (Liberal Democrat Group, 2000). The fact the EU funding problem was much greater than anyone had hitherto realised made the Lib-Dems that much more determined to eschew a deal unless new money was on the table. What seems remarkable in retrospect is that the discussions between the Labour and Lib-Dem Groups were conducted not by the leaders themselves but by intermediaries, Gareth Williams and Michael Hines, the advisers to Michael and German respectively.

On 8 February 2000, when it was clear no deal was forthcoming, Williams asked Hines to tell Michael, who was at that moment anxiously waiting for news with Rhodri Morgan and Paul Murphy. On entering the room Hines felt overawed and uncomfortable. Having accepted a glass of red wine from Morgan he said he was there not to discuss terms but to inform them that what was on offer was "too little, too late". Recalling the fateful encounter Hines said that Murphy and Michael did most of the talking and they reminded him that proportional representation at Westminster might be jeopardised by their failure to agree a deal in Cardiff. Hines agreed to try one more time to get his Group to consider a deal but, when he went downstairs to where they had been meeting, he found they had all forsaken the Assembly for Paradise, an Indian restaurant in the Canton district of the city. The First Secretary's hopes of a life-saving coalition with the Lib-Dems were dashed in the most prosaic way possible, when the potential partners preferred a curry to a deal.

The third factor working against Michael was the refusal of the Presiding Officer, Dafydd Elis-Thomas, to be bullied into accepting procedures that were favourable to the First Secretary. The Michael camp mobilised the full weight of the Assembly's legal officers in its campaign to persuade the Presiding Officer of two things: that he had no right to refuse any number of renominations of Michael as First Secretary and that he had a duty to halt the no confidence motions because they risked bringing the Assembly into disrepute. On the cusp of a constitutional crisis, with no precedent to guide him and with civil servants' independence in question, the Presiding Officer was forced to seek advice on the Standing Orders from *external* legal sources. The heart of the problem, from the Presiding Officer's point of view, lay in the fact that the legal officers to the Assembly were also the legal officers to the administration, a dual role which caused no end of conflict and confusion. Indeed, confusion reigned until the very end of the no confidence debate because, when Michael unexpectedly resigned, it was not clear whether the Assembly would continue with the vote. It was at this point that the Presiding Officer made his dramatic decision to allow the no confidence vote, which was carried 31-27.

But the fourth and most important factor was how rapidly support for Michael melted within the Labour Group after his surprise resignation. He had clearly hoped that the resignation would derail a no confidence vote, allowing him to get re-nominated as First Secretary by his party. But he was told in no uncertain terms that his support had shrivelled to just five members of the Labour Group, and he knew that a secret ballot would expose this fatal fact if he pressed the issue. The resignation gamble had failed.

Throughout his tenure as First Secretary the central issue in the Assembly was Michael's proprietorial political style, a style very much in evidence right to the end. Indeed, the decision not to consult the Labour Group about the resignation was the final straw for the few people prepared to give him the benefit of the doubt. For someone who set such a premium on 'partnership' in his political rhetoric, what was so curious about Michael was that his personal relationships with other leaders in the Assembly left much to be desired, so much so that he was unable to draw on a seam of goodwill when the crisis finally came. This personal situation was of course compounded by the fact that the legitimacy of his leadership, in both the Labour Party and the Assembly, was compromised by the undemocratic route which brought him to power.

When the former First Secretary resigned from the Assembly on 16 March few people in Wales were surprised by the decision. Indeed, for many people it simply confirmed what they had long suspected, namely that Michael felt more at home at Westminster than Cardiff Bay. Whatever the rights and wrongs of the matter, his decision to quit the Assembly signalled the end of one of the most turbulent chapters in Welsh political history, particularly for the Labour Party. But the most worrying aspect of his departure was the way some sections of the press chose to interpret the story: that by opting for Westminster he was in effect "turning his back on Wales". The notion that Westminster is somehow detached from, and irrelevant to, mainstream Welsh politics is a dangerous fiction, not least because the largest decisions affecting legislation and resources in Wales continue to be made in London not Cardiff. From beginning to end Michael's brief career in the Assembly was judged very differently by Labour MPs and Labour AMs, with the former being much more supportive than the latter. This suggests that Wales and Westminster could evolve as parallel political worlds inside the Labour Party, the one becoming less and less comprehensible to the other. Relations within the Labour Party could turn out to be the most important factor in sustaining a healthy relationship between the two.

Resurrecting Devolution: Towards a Popular Assembly?

For committed devolutionists the Alun Michael regime was an incubus on the devolution project, a false dawn which nullified the promise of a new, more inclusive politics in Wales. Rhodri Morgan, the new Labour leader and First Secretary, started his career with something that had always eluded his predecessor, namely genuine popular support. Denied a post in the Blair government, and having shown real dignity when his own party machine branded him a 'maverick' in two leadership elections, there was a widespread feeling in Wales that justice had been done when he finally landed the top job. Addressing the party meeting at which he was unanimously elected as the leader of the Wales Labour Party and its candidate for First Secretary, Morgan identified a new way forward for Labour and Wales without pulling any punches:

> Labour's leader in the Assembly is not there to be a thorn in the side of the UK Labour leader, but not to be a puppet either. Devolution must mean what it says, a defined transfer of power

to Wales. Labour's leader in the Assembly must try to embody the aspirations of ordinary Labour voters and members in Wales, and not be the tool of machine politics. Labour's leader in the Assembly must continue to re-invigorate the traditions of democratic socialism and radical politics of Wales – a politics truly for the many not the few. And Labour's leader in the Assembly must help to inspire our supporters and members with a vision of devolution and democratic politics which involves them in the political process – and starts the task of re-building the bond of trust between the Party and the people in our heartlands (Morgan, 2000).

For devolutionists across the political spectrum Morgan's leadership signalled nothing less than the rebirth of devolution or even the "first day of devolution" as the Presiding Officer put it (Osmond, 2000). Goodwill is a perishable asset, however, and Morgan's administration will be expected to make a more tangible impact, a point he acknowledged in his first party political broadcast when he said that the Assembly had spent "far too much time squabbling and not enough time delivering".

To make a difference Morgan will need to mobilise the modest powers of the Assembly to the full, indeed he seems prepared to fight to extend them if needs be. Closer to Ron Davies than to Alun Michael in his views on devolution, Morgan will need to build a wider and more inclusive coalition in the Assembly, not least because a minority government is inherently unstable. A portent of things to come was a thoughtful paper by Val Feld called *Power-Sharing Options*, the title of which was significant because all five options, not just the idea of coalition, were predicated on the idea of sharing power in one form or another (Feld, 2000). Unlike Scotland, where the Constitutional Convention helped the parties to get to know each other well before the Parliament started, the Welsh parties began this learning process after the Assembly convened. By helping the parties to communicate more freely Morgan's open and engaging style of politics should expedite this process.

The funding problems which triggered Michael's downfall will not be resolved by a change of First Secretary. But, assuming it is not compromised by the 'facts of office', a Morgan administration should encourage a more open and honest debate about Welsh problems and explore more radical solutions. Creating a milieu which values critical debate, where disagreement is not misconstrued as disloyalty, is a vital ingredient in the recipe for democracy and development in

Wales. This milieu was conspicuous by its absence during the Michael regime, a salutary reminder that devolution requires a new political culture and not just a new political structure.

Resonating far beyond Wales the fall of Alun Michael was profoundly embarrassing for Tony Blair since he had personally assumed such a large part in promoting the first First Secretary. Privately, party officers in Millbank freely concede that their crude interventions in Wales were totally counter-productive, not least in alienating ordinary Labour voters. Yet the campaign to install Frank Dobson as the mayoral candidate for London, against the overwhelming wishes of ordinary party members, showed that New Labour was once again prepared to jettison the democratic process – namely one member one vote – when this could not guarantee victory for the machine's favoured candidate. New Labour's deplorable record of manipulating the electoral process in Wales and London had tarnished its claim to be the principled party of democratic devolution.

The trials and tribulations in Wales and London could easily persuade Labour sceptics that devolution is more trouble than it's worth. That would be doubly unfortunate because the real lesson of the Rhodri Morgan case is that devolution and the party can be popular causes so long as the devolved bodies are free to make their own decisions and so long as these decisions are respected by the centre.

On the other hand if New Labour is seen to privilege central control over local autonomy in its designs for the nations, regions and cities of the UK, then people of talent and substance will rightly recoil from these devolved institutions. This would be a political tragedy because the opportunity to re-design democracy in so radical a fashion in the UK occurs perhaps once in a lifetime and the need for democratic renewal is becoming more and more evident. Indeed, when the Westminster Parliament is perceived to be losing power to an ever more centralised Executive, and when New Labour MPs are satirised as pusillanimous 'pager-slaves', the task of extending democracy through devolution becomes more rather than less pressing.

The rejection of Alun Michael imparts a very clear signal to Millbank and Downing Street, namely that a new kind of politics is beginning to emerge in Wales, a politics no longer receptive to a command and control system in which the role of Welsh Labour is to implement decisions taken at head office. Inside the party in Wales initiative and authority are passing, slowly but surely, from unelected party officials to the elected Labour Group in the Assembly. Throughout Wales, not least in the once ultra-loyalist Valleys, traditional Labour voters will continue to experiment at the ballot box if their unpretentious hopes and aspirations go unheeded. What the advent of Rhodri Morgan as First Secretary signals above all, perhaps, is the birth of the National Assembly as a self-consciously *Welsh* institution as distinct from a branch office of a prestigious London address, be it Westminster or Whitehall, Millbank or Downing Street.

Bibliography

Adamson, D (1996) *Living on the Edge: Poverty and Deprivation in Wales*, Gomer, Llandysul

Anderson, D (1992) 'Why I Changed My Mind On Devolution', *Western Mail*, 27 January

Andrews, L (1999) *Wales Says Yes: The Inside Story of the Yes For Wales Referendum Campaign*, Seren, Bridgend

Audit Commission (1993) *Passing the Bucks: The Impact of Standard Spending Assessments on Economy, Efficiency and Effectiveness*, HMSO

Barnett, A (1999) 'An Open Letter to New Labour: Please Stop Patronising Us', *New Statesman*, 28 June

Beaufort Research (1999) *Wales Opinion Poll: Young People*, May, Prepared for BBC Wales, Cardiff

Betts, C (1999a) 'The Weakest Cabinet in the West', *Western Mail*, 14 May

Betts, C (1999b) 'Move Towards Lone Action on Farmers', *Western Mail*, 16 September

Bevan, N (1944) Welsh Day Debate, House of Commons, 17 October

Bevan, N (1947) *The Claim of Wales*, Wales, Spring, pp.151-53

Blair, T (1996) Speech to the Campaign for Freedom of Information, London

Bogdanor, V (1999) *Devolution in the United Kingdom*, Oxford University Press, Oxford

Caines, Sir John et al (1993) *Inquiry into the Findings of the Committee of Public Accounts Concerning the 1991-92 Accounts of the WDA*, House of Commons Library, London

Cohen, N (1993) 'What Happened To Democracy?', *Independent on Sunday*, 28 March

Council of Welsh Districts (1995) *Quangos in Wales*, CWD, Cardiff

Committee of Public Accounts (1993) *WDA Accounts 1991-92*, HMSO

Crossman, R (1976) *The Diaries of a Cabinet Minister*, Cape, London

Davies, G. Talfan (1999) *Not By Bread Alone: Information, Media and the National Assembly*, Wales Media Forum, School of Journalism, Cardiff University

Davies, H (1995) *Regional Government*, Speech to Regional Newspaper Editors, 6 January, Newcastle

Davies, J (1994) *A History of Wales*, Penguin, London

Davies, R (1999) *Devolution: A Process Not an Event*, The Gregynog Papers, Volume 2 (2), Institute of Welsh Affairs

Economist, The (1999) 'Undoing Britain', 6 November

Evans, C & George, E (1999) *Swings and Roundabouts: What Really*

Happened on May 6th, Welsh Labour Action, Cardiff

Feld, V (2000) *Power-Sharing Options,* Labour Group, National Assembly, Cardiff

Foulkes, D et al (eds) (1993) *The Welsh Veto,* University of Wales Press, Cardiff

Francis, H & Smith, D (1980) *The Fed: A History of the South Wales Miners in the Twentieth Century,* Lawrence and Wishart, London

Gould, P (1997) *Assembly for Wales Referendum: Polling,* 14 June

Gould, P (1998) *The Unfinished Revolution: How the Modernisers Saved the Labour Party,* Little, Brown and Company, London

Griffiths, J (1944) *Welsh Day Debate,* House of Commons, 17 October

Griffiths, J (1969) *Pages From Memory,* Dent, London

Griffiths, J (1978): 'Welsh Politics in My Lifetime', in B. Smith (ed) *James Griffiths and His Times,* Wales Labour Party, Cardiff

Griffiths, R (1978) 'The Other Aneurin Bevan', *Planet,* No. 41, pp. 26-28

Griffiths, R (1980) 'Turning to London: Labour's Attitude to Wales 1898-1956', *Y Faner Goch,* Abertridwr

Hall, W & Weir, S (1996) *The Untouchables,* Democratic Audit, Essex University

Hardie, K (1912) *The Red Dragon and the Red Flag,* Merthyr

Harris, W (1923) 'The Political Labour Movement in Wales: Regional or National Organisation?' *The Colliery Workers' Magazine,* Vol.1 (12) pp. 305-07

Hencke, D (1999) 'House of Straw That Jack Built', *The Guardian,* 21 June

Hetherington, P (1999) 'Fight For Regional Bodies Being Lost', *The Guardian,* 4 August

Hornung, R (1999) 'Go to the Council Protesters Told', *Western Mail,* 30 September

House of Lords (1996) *Rebuilding Trust,* Select Committee on Relations Between Central and Local Government, 2 July

Jacobs, K (1993) 'Barons Face Losing Housing Role', *Western Mail,* 8 September

Jones, B & Keating, M (1985) *Labour and the British State,* Clarendon Press, Oxford

Jones, R.M. & Jones, I.R. (2000) 'Labour and the Nation', in D. Tanner et al (eds) *A Mighty Human Structure,* University of Wales Press, Cardiff

Jones, R.M. (1986) *The North Wales Quarreymen,* University of Wales Press, Cardiff

Jones, R.W. & Lewis, B (1998) *The Wales Labour Party and Welsh Civil Society: Aspects of the Constitutional Debate in Wales,* Dept of International Politics, University of Wales, Aberystwyth

Jones, R.W. & Trystan, D (1999) 'The 1997 Referendum Vote', in B. Taylor & K. Thompson (eds) *Scotland and Wales: Nations Again?,* University of Wales Press, Cardiff

Kavanagh, D (ed) (1982) *The Politics of the Labour Party,* Allen & Unwin, London

Kellner, P (1999) 'Core Voters Give Blair A Warning', *The Observer*, 26 September

Kilbrandon, Lord (1973) *Report of the Royal Commission on the Constitution*, HMSO, London

Kinnock, N (1990) Speech to the Regional Government Conference, Newcastle

Labour Party (1995) *A Choice for England: A Consultation Paper on Labour's Plans for English Regional Government*, Labour Party, London

Lewis, N (1993) *How to Reinvent British Government*, European Policy Forum, London

Liberal Democrat Group (2000) *Trust Tony: £250m Matched Funding Cover-Up*, Liberal Democrat Group, National Assembly, Cardiff

McAllister, I (1981) 'The Labour Party in Wales: The Dynamics of One-Partyism', *Llafur*, Volume 3 (2), pp. 79-89

McGhie, J & Lewis, P (1993) 'Tories Put Friends in High Places', *The Observer*, 4 July

McGregor, S (1995) 'Senior Party Figure Attacks Assembly Plan', *The Herald*, 27 July

McKibbin, R (1974) *The Evolution of the Labour Party 1910-1924*, Oxford University Press, London

Massey, D (1995) *Spatial Divisions of Labour*, Macmillan, London

Mawson, J (1997) 'The English Regional Debate', in J Bradbury & J Mawson (eds) *British Regionalism and Devolution*, Jessica Kingsley, London

Mawson, J & Spencer, K (1997) 'The Origins and Operation of the Government Offices for the English Regions', in J Bradbury & J Mawson (eds) *British Regionalism and Devolution*, Jessica Kingsley, London

McSmith, A (2000) 'PM Pleaded With LibDem Leader To Save Michael', *The Observer*, 13 February.

Morgan, B & Morgan, K (1998) 'Economic Development', in J. Osmond (ed) *The National Assembly Agenda*, Institute of Welsh Affairs, Cardiff

Morgan, K (1985) 'Regional Regeneration in Britain: The Territorial Imperative and the Conservative State', *Political Studies*, 4, pp. 560-77

Morgan, K (1994) 'The Fallible Servant: Making Sense of the Welsh Development Agency', *Papers in Planning Research* No, 151, Dept of City & Regional Planning, Cardiff University

Morgan, K (1997) 'The Regional Animateur: Taking Stock of the Welsh Development Agency', *Regional and Federal Studies*, Volume 7 (2), pp. 70-94

Morgan, K (1999) 'Towards Democratic Devolution: The Challenge of the Welsh Assembly', *Transactions of the Honourable Society of Cymmrodorion 1998*, New Series, Volume 5, pp 182-202

Morgan, K & Roberts, E (1993) 'The Democratic Deficit: A Guide to Quangoland, Papers' in *Planning Research* No. 144, Dept of City & Regional Planning, Cardiff University

Morgan, K & Price, A (1998) *The Other Wales: The Case for Objective One Funding Post-1999*, Institute of Welsh Affairs, Cardiff

Morgan, K and Murdoch, J (2000) 'Organic versus Conventional Agriculture: Knowledge, Power and Innovation in the Food Chain', *Geoforum*, Vol.31(2)

Morgan, K.O. (1970) *Wales in British Politics 1868-1922*, University of Wales Press, Cardiff

Morgan, K.O. (1982) *Rebirth of a Nation:Wales 1880-1980*, Oxford University Press, Oxford

Morgan, K.O. (1997) *Callaghan:A Life*, Oxford University Press, Oxford

Morgan, K.O. (1989) *The Red Dragon and the Red Flag*, The Welsh Political Archive Lecture 1988, The National Library of Wales, Aberystwyth

Morgan, R (2000) Speech to Wales Labour Party Executive Committee and the National Assembly Labour Group, Transport House, Cardiff

Mungham, G & Bromley, M (1999) *The Welsh Press and the Welsh Media:A Preliminary Report*, Wales Media Forum, Centre for Journalism, Cardiff University

National Consumer Council (1993) *Paying the Price*, NCC, London

NEDC (1963) *Conditions Favourable to Faster Growth*, HMSO

Nolan, Lord (1995) *First Report of the Committee on Standards in Public Life*, HMSO

O'Leary, P (1998) 'Of Devolution, Maps and Divided Mentalities', *Planet*, No. 127

Official Report of the Welsh Assembly (1999) *Partnership With Business*, 18 October

Osmond, J (1974) *The Centralist Enemy*, Christopher Davies, Llandybie

Osmond, J (1977) *Creative Conflict:The Politics of Welsh Devolution*, Gomer, Llandysul

Osmond, J (1995) *Welsh Europeans*, Seren, Bridgend

Osmond, J (1998) *New Politics in Wales*, Charter 88, London

Osmond, J (1999) *Welsh Politics in the New Millennium*, Institute of Welsh Affairs Discussion Paper 11, Cardiff

Osmond, J (2000) *Devolution Relaunched*, Institute of Welsh Affairs, Cardiff

Patten, J (1993) *Rolling Constitutional Change:The Conservative Approach to the Constitution and Constitutional Change*, European Policy Forum, London

Perry, S (1993) 'Quangos Out Of Control', *Western Mail*, 9 July

Prothero, C (1982) *Recount*, Hesketh, Ormskirk

Putnam, R (1993) *Making Democracy Work*, Princeton University Press, Princeton

Rhodes, R (1988) *Beyond Westminster and Whitehall*, Unwin Hyman, London

Rhondda Cynon Taff County Borough Council (1999) *Report of the Chief Executive*, 23 June, RCT

Rentoul, J (1996) *Tony Blair*, Warner Books, London

Rogaly, J (1993) 'Where Comedy is King', *Financial Times*, 7 May

Rokkan, S & Urwin, D (eds) (1982) *The Politics of Territorial Identity*, Sage, London

Rose, R (1982) *Understanding the United Kingdom*, Longman, London

Rowlands, E (1972) *The Politics of Regional Administration:The Establishment of the Welsh Office*, Public Administration, Autumn, pp. 333-351

Settle, M (1998) 'Half of Council Arrested in Expenses Investigation', *Western Mail*, 11 September

Settle, M (1999) 'Home Rule For Wales Vote That Never Was', *Western Mail*, 1 January

Shipton, M (1999) 'Yes Minister, Leave It To Me', *Wales On Sunday*, 5 September

Smith, D (1997) 'The Ashes onto the Wind: Bevan and Wales', in G. Goodman (ed) *The Political Legacy of Aneurin Bevan*, Gollancz, London

Sparrow, A (1995) 'Day of the Quango Over If Labour Wins', *Western Mail*, 12 May

Starling, P (1999) 'Plaid Takes Off The Mask', *Welsh Mirror*, 30 September

Stead, P (1985) 'The Labour Party and the Claims of Wales', in J. Osmond (ed) *The National Question Again*, Gomer, Llandysul

Stephens, P (1999) 'Real Power is Wielded Quietly', *Financial Times*, 5 November

Stewart, J (1992) *The Rebuilding of Public Accountability*, European Policy Forum, London

Straw, J (1995) *Labour and the Regions of England*, Regional Studies Association Guest Lecture, London, 28 September

Thomas, B (ed) (1962) *The Welsh Economy: Studies in Expansion*, University of Wales Press, Cardiff

Thomson, R (1998) 'Council Slated For Tribal Inefficiency', *Western Mail*, 20 June

Travers, T (1999) 'The Civic War', *The Guardian*, 27 January

Waldegrave, W (1992) House of Commons Speech, 5 November

Waldegrave, W (1993) Speech to the Public Finance Foundation, 5 July

Walker, P (1991) *Staying Power*, Bloomsbury, London

Wales Labour Party (1969) *Draft Evidence to the Royal Commission on the Constitution*, WLP, Cardiff

Wales Labour Party (1970) *Evidence to the Royal Commission on the Constitution*, WLP, Cardiff

Wales Labour Party (1990) *A Statement on the Future of Local and Regional Government in Wales*, WLP, Cardiff

Wales Labour Party (1995) *Shaping the Vision*, WLP, Cardiff

Wales Labour Party (1996) *Preparing for a New Wales*, WLP, Cardiff

Wales Labour Party (1999) *Working Hard For Wales: Labour's Election Manifesto for the National Assembly for Wales*, WLP, Cardiff

Welsh Affairs Committee (1993) *The Work of the Welsh Office*, HMSO

Welsh Parliamentary Labour Party (1999) *Analysis of Labour Results in Welsh Assembly Elections*, Report to the WLP Executive Committee, Cardiff

Welsh Office (1967) *Wales: The Way Ahead*, HMSO

Welsh Office (1997) *A Voice for Wales*, HMSO

Welsh Office (1998) *Local Voices: Modernising Local Government in Wales*, The Stationery Office, Cardiff

Welsh Office (1999) *Making the Difference in Wales*, Welsh Office, Cardiff

Wigley, D (1999) Speech to Plaid Cymru Annual Conference, Aberystwyth

Williams, G.A. (1979) *When Was Wales?*, BBC Wales Annual Radio Lecture, 12 November, Cardiff

Williams, G. A. (1982) *The Welsh in Their History*, Croom Helm, London

Williams, G. A. (1985) *When Was Wales? A History of the Welsh*, Pelican Books, London

Williams, K (1999) *Claiming the National: Welsh Devolution and the Media*, Paper presented at the Stirling University Media Institute, 29 April, Stirling

Williams, R (1989) 'Wales and England', in R. Williams, *What I Came To Say*, Hutchinson, London

Willis, C (1999) Letter to WLP General Secretary on Behalf of the Rhondda Cynon Taff Labour Group, 10 June

Willman, J and Court, S (1993) 'Patronage Determines Who Serves at the Top', *Financial Times*, 14 January

Wright, M & Young, S (1975) 'Regional Planning in Britain', in J Hayward & M Watson (eds) *Planning, Politics and Public Policy*, Cambridge University Press, Cambridge

INDEX